THE BLUE COLLAR SCREENWRITER

and

The Elements of Screenplay

by Robert Gosnell

Text Copyright © 2013 Robert E. Gosnell

All Rights Reserved

Cover by Joleene Naylor

eISBN: 978-0-9911656-0-5
ISBN: 978-0-9911656-1-2

Dedication

For my wife, Elaine, who made it all possible.

THANKS....

...to Leslie Ann Sartor for her support, encouragement and valuable assistance in the creation of this book.
...to Danny Mora, my mentor, who gave willingly of his time, knowledge and wisdom when I needed it most.
...to Danny Morris, my sitcom partner, for being such a joy, such a pain and such a good friend.
...to Raul Carrera, my brother-from-another-mother, who taught me to never stop believing in magic.
...to Rich Lerner, my buddy and co-conspirator, who helped me keep the flame burning "post Hollywood."
...to all those who said I could, for believing in me.
...to all those who said I couldn't, for the motivation.

Table of Contents

FORWARD..1
CHAPTER 1: Escape From The Mundane.........................3
CHAPTER 2: Disclaimer..8
   The Gurus - Who is the Walrus?......................................9
   When Is a Rule Really a Rule?..10
   The Elements in Action..12
   How This Book Works..12
CHAPTER 3: To Be or Not To Be a Screenwriter...............14
   Ups and Downs..16
   The "Spec" Script..17
CHAPTER 4: Breaking In...20
   Suggestion #1: Make Contacts......................................22
   Suggestion #2: Find a Mentor..24
   Suggestion #3: Nothing Beats Being There...............25
   Suggestion #4: Be Creative...27
   Suggestion #5: Build a Circle of Peers.......................29
   Suggestion #6: Don't Drive Yourself Crazy!...............30
   Suggestion #7: Keep Cranking Them Out!................31
   Suggestion 8 - Give Them Your Best Work................32
CHAPTER 5: What Hollywood Wants....................................34
CHAPTER 6: The Un-Hollywood Screenwriter....................41
CHAPTER 7: The Cogs In The Hollywood Machine.........45
   Actors...45
   Agents...48
   The Writers Guild of America..52
   Producers...57
   Studio Executives..58
   Attorneys..59
CHAPTER 8: Form and Format...61
   Form..61
   Format...63
   The Title Page..65
   Credits...66
   Contact Information...69
   Registration/Copyright..70
   Title Page Example..72

Page One	73
The Scene Heading	73
The Action Block	78
Keep it Concise	78
DON'T SHOUT!	79
Keep Them on the Hook	81
The Dialogue Block	83
The Character Heading	83
Character Direction	83
Dialogue	85
Transitions	86
CUT TO	87
DISSOLVE TO	88
SMASH CUT	88
MATCH CUT	89
INTERCUT	89
(Flip To)	90
WIPE TO	91
Internal Transitions	92
Flashback	92
Montage	93
Series of Shots	94
Dream Sequence	94
Insert	95
Camera Direction	96
The Credit Roll	97
Script Page Example	99
PART TWO - CHAPTER 9: The Elements of Screenplay	**101**
Theme	101
The Master Theme	102
The Active Theme	104
The Character's Take on the Theme	108
Theme in Review	111
CHAPTER 10: Story	**113**
Keeping it Real	114
Story Logic	115
Story Devices	117
The Ticking Clock	118
Irony	118

- The Twist 119
- The Maguffin 121
- The Cliffhanger 121
- Symbols 122
- Conflict and Complications 125
- The Forces of Antagonism 125
  - Man vs Man 126
  - Man vs the Elements 126
  - Man vs the System 127
  - Man vs Himself 127
- Complications 129
- Subplots 130
- CHAPTER 11: Character 132
  - Backstory 134
    - Backstory Through Dialogue 135
    - Backstory Through a Flash-Forward 136
    - Backstory Through a Flashback 136
  - Physical Proxies 136
  - "Rocky" Again 137
  - External and Internal Conflicts 140
  - Archetypes 143
  - Characteristics 144
  - Opposing Characteristics 147
  - Character Traits 149
  - Character Goals and Conflicts 152
  - The Villain 153
  - Supporting Characters 155
  - Protagonist as Antagonist 157
- CHAPTER 12: The Acts 159
  - The Three Act Structure 160
  - Act One - The Setup 161
    - Act One Beat Sheet 164
  - The Opening Scene 164
  - The Hook 167
    - The Action Hook 168
    - The Curiosity Hook 168
    - The Suspense Hook 169
    - The Misdirection Hook 169
  - Act One - Introductions 171

The Act One Break...176
Act Two - Obstacles and Complications.....................177
Page 60..180
The Act Two Break..182
   Act Two Beat Sheet..183
Act Three – Crisis, Climax and Resolve......................184
The Crisis..184
The Climax..185
The Resolve...185
   Act Three Beat Sheet..187
Script Length...187
CHAPTER 13: Scenes and Sequences.............................192
Scenes..192
Sequences...198
Motivating Factor...200
Sequence Resolve...201
CHAPTER 14: Dialogue..208
Dialogue Issue Number One......................................209
Dialogue Issue Number Two......................................211
Dialogue Issue Number Three....................................212
CHAPTER 15: Story Types...214
The Fish Out of Water..215
The Ensemble..216
The Buddy Story..217
The Poor Fool..218
The Character Study...218
The Coming-of-Age Story (Rites of Passage)...............222
CHAPTER 16: Genres...224
The Common Genres..227
The Action Genre...227
   The Action Hero...230
   The Action Villain...230
   Martial Arts Action...231
The Adventure Genre..232
   The Adventure Hero..233
   The Adventure Villain...234
Fantasy/Adventure...235
   The Fantasy/Adventure Hero...............................235
   The Fantasy/Adventure Villain.............................236

Nature/Adventure..236
The Caper (or Heist) Genre..237
    The Caper Hero..238
    The Caper Villain..238
The Comedy Genre...239
Romantic Comedy..242
    The Romantic Comedy Hero......................................243
    The Romantic Comedy Villain....................................243
    Romantic Comedy Structure.......................................244
Slapstick Comedy..251
    The Slapstick Comedy Hero......................................251
    The Slapstick Comedy Villain....................................251
Black Comedy..252
    The Black Comedy Hero..252
    The Black Comedy Villain..253
The Youth Oriented "Raunch" Comedy........................253
    The Y.O.R.C Hero..254
    The Y.O.R.C. Villain..255
The Spoof (or Parody) Genre..255
    Spoof Heroes and Villains...256
The Drama Genre...256
    The Drama Hero..257
    The Drama Villain..257
The Melodrama Genre..258
The Science Fiction Genre..258
    The Sci-Fi Hero..259
    The Sci-Fi Villain..260
The Horror Genre...260
    The Horror Hero...262
    The Horror Villain...263
The Suspense Genre..263
    The Suspense Hero...266
    The Suspense Villain...266
The War Genre..267
    The War Hero...268
    The War Villain...268
The Mystery Genre..269
    The Mystery Hero..270
    The Mystery Villain..270
The Crime Drama Genre..271

The Crime Drama Hero	272
The Crime Drama Villain	272
The Western Genre	272
The Western Hero	273
The Western Villain	274
The Musical Genre	274
The Sex Exploitation Genre	276
CHAPTER 17: The Process	**278**
Choices	283
Writing to a Budget	285
CHAPTER 18: Development	**288**
The Outline	289
The Beat Sheet	291
The Six Starting Points of a Beat Sheet	292
Man Bites Dog	293
"Man Bites Dog" Beat Sheet	295
CHAPTER 19: Rewrites	**297**
Notes	297
Edits	301
CHAPTER 20: Marketing	**306**
The Treatment	306
The Logline	308
The Synopsis	310
The Query	312
Query Letter Rules	313
Sample Query Letter	314
Finding a Buyer	315
CHAPTER 21: Pitching	**318**
10 Simple Rules for Surviving the Pitch	318
In Closing	325
About the Author:	326
Films Referenced in This Book	I

FORWARD

I am a screenwriter. I am proud to be able to say that.

It was my dream, more than thirty years ago, and I've been blessed to see that dream fulfilled. It didn't occur to me, at the time I began to pursue my dream, just how great were the odds against me. I was a blue-collar guy from a working class family. The extent of my education consisted of a high-school degree from a small town in the Ozarks and a hitch in the U.S. Navy, where I was schooled in a trade that would do me no earthly good, on the outside. I had no friends or contacts in Hollywood, had never even seen a screenplay or teleplay, and didn't know there were such things as film schools. And, I was already thirty-two years old.

What I did have was a nagging "I-think-I-can-do-that" bug in my brain, a driving desire and a wife. An exceptional and extraordinary wife, mind you, and I believe the dedication at the beginning of this book says it all.

Oh, and a cat. We had a cat. A very ill-tempered feline, and a really atrocious traveling companion.

Off we went to Hollywood, and I, with star-studded blinders on my eyes and that nagging little bug in my brain, set about making my dream come true. After thirty years of living it, I've arrived at the writing of this book.

But, this book is not about me, except to the extent that my experiences resulted in lessons worth sharing. This book is about you, be you blue-collar, white-collar or otherwise.

It is for those who aspire to the same dream that I embraced; who possess that nagging little bug in their brain, yet are hindered by the same superficial limitations I faced; the mistaken notion that outsiders like us, without the connections, advanced education or contacts, simply shouldn't be there.

Within these pages, you will find the lessons learned by a middle-class, working guy who stumbled blindly into Hollywood, made mistakes, honed his craft, slogged through the trenches and eventually hit pay dirt.

In my somewhat eclectic career, I've had a taste of an array of mediums. More by destiny than by design, I've had my writing produced in network television, syndicated television, basic cable, pay cable, studio features and independent features. And, I'm still in the game.

It's been a career filled with rich and rewarding experiences, colorful stories and memorable characters. Out of it came a philosophy on screenwriting formed and refined by trial-and-error, study, research and writing. Always, writing.

I am not entirely self-taught, mind you. Much of my education came from the books and screenplays I've read, the classes and seminars I've attended, and the generosity of those who would selflessly share their knowledge with me, to whom I owe a debt of undying gratitude.

This book is one writer's view from the trenches, plain and simple. I hope you will find something in the following pages that speaks to you, and I hope it will inspire you to take the next step, perhaps the first step in your screenwriting career.

It's the only way you'll ever get rid of that bug in your brain.

CHAPTER 1

Escape From The Mundane

When I started writing screenplays, there were only two books on the craft, that I can recall: "Screenplay," by Syd Field, published in 1979, followed in 1983 by William Goldman's "Adventures in the Screen Trade." Mr. Field tells us how to structure a screenplay. Mr. Goldman tells us what it is to be a screenwriter. Theirs are still two of the best books available, and together make a fine "bible" for any screenwriter.

The success of these books probably contributed to the deluge of screenwriting books and classes that followed in the early eighties. That trend has proliferated in the 21st century, until now, even people who don't write screenplays are writing books about how to write screenplays. In fact, it's mostly people who don't write screenplays, who are writing screenwriting books...or articles, or blogs, or postings on websites.

So, why another book about screenwriting?

After exploring the market and listening to the messages being delivered, I realized that each one of these books, blogs, articles and websites represents a unique point-of-view, one that is personal and subjective.

That matters, because, while there certainly are some hard and fast rules that apply to screenwriting, it isn't like teaching math or

English, where only hard and fast rules apply. Two-and-two always equals four, but where the first act of a screenplay ends is a subject of debate. Thus, we get methods and labels and definitions and rules coming at us from every angle, and they often conflict, because people don't always see things the same way.

In the early days of film and television, writers mostly just stumbled into the craft. Writers from radio, playwrights and novelists logically shifted into the new medium and helped to develop the form.

These days, many writers earn their chops in film school, where they learn screenwriting as part of a broader curriculum. Those who become successful screenwriters and filmmakers are deserving of high praise. They are a rare and precious commodity.

Other writers are born into the inner-circle of Hollywood, picking up the torch from family members who blazed the trail ahead of them; taking over the family business, so-to-speak. Nepotism thrives in Hollywood, just like anywhere else.

Still others sort of ease into the industry through personal contacts. A friend from college now works for the studio, maybe, or their father plays golf with a high-powered agent.

But, not many screenwriters come from a machine shop in Phoenix, Arizona, or a farm in Nebraska, or a garage in New Jersey. From blue-collar worker to Hollywood screenwriter is a transition that is rare.

I'm here to tell you that it doesn't have to be that way.

Because I was not equipped with the standard prerequisites for a screenwriting career, the path I took into the industry; my learning curve, was radically divergent from the norm, and therefore, my perspective on screenwriting and on being a screenwriter bears a certain uniqueness.

I didn't used to think that was particularly significant, but the heightened interest in screenwriting in recent years has changed the landscape. What was once a relatively confined field of endeavor has morphed into a fad. Thanks in large part to the internet, screenplays from all over the world flood the market.

What has been unearthed are a lot of blue-collar stiffs out there, just like me, and probably some white-collar stiffs, too, who are looking for something creative, fulfilling and fun to do with their lives, and think screenwriting might be it.

Now, I suspect, there are few proud parents who are sending Junior off to college in the hopes he'll become a screenwriter. Doctors, lawyers, engineers and the like bring with them a measure of security past graduation. The choice of screenwriting as a career doesn't guarantee you a damn thing. If you can't put it on the page, no amount of formal education is going to help. If you can put it on the page, then it doesn't matter where you come from.

That's what I believed, when my wife Elaine and I made the trek to Hollywood with much enthusiasm, great anticipation and not much else. It's still what I believe today.

For those of us for whom film school isn't realistic and the wonderland of Hollywood, beyond a Universal Studios tour, seems unreachable, having a natural writing talent and a nagging bug in our brain just isn't enough to shake us into action. There must be a spark. We need an epiphany.

Mine came from a most unlikely source.

From my early teens, I had dabbled at writing, even took a couple of mail order courses. The bug was nibbling at my gray matter, even then, but I had no idea what to do with it, and thus, I never seriously considered it as a profession.

Until that day.

It was like most any other day, on the surface, but a two-inch ad in the newspaper was about to make it special. I was working in a machine shop, at the time, schlepping heavy machinery, sweeping floors and welding blades for band saws. That evening, I scanned the newspaper (another blue-collar mind set: always looking for a better job) and that's when I saw the ad. A melodrama troupe, made up of kids just graduated from high school, was looking for someone to write old time melodramas...make that "Olde Tyme

Melodramas," for them.

You remember those, right? The mustachioed "Simon Legree" villain, the pure-as-the-driven-snow hero. Good, old fashioned save-the-mortgage, tie-her-to-the-railroad tracks, Dudley Do-Right melodramas. These kids even had a "gig," performing shows at the old Opera House in an area amusement park. Something in my brain clicked.

"I think I can do that."

And as it turned out, I could. I believe I was the only candidate who applied, so I had that going for me. And, there was no money up front, so they had that going for them. They gave me copy of a melodrama script to use as a template and I wrote my first one. I believe I got $40.00 for it. They rehearsed it, produced it and performed it.

And, it worked. I mean, it wasn't "Casablanca," but, hey...

That first moderate success led to more melodrama scripts; a half dozen or so, as I recall, along with some sketches and monologues. My confidence in my writing ability began to grow.

The melodrama troupe added some members and evolved into a sketch comedy ensemble, in which I also performed. Mostly, though, I wrote jokes and sketches and created characters and got to see it all performed live, in front of people who either liked it or didn't. I was writing, and my learning process had begun.

It wasn't a living, by any stretch, but it had three of the "big four" elements I was looking for. It was creative, fulfilling and fun, and more importantly, it was the defining event that spawned my journey. The "inciting incident," if you will.

A year or so later, the television series, MASH would unleash the bug, once more. It was a brilliant show, and the writing sparkled. I was watching a rerun over dinner, when the thought struck me, again.

"I think I can do that!"

Well, now, that was a much taller order than writing sketch comedy in Phoenix, Arizona. But, when the bug bites...

It wasn't "MASH" alone, mind you. There were a number of outstanding situation comedies on the air, during that period. "Taxi," "Barney Miller," "All In The Family," "The Bob Newhart Show," "The Mary Tyler Moore Show" and "WKRP in Cincinnati," along with the Garry Marshal dynasty of "Happy Days," "Laverne and Shirley" and "Mork and Mindy." Sitcom was King.

But, it was that "MASH" episode on that night that brought on the epiphany. At that moment, I knew what I wanted to do with the rest of my life, and it was liberating.

It was a blessing that I was too naive to know that what I was thinking was impossible. In truth, it probably wouldn't have mattered, anyway.

For the next couple of years, I applied myself to research. My initial focus was on situation comedy, so I studied the shows incessantly. I subscribed to the Hollywood Reporter, to gain some long-distance insight to the industry.

Through the mail, I finagled a script, generously provided by the talented and prolific writer-producer Tony Sheehan, for the sitcom "Barney Miller." I wrote two rough sitcom scripts and a screenplay to serve as writing samples. Through some diligent digging, I even mined the names of a couple of people who were on the fringe of the industry in Hollywood, whom I could contact.

Meanwhile, Elaine applied herself to the task of making this transition financially feasible. Her natural genius with money finally brought us to the point where we could make the leap.

We packed our belongings, dug the cat from under the bed and headed for Hollywood.

CHAPTER 2

Disclaimer

One thing I want to be clear about at the outset is that what I present, here, is not to be deemed a "method." I am, in no way, telling you that I, and I alone have the best possible formula for writing a great screenplay. If, after reading this book, you choose to call what I present a method, then feel free, but I don't look at it that way. What I've done is gather information from myriad sources, and my approach to all of the rules and methods was simple:

Try it.

It will either hold up, or it won't.

Whatever the source of the information, I took what worked for me, maybe even refined or redefined some of it a bit to suit my personal taste. What didn't help me or felt uncomfortable, I discarded.

Every method; every point-of-view I encountered from working writers, teachers and screenwriting books influenced me in some way. They all gave me a deeper understanding of the process; another perspective to shape my own.

What I also learned from this is that the things I rejected were just as important to my screenwriting development as the things I embraced. Every method from every learned source would eventually reveal flaws; chinks in the armor. Nobody's perfect.

What I offer is my understanding of the process; a sharing of information, having sorted through the chaff to get to the grains of truth and to find what fits my personal style. I've learned from teachers, mentors, classes, seminars, books and peers, but only by applying the information could I uncover what is real and what is effective; what is fact and what is opinion. And, what is just plain baloney.

The bottom line is, if you find something in this book that makes you a better screenwriter, or gives you a clearer insight to the process, then it'll be a win-win situation, and how often do those come along?

If you want to disagree with my approach, feel free. Right for me isn't necessarily right for you. I'm fine with that.

If, however, you're looking for a method; a clear template of rules and guidelines, there are many options out there to choose from.

So, let's talk about them, for awhile.

The Gurus

Who is the Walrus?

Just as there are now many books on screenwriting, there are also a slew of people out there teaching it, and the internet is rife with experts who seem to have sprung from out of nowhere. Unfortunately, there are far more screenwriting "experts" than expert screenwriters.

Now, I'm not here to trash anyone...in particular. There are several different styles and philosophies employed in the teaching of screenwriting. While I may disagree with some of what I've read and heard, that doesn't make it wrong. Where I draw the line is when something is stated as fact, when it clearly isn't.

So, this is a kind of general, if-the-shoe-fits commentary. And, it is a commentary.

At the time I entered the business, there were many fewer sources from which to gather information and guidance on screenwriting than are available today. On top of that, most of those who had the information were much less willing to share it.

Later, they began to realize that they could make a shitload of money by marketing that information, and the rush was on. Today, the information available on screenwriting is mind-boggling. Some of it, though well-intentioned, is just plain wrong.

There are many methods being touted, some delivered by actual screenwriters and others by people who, though they may not be screenwriters by trade, are learned individuals with a valid understanding of the craft. There is something to be taken from each of them, and probably something to be left behind. I like to believe that they enhance, rather than detract from one another.

Once again, the key is application. If something you learn from a screenwriting guru actually helps you write, add it to your process. Just don't consider every word from every teacher to be gospel. How can you, when so many of the "experts" don't even agree with each other?

It's lucrative for a screenwriting teacher to allow the perception that he has "the secret;" that his method, alone is the path to successful screenwriting. It isn't so, not in any case. There are many, many approaches to writing a story, and probably some yet to be created. Don't allow one philosophy to be your only guide.

Beyond that list of highly qualified teachers are a whole bunch of really unqualified, self-proclaimed teachers, who have a point of view they'd love to impress upon you, generally for money, which can be as damaging as it can be helpful.

When Is a Rule Really a Rule?

My biggest pet peeve in this era of screenwriting experts is the number of rules being floated. You must do this and you can't do that, or this story moment has to appear on exactly this page. When I run across one of these, I always test it (I can't believe they don't, before making it up) by applying it to several successful films.

Because a rule doesn't change. A rule is constant. Slightly bendable, perhaps, but basically etched in stone. I beg you to not fall prey to this "rules" trap.

Of course, there are rules to writing a story in a screenplay form, just as there are rules to any writing form. That's what makes it a form. But, I have found very few hard and fast rules to writing a screenplay. There is a relatively specific format, and there are a number of options, choices and tried-and-true devices which you may apply as tools in constructing your story. Many of these become rules in someone's method. That doesn't always make them so.

Now, more than ever, there are plenty of people out there willing to give you a beat-by-beat, fill-in-the-blanks template to follow, and at the end of it, you'll have a screenplay, but it's akin to the old paint-by-numbers process. You'll wind up with a picture, but it ain't art. And, it may not be an accurate reflection of who you are, and what you're trying to say.

Following someone's rigid format, not allowing for variables, inhibits your creativity and stifles your personal voice. If you accept something as a rule, when it really isn't, you're going to try and work it into every script, and it may not always belong there. You'll end up feeling frustrated and wondering what went wrong.

When it comes right down to it, the best teachers out there are the talented, creative screenwriters who have gone before, and who have provided the written material for the greatest films of all time.

In my opinion, nothing serves better as a teaching tool for a screenwriter than a well-made film, produced from a well-written screenplay. How fortunate we are, to have the best motion pictures ever made at our fingertips. No screenwriting class or book will surpass the lessons available to us by studying them.

I strongly advocate this method for the study of film history, as well. If a writer strives to be a novelist, he can do no better than to examine the works of Ernest Hemingway, Mark Twain, William Faulkner or John Steinbeck.

For a screenwriter, the study of films from their very inception and through their evolution to the present day provides a Master's Degree worth of valuable education to enhance our understanding of the medium.

The Elements in Action

We've all learned something about movies just by watching them. On some level, even as a casual viewer, we gain an understanding of the form. Once we know what specific elements to look for, however, we can more intelligently dissect the structure of a film.

Because I have always relied on this method of studying films in order to understand screenwriting, I use this same approach when I teach. I can explain how a plot point works, what constitutes an act break or how to motivate a character, but demonstrating it with an example from a good film; allowing students to visualize the element at work, seems the most concise and effective way of driving the point home.

They have been chosen for their quality and their value as teaching tools. They have also been singled out for their wide popularity, and therefore, their longevity and familiarity. Even if you haven't seen them, you'll probably know the storylines.

How This Book Works

I will use the same approach in the writing of this book as I employ in my screenwriting classes and workshops. As I point out and explain the elements of a screenplay, I will offer examples from some worthy films, many of them Academy Award winners, some of them commercial blockbusters, all of them worth watching. Many of these are older films. I make no apology for that. Regardless of what era it comes from, a great film is a great film, just as relevant today as are any of our classic novels, symphonies or works of art.

The examples I use will be presented in a manner which keeps them in context, so not having seen the film won't detract from your understanding of the point being delivered.

Once you have determined where your screenwriting interest lies, in terms of subject matter, seek out the films which apply, then watch and study them. If you feel that Romantic Comedy is your forte, reach back into the film vaults and select the greatest films of that genre, from early movies like "It Happened One Night" and "The Philadelphia Story" to contemporary examples, such as "The 40 Year Old Virgin" and "Date Night."

If Action movies are your bag, dive in to the early "swashbuckler" films of Errol Flynn and Douglas Fairbanks. Compare those with great films of the genre through the decades, right up to the "Pirates of the Caribbean" or the Jason Bourne series.

See which common elements exist in them all, because there will be common elements. You'll come out of it with a clear understanding of what is required of you in your efforts in your chosen genre.

In Summary: While the urge to lock onto one teacher's method may be tempting, limiting your education to one source just limits your education. Test the rules and methods you encounter, and make certain they work for you, before incorporating them into your process. Read scripts and study film history to gain an understanding of the evolution of the medium, and most importantly, keep writing.

CHAPTER 3

To Be or Not To Be a Screenwriter

Before doing something as foolhardy as dropping everything and rushing off to Hollywood, you should ask yourself a couple of simple questions. The first:

Am I really a writer?

Do you truly have a natural writing talent; an inherent ability to tell a story with words? Techniques can be learned, but natural ability can't. A great many people do have the talent. I've seen it in my peers and in writers who have passed through my classes and workshops, so I know it exists in many of us. I've also encountered those who think they do, but sadly, don't.

Now, we're all creative in some fashion, but not all of us are writers, no matter how much we want to be.

You have to be completely honest with yourself, because if you don't have that inherent writing ability, you're going to find out in some pretty painful ways. Read your work with a critical eye. Compare your screenplay to scripts from successful films. Have it read by people you can trust to be perfectly honest with you.

If the reviews are overwhelmingly bad, or even lukewarm and not terribly encouraging, don't fool yourself into thinking that everybody else just doesn't "get it;" that you're actually standing up, a lone, noble soul, for your artistic integrity.

Maybe, you are. Or, maybe, you just can't write. It's no sin. There are plenty of other outlets to employ one's creativity.

Once you've satisfied yourself that, yes, that little writing bug is present in your brain, it's time to consider question two:

Can you cut it?

And, if you can, do you really want to? Most of the people you'll be competing with can and do. They know something that most aspiring screenwriters have yet to learn:

There is a difference between writing a screenplay and being a professional screenwriter.

In the beginning of my Hollywood adventure, I naively thought that talent was the only real barometer for success. If you had "the gift" you would succeed. The cream rises to the top, doesn't it?

Sure, if it works its ass off. The competition is brutal, and you must always remember why they call it show business. Motion pictures are a multi-billion dollar industry, and everyone wants a piece of that action.

You'll have to be thick-skinned, if you're going to dive into that shark pool. It means dealing with rejection and failure on a fairly regular basis. No one has the time or inclination to stroke your ego or worry about your feelings. For a variety of reasons, some people will just not like what you do. You have to wade through it, keep your head on straight, keep plugging away and improve your craft.

If you get a project produced and it fails, consider it a lesson learned, lick your wounds and forge ahead to the next one. And, look on the bright side. Even if your project falls flat, you'll still have a produced credit, and produced credits are gold.

Ups and Downs

Like anything else in life, there are up sides and down sides to being a screenwriter. On the positive side, you can work at home! You don't have to shave or comb your hair. You can hang around in sweat pants and flip-flops. Start when you want to, quit when you want to. How great is that?

On the down side, you can work at home!

While it's a luxury to set your own schedule, it's also a responsibility. The distractions can be deadly. It's a lot more fun to play a video game than to stare at a blank computer screen. You can watch a movie and tell yourself you're doing research, but what you're really doing is watching a movie, and though there is something to be learned from watching a well-constructed film, it still isn't writing.

I've had friends; people whom I love dearly and enjoy spending time with, call me in the middle of the day with a conversation that goes something like this:

"Hey, what are you doing?"

My response: *"I'm working."*

"Wanna go see a movie?" (or "grab some lunch" or "hang out")

"No."

"How come?"

"Because...I'm working."

It's just hard for them to accept. After all, I'm home. I'm on my own time. I can go "do something" if I want to.

It's no sin to cave in, once in awhile and go have lunch with a friend to give yourself a break, but it's also an all-too-tempting opportunity to procrastinate.

This perception that you're always available will prevail, even when you've actually sold something to prove you're a working screenwriter. Rides to the airport, errands to the grocery store, taking the cat or dog to the vet, picking up the kids from school, entertaining out-of-town visitors...all things you'll be expected to do, sometimes want to do, often have to do. And, they don't come when it's convenient. They come when they come.

Your schedule is flexible, so it only makes sense, doesn't it? It also makes it more difficult for you to do your job. You must find ways to make up for that lost time. Re-work your schedule. Work in the evening, late at night or on weekends, if need be. Write as much as you can, when you can. Just make sure you write.

Another bane of the screenwriter's life is the never-ending search for motivation. Anyone who has ever started a small business will tell you that you must be self-motivating if you are to have any chance of success.

As a screenwriter, you are a small business. You can have a host of great ideas, but if you don't have the will-power to sit down at the keyboard and forge those ideas into scripts, then hone those scripts to their maximum potential, you're sunk.

There is no pre-set routine for you to follow, no supervisor to assign you a task; nothing tangible to structure your work day. It's just you and your imagination. On top of that, there's no paycheck waiting for you, at the end of the week, or month.

Your small business has no product, unless you generate it on your own initiative.

They call them "specs."

The "Spec" Script

The term "spec script" means you're writing it on speculation, and that means, you'll spend a lot of time and energy doing work with no promise of any reward at the end, aside from personal satisfaction. Maybe, it'll sell, maybe it won't. Maybe, it'll serve as a great writing sample that will lead you to a paid assignment. Maybe it won't.

I can tell you what it will do. It will make you a better writer.

Every script you put behind you provides an education, whether or not it ever gets produced. A half-dozen spec scripts that go nowhere can be just what you need to take your talent to a level that finally gets your great American screenplay on the screen.

If what you want to be is a professional screenwriter, you must remain diligent; constantly married to your keyboard, constantly churning out new work. It takes commitment.

The great satirist Art Buchwald once told the story of a man who wanted so much to win the lottery, he prayed every night for it. Each evening before bed, he would fall to his knees and beg God to *"Please, let me win the lottery!"* Finally, after months of this, he was in the midst of his ritual prayer, when he suddenly heard a big, booming voice from out of the heavens:

"Give me a break! Buy a ticket!"

The hapless fellow in Art Buchwald's story discovered that God himself couldn't determine his fate. Winning the lottery requires an investment. In that case, it's only a buck. In your case, it's time, effort, commitment, dedication, brain-drain and sweat equity. And, a little talent doesn't hurt.

Unfortunately, some aspiring writers see their first spec screenplay in a "lottery ticket" light.

"I'll dash out a great story," they imagine, *"submit it to the market and wait for fate to sweep me up in its arms and propel me to fame and fortune!"*

Okay, anything is possible. Maybe, they'll write that script, land a major agent from ICM who will get it directly to the green-light guy at a big studio, make a quick sale, deposit a huge paycheck and revel in glory on opening night as Tom Cruise and Meryl Streep bring it to life on the big screen, (probably in 3-D) amid whispers of Oscar nominations. Maybe, it will happen that way for them.

Or, maybe they'll win the lottery.

If you submit your spec script to an agent, and he likes your work, one of his first questions to you will be *"Do you have more?"* Maybe, it took you a year or two to get that first hot script sharpened to perfection. It can't take you a year or two to write the next one, but it has to be at least as good.

Also consider that the medium is collaborative. You'll have to take notes; volumes of notes from lots of people. You'll have to exchange ideas and argue story points and learn to juggle fragile temperaments and creative conflicts with tact and diplomacy.

At the end of all that, should you survive, you will be worthy of the best compliment any writer can hope for; you'll be regarded as a "pro." Disciplined. Reliable. Consistent. Seasoned. Someone who can handle any writing task thrown at them: Writing, rewriting, co-writing, adapting; pitches, concepts, treatments, punch-ups, outlines, loglines and picket lines.

And meetings! Meetings with agents, producers, directors, actors, lawyers and executives, and getting through those meetings without pissing somebody off.

In Summary: You may consider that I've painted a pretty bleak picture of the lifestyle, but none of it is insurmountable. Forewarned is forearmed, and while the demands of a screenwriting career are daunting, the rewards, both financial and personal, can be every bit worth the journey. It isn't your average lifestyle, and for some of us, that's exactly what we're looking for.

So, is screenwriting the life for you?

Have I scared you away, yet?

No?

Great.

Read on.

CHAPTER 4

Breaking In

Well, it's what everyone really wants to know, right? How to to get that first big break? It's certainly among the top ten questions I'm asked. Here are a few thoughts on that subject.

First, be born into the industry.

Too late? Yeah, me too.

Those of us who sweat and toil for our breaks often feel a sense of resentment toward those who got theirs through nepotism. The first lesson I learned about that is to *get over it*. If I were in their place, wouldn't I take advantage of it? Absolutely!

If you have relatives or contacts in the business, exploit the hell out of them. Just because you have an easier road in doesn't necessarily mean you don't deserve to be there.

Would Michael Douglas have become a great actor if his dad had been a shoe salesman? Who knows? Maybe those lucky few with a birthright deserve to be there and maybe they don't. Most of the time, that works itself out. The bottom line is, it has nothing to do with you.

If I were pressed to break my covenant regarding rules and define the rules for breaking in as a screenwriter, there would be three:

1. Write your ass off.
2. Learn your craft.
3. Hustle your work, any way you can.

Consider that for virtually every job title in the motion picture and television industry, people don't work unless someone hires them. The only exception is the writer. No one can stop us from writing. They may not always pay us for it, mind you, but they can't stop us from doing it. The entire entertainment food-chain starts with us. That's an advantage we must exploit.

The third item on that list, hustling your work, is a critical piece of the puzzle, of course, and the most elusive. There are no set formulas for accomplishing this.

The easiest way to get your screenplay read is to submit it to a screenwriting contest, or one of many internet sites offering reading and coaching services. There are some reputable sites out there, with sincere intentions, and writers do, on occasion, find work or gain recognition through them.

There are others, just as sincere, but less qualified in nearly every respect to judge your work. They have or had some limited experience in the industry, at some level, and therefore feel qualified to counsel you, or evaluate your writing talent. They want to help you. They think they are, but they really aren't.

And, there are still others who approach the whole thing purely from a business perspective. You pay them money and they read your script, with the promise to pass along to their industry contacts. Those industry contacts, generally elusive, faceless, nameless individuals, will then do something wonderful with the script, once it is, in their view, "ready." In most cases, these businesses aren't really looking for the next great screenplay. They're looking for the next paycheck.

The problem with all of these submission sites, good and bad, is this: It's a volume business. Anybody can play, and therefore, it's pretty easy to get lost in the crowd.

If you're more inclined to take the job of hustling your work to a higher level, thereby increasing your odds, I can offer some suggestions that may help you create opportunities.

Suggestion #1: Make Contacts

I know, it's a pretty obvious note, but it's important. The way almost everyone gets that first major break, meaning a produced credit, is through contacts. If you have no contacts at the outset, you must create them from scratch.

The best way, maybe the only way to do that effectively is through your work. You have to get noticed, and your script is all you have to make you a viable commodity.

Yes, you can schmooze at industry parties, if you're fortunate enough to get into one. You can schmooze your way into a lot of things, if you're charming and witty and good-looking, but if you were all of that, you'd probably want to be an actor.

You can network and make cold calls and create an internet site and take classes until you're blue in the face. I don't disparage any of that. I've done it all myself. But, if you're not writing, and constantly working to improve your writing, you're wasting your time.

Your script is your calling card. You live and die by it. You can tell people you're a writer, but they aren't going to believe it until they read what you've written, and maybe not then, if your script doesn't cut it.

While the internet is a wonderful tool which has greatly expanded our horizons, it can't replace the old-fashioned, face-to-face approach. You need to get out there and shake some hands. Writers tend to be less gregarious in nature than the people we deal with in the industry, and we aren't always comfortable in social surroundings. Let's face it, writing is a highly personal, private matter.

You just have to suck it up, put a smile on your face and go for it. Get yourself around and in front of as many people as you can.

Develop relationships, exchange thoughts and ideas and solicit advice.

"How," you might ask, *"when I don't live in Hollywood?"* It's a fair question.

First, do what you can locally. When classes, seminars or lectures come to your town, attend them. Query the instructors or speakers, making it clear that what you're looking for are contacts, or at the least, advice on how to gain new contacts.

Attend screenwriting conferences and pitch festivals, and don't just "sit in." Get active. Network, and as distasteful as I find the word and the activity itself, schmooze. Maybe, you don't like schmoozing. Neither do I. So what? I didn't like giving book reports in front of the class in high school, but if I wanted to pass the class, I did it. I imagine you did, too. And, it didn't kill us, did it?

Do you take a vacation every year, or couple of years? Fine. Forgo Disney World or the beach and take a working vacation to Hollywood, and do so armed with every script and/or pitch idea you can muster. Make some phone calls and do some research before you go. Try lining up a meeting or two with someone, anyone who will take a few minutes to talk to you.

Have you met someone on line, perhaps in a screenwriting blog site, who lives there? Let them know you'll be in town and offer to buy them lunch for an opportunity to pick their brain.

Check out a couple of TV shows, while you're there. Tickets to the tapings of many TV shows are free, and they're always soliciting audiences. I learned, first hand, the value of watching the process in action. Most people go there to be entertained. You should go there to learn.

If you remain diligent, you will encounter opportunities to have your work read, and that, more than anything, will lead to more lucrative contacts.

Contacts come through many avenues and manifest in many forms, so when you encounter anyone who is, at any level, connected with the film industry, don't take them lightly. They may be a rung on the ladder you're attempting to climb.

Suggestion #2: Find a Mentor

Easier said than done, I'll grant you, yet it happens all the time. While what you'll encounter from most of those above you in the industry is, at best, indifference, there are people out there who are willing to give a "newbie" a hand up.

The three basic requirements for hooking a mentor are talent, commitment and a touch of unbridled enthusiasm. It's okay to be naive. In fact, they like it that way. They want to start with a clean slate; an unsoiled mind. If you show you're not just willing, but anxious to learn, your odds increase.

Since I had no contacts of any kind in the Hollywood industry before I made the leap, I quickly set out to acquire some. I made several scouting excursions to Hollywood. On one such excursion, a minor contact led to another minor contact, who then turned me on to the gentleman who would become my mentor and friend, Danny Mora.

Danny is a Hollywood renaissance man: Actor, writer, comedian, producer, voice artist, radio personality and acting coach, with a few other trade specialties thrown in. He was all of that when I met him, and he's all of that at the time of this writing.

After an introduction by a friend-of-a-friend, I approached him with a spec sitcom script, and he was kind enough to take time from his frenzied schedule to read it and give me notes. At the time, I'm certain that neither Danny nor I had any idea that he would become my mentor, but that's what would eventually happen, and it was my spec sitcom script that opened the door.

A mentoring relationship is personal, as much as business, and must develop naturally. Understand, however, that even if you meet your potential mentor face-to-face and bowl him over with your charm, initiative and sincerity, if you then present him with a mediocre script, it's game over.

Having someone who is in a superior position to you, industry-wise, solidly on your side is an immense advantage when you're trying to break in. When you encounter an individual who is willing to take you on, consider it a blessing and treat it as such. Strive to return something of value to the relationship, even if it's only by validating your mentor's faith in you. And, pass that kindness and wisdom along to someone else, once you've earned your stripes. It's about as rewarding as anything in this business can be.

Suggestion #3: Nothing Beats Being There

"Do I have to live there?"

It's one of the most frequently asked questions I hear from aspiring writers. "There" is, of course, Hollywood. In the back of the questioner's mind, she's hoping I'll say "no." I wish I could.

Generally, I refer to the Willie Sutton story. Actually, it's more of an urban legend, and may not even be true, but that doesn't matter. It's a great story, and more importantly, it makes my point.

Willie was a famous bank robber, who had a prolific career, primarily in the 20's and 30's. When he was finally captured, the legend goes, he was asked:

"Willie, why do you rob banks?"

Willie's reply?

"Because that's where the money is."

In the case of a screenwriter, Hollywood is still the bank. True, things have evolved, somewhat, with the advent of the internet. Suddenly, there is access from places where it never previously existed.

There are more contests than studios, these days, along with expos and classes (both online and probably in your local area) and seminars and the like. It's almost overkill, and that's the problem. It isn't a very selective process. As I've already pointed out, it's an "anyone can play" game, and so rising above the crowd is difficult.

In feature writing, there is also an option for a writer to work in the independent market in her home town, or at least home state. That can provide great advantages, not the least of which is a choice of lifestyle.

However, in the major commercial screenplay world, even if you successfully market your first script from the hinterlands, you're going to have to make that Hollywood commitment eventually, if you want a career and not just a one-shot deal.

Yes, it's possible to sell a screenplay from the fringe, but those who are there, making face-to-face contact on a daily basis will always have a substantial advantage.

The demands to be physically in the mix are even greater in television. Most television production is still limited to Hollywood and New York, and while there have been a smattering of programs produced in other large cities in recent years, these aren't considered hubs, which is what you're looking for.

At that time I made that precious Danny Mora contact, I was still living in Phoenix, Arizona. Once Danny satisfied himself that I possessed the raw material to be a television writer, his first major piece of advice was this:

"If you want to do this, you have to move to Hollywood."

Three months later, I did just that. For more than two years, I worked with Danny at his small production company, trading my time for his expertise. I answered phones, ran errands, did whatever was needed. In return he guided, counseled and taught me in the ways of Hollywood, from the politics to the page.

I took full advantage, not only of his knowledge, but of Danny's long list of industry contacts. By my calculations, my time spent with him shaved a good five years from my journey. I worked hard to reach the point where I could consider myself his peer, and I'm still not certain I've accomplished it. But, his friendship alone is reward enough.

None of that would have happened, had I spent those two years sitting in my little apartment in Phoenix, banging away on my typewriter. (Yes, I said typewriter.)

Screenwriting can be done from anywhere, but there is no doubt, being there is better.

Suggestion #4: Be Creative

I'm not talking about pulling some lame P.R. stunt to get you noticed, like gluing yourself to the Hollywood sign buck naked for the evening news. I'm talking about finding creative ways to gain access to the people you need: those who can hire you or buy your screenplay.

You'll hear all kinds of stories about tricks people have used to create that first break. I knew of an actor who took a menial job, making deliveries. As fortune would have it, part of his route took him to several of the studios. Now, getting onto any studio lot is a gem of an accomplishment, and an opportunity that should not be wasted.

This actor had access to the lot through his job, so along with his deliveries, he would bring manila envelopes with his head shot photo, resume and contact information inside. After completing his obligatory delivery, he would make a pass through the individual production offices on the lot and drop his manila envelopes at the appropriate desks, announcing, *"Here's the picture and resume Mr. So-and-so asked for."* I don't know if it ever worked for him, but I hope so.

Another story concerns a writer who posed as his own agent. Using a fictitious agency name, he would set up meetings for his talented new writer. Rarely did anyone check to see if his "agency" was actually legit.

Yet another writer would call various agencies asking if they represented a great, new writer he was trying to locate. Of course, the great new writer was him. Then, after a cooling off period, he would call back the agencies as himself, the great new writer, seeking representation. Often, the comment he got back would be, *"I've heard of you!"* Of course they had. From him.

My sitcom writing partner, Danny Morris (not to be confused with Danny Mora - I know, it's eerie, huh?) had fine-tuned the art of sneaking onto studio lots before we hooked up. His problem was, he had difficulty approaching producers and opening up a conversation with them. That became my end of the deal.

Danny was not adverse to climbing the fence to gain studio access, but I'll confess, I never tried that. Besides, there were other ways. Sometimes, a friend or acquaintance would be working on a production at a particular studio. In that case, we would cajole them into getting a pass for us, which would get us on the lot. Other times, we would go in with an audience that was bused in to watch a taping.

Once on the lot, Danny and I would visit every sound stage where a sitcom was being produced. We watched run-throughs and tapings, and often managed to lift a random script for that week's show.

We weren't there to cause any trouble or get in anyone's face. We were there to watch and learn. We kept a low profile, and that's what kept us from being discovered and unceremoniously thrown out on our keisters.

Paramount was our favorite target, because so many sitcoms were produced on that lot at the time. We would find a way on, then leave through the employees exit, our scripts tucked under our arms, looking like we belonged there and always making certain to say goodnight to the guard. Eventually, the guards thought we worked there, and we could come and go at will.

The only times we made our presence known at any of the shows we frequented was during social events, like wrap parties or Christmas parties. In that case, family and friends were often invited, so it wasn't unusual to see strangers in their midst.

We attended Christmas and wrap parties at "Mork and Mindy," "Taxi" and "Cheers," among others. We would wait for the Producers or Story Editors to get a couple of drinks in them, then introduce ourselves and hit them up for a pitch meeting. We got a couple, too. I would imagine that, in these more precarious times, security is tighter than it was then, but you get the idea.

Creativity can reap rewards, but the key is to use common sense and not do anything too radical. These tactics I've mentioned and others like them come with risks. Creativity gone awry can damage your reputation before your career ever gets off the ground. Use discretion.

Suggestion #5: Build a Circle of Peers

And work them. Share contacts and information with those on the same level as you. Maybe, they can turn you on to an opportunity that is a better fit for you than for them, or vice-verse. When one of you breaks in, it can open the door for others.

An actor friend of mine spent his early days in Hollywood at one of those franchise copy places, where he worked with a couple of "wannabe" filmmakers, Chris and Bryan. They were all making copies on the late shift.

Knowing my friend was an aspiring actor, Chris and Bryan asked him to perform in a couple of student films they were producing. No money, of course, but my friend was happy to help out, and to get the exposure, however limited.

Some time after he left that job, my friend got an excited call from Chris.

"Hey, man, guess what?"

"What?"

"I've been nominated for an Academy Award!"

My friend had been making copies with Christopher McQuarrie and Bryan Singer. McQuarrie had been nominated, and ultimately won the Best Screenplay award for "The Usual Suspects," which Singer directed. Both men have gone on to stellar careers. You just never know.

The "buddy system" has always worked for entertainment-related college grads. The class of "whenever" enters the field at the same time, and often maintains contact with one another. When one gets a high-profile studio position, the first thing they want to do is bring one or more of their old college chums into the fold.

No doubt, you've heard the mail room stories; low level positions working in the mail room or as an assistant or intern at an agency or studio, from which they work their way steadily up the ladder.

Believe it or not, a great number of those people are college grads, often film school grads. If you're a blue-collar guy or gal with no connections, your chances are slim, but each situation is unique, so don't rule it out. A bright, talented person can rise quickly through the ranks of these organizations.

Speaking of organizations, there are all kinds for a writer to get involved in to generate a circle of peers. There are writers groups, improv groups and theater groups everywhere, and they all have room for new blood. Taking classes and attending seminars can also lead to connections with those on your level.

You'll also find small, nascent production companies struggling for a foothold in the industry. When you find them, don't be afraid to offer your talents for free, initially, in exchange for your involvement. If that little production company breaks out, the rewards down the road can more than compensate for a lack of up-front pay. If it doesn't break out, you'll still walk away with some valuable experience and education.

Suggestion #6: Don't Drive Yourself Crazy!

There are numerous ways to drive yourself crazy. I've tried them all, and each is quite effective. It's exciting to get a story meeting or pitch session somewhere, but for God's sake, don't sit around afterward, waiting for the phone to ring. It's a habit that's easy to acquire and hard to break.

The least stressful thing to do is release it to the universe with positive thoughts, then put it behind you, hope for the best and keep writing. Very Zen, I know, but doing so will make your life so much easier.

And, don't envy another writer's success. It's tough not to, when that classmate or workshop buddy lands a lucrative deal and leaves you eating dust, because, you know, his writing isn't really that good. Well, maybe it is, but it certainly isn't as good as yours. So, why him and not you? Bastard! He got lucky, that's all.

What a huge waste of time, energy and emotion that should be going into your writing. You have to use those situations for motivation. So, you're better than he is? Fine, then this just proves that you're going to get your shot, right? I mean, if he can do it...

And, take another slant on the situation. If you replace your envy and frustration with genuine support and encouragement to your cohort, you may be developing a great industry contact from within your own circle.

If things work right, those who rise up the ladder should take any opportunity to extend a hand to those below. I mean, in a perfect world. And, it happens. Your attitude toward that awkward situation can make the difference. Maybe next time, it's you who "gets lucky." Believe it or not, that can be uncomfortable, too, when it comes to relating to your peers.

Suggestion #7: Keep Cranking Them Out!

In other words, stockpile! This goes right back to my primary suggestion, which is to write, write more and keep writing.

You may want to try your hand at different genres to see which is the best fit for you, which means you'll end up with, maybe a sci-fi script, a romantic comedy and an action piece. Or, maybe you've found your niche and you'll have six or seven suspense screenplays on hand.

Don't be disheartened if they don't sell right away, because somewhere, down the line, someone is liable to say, "*I wish I had a good action piece with a strong female lead,*" and you'll be able to pipe up, "*I have one of those!*"

Okay, you wrote it five years ago. So what? Maybe, five years ago wasn't the right time, but now is. You'll have it in your arsenal. Dust it off, punch it up and submit it.

The simple truth is, you can never hurt yourself by writing more.

Suggestion 8 - Give Them Your Best Work

While I advocate continually writing new scripts, make sure each one is polished to a high sheen, before you shop it. Just because you've reached that blessed "Fade Out" point you've worked so hard for, doesn't necessarily mean you're done. As Ernest Hemingway once quipped:

"The first draft of anything is shit."

It's fine to set your first draft aside and move on to the next project. It's often quite helpful, in fact, to let a script sit for awhile before diving back into it.

A passage of time of a few weeks or even months can give you a fresh and more objective take on the story, and make the rewrite or polish stronger. Just, make sure you've fine-tuned it before you put it on the market, and when you market, be discerning.

Beware of the "shotgun" approach; sending your script out to every company you can get to at once. It can kill a good script, and here's why: When a studio executive reads your screenplay and there's a flicker of interest, he'll invariably ask this question:

"Who else has read it?"

What he wants to know is, who else did you shop it to, and how did they respond? Studio story execs tend to be insecure. It's always easier for them to say "no," because it's risk free. If they say "yes," and the thing turns out to be a bomb, it can cost them their jobs. So, if they discover that you sent the script to Paramount, Fox, Castle Rock and Columbia and they all passed, what makes you think this guy is going to want it?

In Summary: Employing some or all of the tactics I've touched on may appeal to you and may help you. You may have an entirely new approach for yourself. Key is to be true to yourself. Be who you are. If any of the suggestions I've given make you uncomfortable, don't use them. The idea is for you to find the niche in this industry where you belong. Don't try to force yourself into a relationship or situation that requires you to stifle your true nature.

CHAPTER 5

What Hollywood Wants

Okay, you've decided, despite of all of my warnings, that you want to be a screenwriter. Next question:

What should you write?

In writing any book, screenplay, stage play, short story, song, etc., the trick is to have an angle. A fresh look at an old story, because, in reality, they're all old stories. They may have new settings, new characters and different complications, but when you boil them down, they've all been told before, probably numerous times, simply wearing different costumes.

And, let's go a step further. Not only have we known these stories for centuries, but we've known how to write them for almost as long. It was that astute philosopher and scribe Aristotle who defined the staples of storytelling: plot, theme, character, dialogue and the rest. Notice, I said storytelling, not screenwriting. That's because, the first step when you sit down to write a your script is to tell yourself this:

"I'm telling a story."

It's a different mindset than:

"I'm writing a screenplay."

The screenplay is the medium...the format. The more you think "screenplay," with all of its formatting requirements and structural constants, the less you think "story," and that can be a trap.

I'll grant you, it's true that industry executives are looking for marketable elements, like unique concepts, stunts, CGI and exotic locations. That's only fair, since their job is to sell. However, what they sell are elements. What you will sell is a story.

At some point, it will also be your job to sell, but the best tool you have to make that sale is not the stunts, CGI or locations, but a great story.

Before your screenplay gets a green light, every executive at every level of film production at a studio has to "sell" it to someone else. Several people, up the ladder to the top, must buy into your script, and trust me, they see commercial elements all the time. It's how those commercial elements are handled that sets them apart.

In his book "Adventures in the Screen Trade," William Goldman emphatically states that "Nobody knows anything." His reference is to Hollywood, of course, and he's absolutely right. If they knew, there would never have been an "Ishtar," "Howard the Duck," "Gigli," or any number of major box-office flops. Those films all had commercial elements, concepts and stars, and a lot of good it did them.

I once heard a producer quoted as saying:

"If I had made all of the films I passed on, and passed on all of the films I've made, the end result would probably be about the same."

He's probably right.

Okay, so they don't know, and that means, all they have to work from is perception. Whether a perception in Hollywood is valid or not, it is a perception that you, the screenwriter, have to deal with.

The problem here is, the perceptions change like the seasons in

Hollywood, and there is no rational way to stay ahead of them. When "Jaws" became the first blockbuster; "tentpole" in today's lingo, everybody wanted blockbusters. It was the first film to break one-hundred-million-dollars in box office receipts, and studios rushed to grab a seat on the bandwagon.

In this case, it began a trend which is not only still with us today, but dominates the market. Will it be the trend next week or next year? There's no guarantee. The industry is already seeing the beginning of Superhero burnout at the box office.

Once upon a time, Westerns ruled the Hollywood landscape, both in theaters and on television. Getting a Western marketed today is, to say the least, an uphill climb.

In the 1950's and '60's, zombies, werewolves and vampires were frequently showcased in horror films, a trend that ebbed for a couple of decades, and now is back with a vengeance. How long will it stay in vogue, though? If you write one today, will it be marketable tomorrow?

And, if you do write one today, do you think it will be unique in the marketplace? How many hundreds of zombie, werewolf and vampire scripts do you suppose are out there, in the middle of this trend? The task to set yourself apart becomes that much more challenging.

Shortly after my entry into the industry, "Cheers" rose to the top of the sitcom heap. Every aspiring sitcom writer wanted a seat at their table. When I inquired of my agent what type of spec script they might consider reading, this was his reply:

"Anything but a "Cheers" script."

As it turned out, they had been assaulted by a flood of spec "Cheers" scripts, and had no interest in reading more of them from outside writers. Besides that, sending a spec script of a particular show to that specific show is always a bad idea. These are the people who write the show, and they're more likely to be hypercritical of an outsider's attempt to fully grasp the characters and concept.

A few years later, the sitcom trend began to wane. Soon, we were hearing the death rattle within the industry. Sitcoms were dead!

Then, along came Bill Cosby with "The Cosby Show," and sitcoms were back. Then, they began to fade, once more, and in a couple of years, sitcoms were dead, or at least dying, again. And, what happened? Along came "Seinfeld" and changed the perception, once more.

I heard it again, not so many years ago, and guess what? Sitcoms are back and currently doing quite well. Give it some time and they'll probably be dead again, but it's just that old pendulum swinging. And, as the pendulum swings, the perceptions change.

But, who generates the perceptions? They have to come from somewhere, don't they? Indeed, they do.

I want to qualify my next statement, before I state it. It's going to sound a lot like I'm dissing Hollywood, and I'm not. I love Hollywood. The years I spent there were some of the most exciting and fruitful of my life. And, it really isn't fair to lump everyone there into one category and declare: "That's Hollywood."

There are some brilliant, creative minds out there, doing some extraordinary work. Maybe "nobody knows anything," but there are some people on the creative side who come a lot closer to knowing than most. It's just a matter of having better creative instincts.

But, the business side of things; the selling and the spinning, the wheeling and dealing has evolved. In the early days, studios were owned and operated by filmmakers. By their nature, filmmakers are risk-takers; visionaries, driven by artistic goals and desires. They brought to the screen a wide array of story choices for audiences to consider.

Today, studios are owned by corporations and operated, not by filmmakers, but by deal makers. Because of this, the decision-making process within the studio structure is generated from a corporate mindset, rather than a creative one. Their perceptions are based on numbers, and whether we like it or not, their perceptions create our reality.

Since it is the business of show, commercial viability is a critical requisite. That's a huge contributing factor in the reason we see so many franchises, sequels and prequels. Every comic book hero imaginable becomes franchise fodder, because it brings with it an established profile. Same goes for a best selling novel. It has a market coming in, and that makes it a safe, or at least safer bet.

So, what are they looking for? What does Hollywood want? After years of study and deliberation, I finally found a couple of constants from within the ever-shifting sands of perception and came to this conclusion.

Hollywood wants movies that are uniquely familiar.

I know, it sounds like a contradiction. Stay with me. The fact is, they don't want you to frighten them with new ways of telling a story. They like the old way just fine. They understand it, at least enough to know it when they see it. They've all had the structure burned into their brains, so they're looking first for familiarity. They want a hero, a goal and complications.

Yes, they want you to mess with their emotions and yes, they want you to surprise them, but only in an old-shoe-comfortable form. They want elements which have worked in the past. It's the closest thing to security the business can offer them.

At the same time, they want it to be fresh and unique. A new twist. An angle. A concept. Something that jumps out at you from a movie poster. Scenes that make a great trailer for television. They want an element that other people will want to copy.

They want uniquely familiar.

I'm not promoting, just reporting.

Once, when discussing with Danny Mora a sitcom episode I had seen, I said to him, *"I can write that well."* His reply surprised me.

"Then, they don't need you."

Of course, they don't! They already have people, lots of people, who can write "that well." People they have relationships with.

People who they know can deliver. Why should they take a chance on me?

In order to break through that wall and get noticed, you have to give them something fresh and compelling; a story that engrosses them, a style that captivates them and characters that thrill them. "Average" doesn't excite them. "Just as good" doesn't cut it.

When we write for Hollywood, our creative freedom tends to diminish as the dollar values go up. It isn't that we can't generate great stories within the confines of the studio guidelines, but it certainly is tougher. That's why it's worth so much.

On the up side, they don't mind spending money. They want to spend a lot of money, because that buys more commercial elements, like big stars, splashy CGI effects, elaborate stunts and 3D.

It also buys more perks for the multitude of producers and executives who will be employed.

An associate of mine once approached a producer he knew in Hollywood, who had been a childhood friend. My associate had packaged a small movie project for local production, budgeted at one million dollars. He pitched the project to his producer friend, hoping to acquire funding from his company. The conversation went like this:

Producer (shaking his head): *"Hollywood doesn't make million-dollar movies."*

My Associate: *"Why not?"*

Producer: *"Because, you can't steal a million dollars from a million-dollar movie."*

A pretty cynical reply, but generally accurate, at the studio level. The positive side of this for the writer is, if you have a screenplay they truly want, they will reward you handsomely for it.

They will, because they realize that while it's quite possible to make a bad film from a good screenplay, you simply can't make a good film from a bad screenplay. That's the crap-shoot payoff screenwriters are looking for in Hollywood.

While I don't recommend to any writer that they come into this business with a goal of getting rich quick off of one script, I can't deny the possibility of that miracle deal. It's always present in the back of every screenwriter's mind. Who wouldn't want that? Just, make sure you temper that desire with a large dose of reality. Prepare yourself for the long-haul.

In Summary: The resolve of all of this is, instead of asking *"What does Hollywood want?"* the question should be *"What will Hollywood want tomorrow, or next week, or next year?"*

The answer is, your guess is as good as anyone else's. Your only defense is to write a story you're passionate about and let it find its market.

CHAPTER 6

The Un-Hollywood Screenwriter

Generally speaking, Hollywood will shrink in fear from an idea that requires them to take risks on a form they don't recognize. If you want to do something really different; truly cutting-edge, or a powerful story that doesn't have the necessary commercial elements for Hollywood, you either have to make it yourself or find an adventurous independent producer who's in love with your story and respects your judgment.

That may not be a bad thing, because the independent producers in your home town can be every bit as important to your career as any Hollywood studio.

It's the independent producers who take creative risks, and that may provide the best opportunity for your screenplay to become a reality. Witness "Being John Malkovic," "She's Gotta Have It," "The Blair Witch Project," "Sex, Lies and Videotape," "Clerks," "Napoleon Dynamite," "Reservoir Dogs," "Little Miss Sunshine" and "Paranormal Activity" as a few examples.

There are also countless independently produced, straight-to-DVD genre films out in the market. Certain genres, like Action, Adventure, Horror and Sci-Fi have a strong enough fan base to support the distribution of a film, even when produced on a limited budget. Check out the listing of films presented at a confab such as the American Film Market, some time. There will be scores of small distributors selling hundreds of independent films in these genres.

Another up-side to the independents is that the experience is quite different from that of dealing with the majors, usually in a positive way. Often times, a writer of an indie production will have an opportunity to stay close to the process; actually be on the set, even participate. All things that help you learn your craft and get your vision on the screen. All things which are very much frowned upon in Hollywood.

Writing for independent film production is a wonderful training ground, an easier venue for a screenwriter to penetrate than Hollywood, and an opportunity for a new writer to see her work produced and acquire a credit.

Besides, maybe the grind and bureaucracy of the Hollywood maze isn't for you. Maybe, you could go there, break in, find work, make tons of money and be the world's most miserable sonofabitch.

Perhaps the kind of stories you enjoy aren't generally Hollywood's cup of tea, but you still want to write them. Well, small films do break out. There are festivals that attract distributors, and risky indie films that win Academy Awards, and any of that can skyrocket you to the top of Tinseltown's "A" list.

The greatest obstacle faced by independents is the ultimate commercial appeal of their films. Fulfilling an artistic vision may be personally rewarding, but those rewards can't truly be realized unless people see the movie.

There are basically only two options to overcome that obstacle, that is, to attract a viable distribution deal. The first is a killer concept. That means, taking the gamble that a fresh, quirky or untried vision will appeal to a mass audience, as "The Blair Witch Project" did, when it spawned the popular found-footage genre, and the truly unique "Being John Malkovic" did, when it hit a home run with its offbeat concept.

Option two is to attach a recognizable actor with a profile to the project. While this option is not an easy one to fulfill, particularly with the budget limitations indie producers face, it also isn't as hard as it may seem on the surface.

There is only one thing an actor values above his paycheck, and that is a great part; a chance to stand out in a role that will make the industry and the world take notice. That fact is your ammunition.

Actors with a television profile will often leap at the opportunity to do a small, well-written indie film with a juicy role. It's a chance to show his chops, get noticed and get a shot at a major film. Besides, TV pays well, so if this television actor is anywhere near star-level, the money won't be the issue. Convincing their agents that they want to do a small film for crap money will be a bigger challenge.

The antidote to this for the indie producer is to offer the actor a generous back-end deal; a sizable chunk of the picture's gross profits. Offering your star scale wages up-front guarantees that he won't be completely wasting his time, while the possibility of break-out profitability is oft-times a risk worth taking.

Seasoned actors on the wane will also take a great part for some of the same reasons as TV actors. They may be household names, but they aren't getting the offers they used to get. In this case, they're looking for redemption, possibly trying to revive a fading career, and sometimes, it works. Ask John Travolta, before "Pulp Fiction," or Mickey Rourke before "The Wrestler."

There are also some wonderful character actors, those whose faces we've seen in numerous films, but whose names don't always leap to mind. These folks keep showing up in movies, year-after-year, because they are solid, experienced, relatable and professional. Yet, they're never likely to be offered a starring role in a studio-level film. Independent films give them that opportunity, and their involvement in the project provides distributors with some level of comfort.

And then, there are many "A" level actors who simply live for a great role. They don't need the money. They turn down money jobs every day, but offer them a dynamic, unforgettable character and they're on board.

The problem, in this case, will be getting to them, and if you get to them, getting into their schedule. That's a task left to the producer, obviously, but it will be the role you've written in your screenplay that makes the difference.

In order to get that actor to play a part you've written, other factors come into play. The actor will also need to be comfortable with the director and supporting cast, and the technical proficiency of the crew.

Quite often, when we see a big star in a small film, it's because the people making that small film are known to the actor. They are friends or associates, with proven track records, at least at some level.

For a struggling, unknown indie producer to get your script to a high-profile actor is a challenge, at best. Yet, it can and does happen.

In Summary: We often make screenwriting synonymous with Hollywood, as if Hollywood is the only option, yet movies are made all over this country; all over the world by independent filmmakers. Granted, the big corporate money isn't there. You won't get rich from one screenplay deal, but it can easily lead to bigger and better opportunities. Just because you don't feel like knocking down Hollywood's door, don't think that means the door is eternally closed. It ain't necessarily so.

CHAPTER 7

The Cogs In The Hollywood Machine

The film and television industry is made up of many parts, all of which are of significance to a working screenwriter. The screenwriter can be considered one of the cogs in this machine, but I prefer to think of us as the fuel that runs the beast. Nothing happens without the written word. There are those who would argue that the much overdone "reality" genre invalidates that statement. I disagree, but that's a conversation for another day.

The point is, we're not alone, out there. There are people who work around us, for us, over us and because of us, and at some point, a working screenwriter will encounter and deal with them all. With that in mind, I've constructed a short list of those who will play the most prominent roles in a writer's career, and some brief thoughts on their function.

Actors

"Have you read the script?" asked the writer.

"Part of it," replied the actor.

"Which part?" the writer inquired.

"My part," the actor answered.

Alfred Hitchcock was once credited with the quote:

"Actors are cattle, and should be treated as such."

Perhaps, for dear old Al, the actors were only tools to use in fulfilling his vision. I don't believe that does them justice. I get the "cattle" part. They must feel that way a lot, judging by the humiliations I've seen them subjected to, smiling all the while. The frustrations must be staggering.

Some writers write parts with specific actors in mind. It's done more as a visualization tool for the writer, I think, than any real thought of getting that actor for the role. The odds are simply too astronomical to logically write a part for the only actor who can play it.

It's not inadvisable to write for a "type," however. It plays into the familiarity aspect of the uniquely familiar equation. Writing a role that can be filled by any of several action stars is just good judgment. If Bruce Willis can carry an action film, so, too can Tom Cruise, Hugh Jackman, Jason Statham, Will Smith or Denzel Washington.

There is often a certain level of insecurity within many actors. Don't ask me why that is, because I can only speculate. Perhaps, it's as simple as the fact that they are putting themselves "out there," their faces in giant close-up on the screen, vulnerable to the slings and arrows of outrageous critics, both professional and amateur. It's hard to blame them for that. I know, it would scare the bejesus out of me.

That insecurity can manifest itself in a number of ways, but where its effect on a writer is concerned, it usually boils down to the actor taking it upon himself to change an action or a line of dialogue. Sometimes, the change is insignificant, and not worth fighting over. You wrote a red car, he wants a blue car. Go for it.

Other times, the change is devastating, at least from the writer's point-of-view. It may change the entire tone or intent of the original scene. It may establish some trait or characteristic in a character that is counter-productive. The sad fact is, there is rarely anything a writer can do about it. The higher the profile of the actor, the more our opportunities to argue over a change diminish.

The comment I've heard most frequently from actors in this circumstance is this:

"I don't think my character would say (or do) that."

They rarely take into consideration that their character is actually our character. A character we created. A character we developed. A character to whom we are God.

In most cases, whatever the actor's objection to the line or action, it has already been considered by the writer, if the writer has done his job. However, a screenwriter should never close himself off, completely, to additional notes, from wherever they may come. The form is, after all, collaborative. It certainly does no harm to listen to the actor's objection, or suggestion. When an actor truly embraces a role, he may indeed, have helpful ideas which will improve the part.

In any event, on those infrequent occasions when the writer has a chance to defend the choice he has made, doing so with tact and diplomacy is an absolute must. Remember, there are fragile temperaments at work, on both sides of this issue.

Gently explaining to the actor why the line reads as it does may be fruitful. Finding a compromise is the next best option. Just be prepared to accept defeat. By the time your screenplay reaches the actor, odds are, it is already in production, and the screenwriter is out of the picture; essentially powerless. Unless we are directing the film, our influence is minimal, at best.

In Summary: The quality of an actor's performance is critical to the success of a screenplay. They bring our characters to life, and we are trusting them with our "children." A poor performance can be awfully disheartening, to be sure, but a good performance from an actor who embraces and enhances the role can fill a writer's heart with joy.

Agents

Hollywood agent: "Hello," he lied.

Agents are a fact of life for a screenwriter. If you are successful in your quest, at some point, you will have to deal with them, and you will want to.

Agents are often the subject of ridicule and scorn in Hollywood. Their image is probably on a par with attorneys, who, by the way, you will also need at some point.

Producers and studios see agents as bloodsuckers, who try to drain every penny and perk they can from them. Writers use them as excuses for why they aren't getting work. Much of the derisiveness leveled at them is unwarranted. Not all of it, mind you, but much of it.

The reality you must embrace is that you are in charge of your career. Don't make the mistake of thinking that because you have an agent, you can kick back, pop a beer and wait for the offers to roll in. They'll work for you only if they see you working for yourself.

Agents get ten percent of your script fee because they only do ten percent of the work. That's all they should do. They represent you. If you want them to do a good sales job, then give them a good product. The right agent can be your best friend, regardless of how you might feel about them, personally.

When you're trying to set up a pitch with a producer or development executive, you'll be asked two questions, and one of them is, *"Do you have an agent?"* If you can say yes, chances are, the conversation will progress. The other question: *"Are you WGA?"* We'll talk about them later.

I've had four agents in my career, and only one of them ever actively sought and acquired work for me, but all of them were important to my growth.

My first agent worked at a small boutique agency which represented a couple of prominent television actors, but didn't have much in the way of a stable, or high visibility. The agent I dealt with was almost a caricature of a Hollywood agent. At one meeting, he actually talked with me while carrying on two simultaneous telephone conversations, with a phone at each ear.

But, the company was legitimate, and that, in turn, made me legitimate. I was a novice, early in the business, and having an agent of any kind was a major first step.

My second agent was even more important to me than the first. He worked for a major agency that handled writers, actors and directors, primarily in the television market. That worked perfectly for me, because my first foray into writing for Hollywood was in situation comedy.

I was writing with my sitcom partner, Danny Morris, who, like me, was on the "bunny slopes" of the breaking-in process. We had nothing in common, were ten years apart in age, had completely different writing styles and argued over jokes and stories constantly. In other words, we were perfect for each other. Danny had encountered our agent-from-a-big-TV-agency, laid a couple of our spec scripts on him and got a bite.

He was a young upstart at the agency, without much of a client list or established industry contacts, but if he hadn't been that, we probably would not have landed him. He never actually got us a job, but the agency name opened bigger doors and got phone calls returned, and here's the thing: At the top of this agency is someone who is plugged securely into the highest levels of the industry.

The agent may not be a "big dog," but the agency, itself, has clout. If the project is right, all of the agency's contacts become your young upstart's contacts, and that is invaluable to you. Once you start selling, your profile raises, and you begin to draw the attention of higher level agents within the company.

Danny and I applied a little creativity to secure this relationship. We worked a deal whereby the agent didn't have to sign us, right away. We just wanted to use the agency's name and profile to set up meetings. If a company called the agent to check us out, he would verify that we were his clients. When we got a job, then we'd sign contracts and give him his cut. It was pretty much of a no-risk situation for him, and it worked.

When Danny and I were hired onto the writing staff of a new ABC sitcom, "Baby Makes Five," this was the agent who represented us. He didn't find the job and he didn't secure the job. We did that. But, his name, or rather that of the agency, got us in the door. Once we landed the job, he signed us, as agreed, and of course, took his cut.

Agent number three was my "real" agent. I moved with him, over the years, through two major agencies and into his own independent agency. He sent me on meetings that produced work. He gave good advice, we clicked on a personal level, and he was good at his job.

I once had a producer I was working with say to me, *"Man, your agent is tough."* I replied, *"No offense, but that's because some of you guys can be assholes."* Fortunately, the producer to whom I made this comment had a sense of humor, and wasn't one of those aforementioned assholes. But, he was right. My agent could be tough. Better him than me.

You, the writer, certainly don't want to be portrayed as the bad guy in any negotiation. That is a role your agent fills, sometimes with gusto. Sadly for me, this agent burned out on the industry and moved on to greener, and no doubt less stressful pastures. He is my one example of having the right agent.

I say that not only because I got a lot of work through him, but because he understood my strengths, took my personality into account when he made his choices for meetings to send me on, and he genuinely liked my writing style.

He told me what was working; what was currently hot. He evaluated the scripts I gave him and determined their commercial viability, or lack of same. He told me what studios and producers were looking for, and he often made suggestions, but he never told me what to write. That's the kind of agent you want.

Agent number four was acquired through a recommendation from agent number three. He, too, was an independent. We didn't really gel, but never actually had the chance. I took a couple of meetings he set up, but by that time, I, too, had grown weary of the Hollywood grind, and my wife and I had made a lifestyle choice, partly for family reasons, to move to Colorado, where we had both lived in a previous life.

By this time, I had crossed that critical Hollywood line in the sand. I was now over forty, and though it may seem irrational, ageism is, indeed a factor for writers in Hollywood. The logic of that has always escaped me, but there it is.

At any rate, once agent number four discovered I was leaving town, he lost any interest he may have had and soon dropped me from his client list. At least, he had the courtesy to let me know that, up front.

Acquiring an agent from outside of Hollywood, especially if you have no track record, requires a lot of luck and determination. There are legitimate reasons why, but it mostly boils down to the fact that you're not there.

While sending spec screenplays to prospective employers or buyers is certainly part of an agent's job, it is only one part. They want to send you on meetings, because personality plays a part and personal contact is a big plus when you're trying to develop a relationship. My "good" agent frequently arranged "get to know you" meetings, with people whose needs might mesh with my style.

Agents also want to be able to shop you for assignments and rewrite opportunities. None of that can happen when you're a couple of thousand miles away, and Skype doesn't effectively fill the void.

It's understandable that an agent wouldn't want to take on a client with such limitations. It is possible to change their minds, though, and, you already know how, don't you? Yep. The right script. Bowl them over with the material, and all things are possible.

In Summary: Agents are a special breed and can be invaluable to you, if for no other reason than to release you from the burden of business requirements that you can't, and shouldn't have to deal with. It may be a profession that tends to be looked down upon, but it's a profession we in the industry rely on. They get bad-mouthed, because part of their job is to be the bad guys when they negotiate on your behalf. You want a bad guy in the room, hammering out your deal, and you want him to be good.

The Writers Guild of America

"The fact of the matter is that for many, many members of the Writers Guild, being on strike represented a career step up. They weren't unemployed [because] they could now say they were on strike." - Aaron Sorkin

There are two branches of the Writers Guild of America: the WGA East and the WGA West, with jurisdiction divided by the Mississippi River. They are separate entities with their own governing bodies, but of course, work in tandem on most issues, including strikes and collective bargaining.

The Screen Writers Guild was formulated in 1933, and a merging of groups representing writers on both coasts created the Writers Guild of America, East and West, in 1954. Their mission, as with any other labor organization, is to present a unified position of strength in bargaining with employers, in this case networks, studios and producers.

Similar to agents, the WGA has a long-standing love/hate relationship with its members, but there are two undeniable facts to consider: You want to join, and you have to join.

In the early days following my arrival in Hollywood, people were constantly asking me, *"Are you WGA?"* I figured it must be important, so I finally shrugged and said, *"Okay, I'll join."*

That's when I discovered the old WGA Catch 22. You can't just join, you have to qualify, and in order to qualify, you must sell something to a company which is signatory to the WGA's Minimum Basic Agreement.

What raises the level of difficulty is that producers and studios are reluctant to hire you, unless you're a WGA member, but you can't become a member until somebody hires you.

There's the old brick wall. That's why people kept asking me, *"Are you WGA?"* What they were really asking was, *"Are you real?"*

Here's how it works:

The value of each covered writing service; screenplay, story, rewrite, bible, staff position, etc. is broken down into units. In order to qualify for WGA membership, a writer must accumulate 24 units, which is equivalent to the minimum fee for the writing of a screenplay or teleplay of 90 minutes or longer. Those 24 units must be acquired over a period of three years prior to joining. That, plus a $2,500.00 initiation fee will get you in.

Once you have attained membership eligibility, you won't have to run to the Guild office and lobby for membership. They will kindly send you a letter, congratulating you on your success and telling you, in somewhat diplomatic terms, that if you don't join, you'll never work in this town, again.

I stated, earlier, that you *have* to join, but that isn't really true. No one can force you to join a union. Any signatory company is allowed to hire a writer who isn't yet a member of the WGA. *Once.* After that, a writer who doesn't join the union will no longer be allowed to work for any signatory company.

Technically, they aren't telling you that you can't write for such a company, they are telling the company that they can't hire you. That's the agreement the company signed with the Guild. Beyond that, though, odds are, if you aren't a WGA member, these companies don't want to hire you. They'd rather just play it safe.

Those employers are ever-guarded and timid in the decisions they make, because any wrong decision can get them axed in an instant. As a result, they are always seeking validation, particularly when it comes to who they are cutting big checks to. If you're in the WGA, you're a screenwriter. If you aren't, well, then, it's questionable. Just another second-act complication to overcome in a screenwriter's story.

There are some definite positive aspects to membership in the Writers Guild of America, East or West. They negotiate, on your behalf, with huge and powerful conglomerates, against which an individual writer would never stand a chance. In doing so, they acquire increases in wages, employer contributions to health insurance, a well-managed pension plan, clearly defined working conditions and those precious residuals.

Residuals, if you aren't familiar with them, are similar to royalties for a novelist, in that they represent payment for work done at an earlier date, but they differ in one major way. Novelists own the copyright for their work. Screenwriters do not.

When a screenwriter makes a sale, he signs over the copyright to his script to the purchaser, and no longer owns it. Residuals were negotiated by the Writers Guild in 1953 to establish payments to writers for the rebroadcasts of their work, initially on TV. The formula has been modified since, to include other forms of transmission.

In the case of the WGA, a writers residuals are calculated on a percentage of every sale by the employer of a produced work which was written by a credited WGA writer. So, if your movie goes to TV or cable, you get paid. If your TV episode reruns, you get paid. If your series episode sells in France, you get paid. How much you get paid is determined on a sliding scale, based on the number of airings and the media on which the project is aired.

This is a critical financial issue for screenwriters, who are often out of work for long stretches of time. A steady flow of residuals can substantially ease the pain, maybe even assure survival. Without them, a great number of writers would be unable to make a living.

Residuals are collected by the Writers Guild, which passes them along to the writer. The Guild will also represent writers in disputes with producers over pay or working conditions, and can match a company's battery of attorneys with its own.

Of course, if there are up-sides to membership in the WGA, there must be down-sides, and there certainly are. For one thing, the Writers Guild is not in the business of obtaining work for its members. No offers come through them or are negotiated by them. That's the responsibility of you and your agent and/or manager. The Guild will take its cut when you get paid, along with annual dues, but getting you jobs is not their function.

A Guild member is also restricted to working only for those companies who have signed on with the Writers Guild, i.e. signatories. Every major domestic entertainment entity has done so, along with many small, independent producers.

That proved to be a major hassle, I discovered, when making the move from Hollywood to Colorado and becoming involved in independent production. None of the companies who wanted to employ me or purchase my screenplays were signatory to the Writers Guild of America, West. That meant, if I wanted to deal with them, I had to guide them into and through the process of becoming signatory.

There is no cost attached to becoming signatory for the producers, but their financing sources and other details must be revealed, and they then become obligated to adhere to the requirements laid out in the Guild's Minimum Basic Agreement. That means pension and health contributions, determination of credits, working conditions and the rest. It can get sticky, for a WGA member working and living in the heartland.

The negative attached to that negative is the fee requirement. Independent producers don't have the resources of a Paramount or CBS, but a writer is not allowed to take less than the minimum wage determined by the WGA.

To its credit, the Guild has designed a couple of low-budget contracts which are sanctioned by it, and allow much more flexibility for the indie producer and the screenwriter. The details of this, found in the WGA Schedule of Minimums, and all other Guild functions are readily available on the WGA website at www.wga.org.

Another detriment to membership in the WGA is the constantly looming possibility of a strike. The writers strike of 2007-2008 was a rancorous one, and I had the somewhat dubious distinction of participating in an even more rancorous one in 1988, which turned out to be the longest strike in Guild history at five months. I walked picket lines and manned the informational "warm lines" at Guild headquarters.

What I didn't do was work, and to say that five months of that grew tedious would be an understatement, but where there are unions, there are strike possibilities. At least, when it happens, as Mr. Sorkin pointed out, it gives us an excuse for being out of work.

As a side note, I should mention the Writers Guild of Canada. I am also a member of this Guild, and I've never even been to Canada. One screenplay I wrote, a Showtime original family film titled "Escape from Wildcat Canyon," was produced by a Canadian company and filmed in Canada. Therefore, the WGC held jurisdiction.

It is not at all unusual for the two unions to cross paths in instances such as this. Officially, it requires a waiver from the Writers Guild of America, allowing one of their members to work under the auspices of the Writers Guild of Canada. In this case, and in most, I suspect, this was simply a formality. As a result, however, I was faced with the same issues which I faced when qualifying for WGA membership. I wrote a WGC covered project, and therefore was expected to join that union.

Now, I could have chosen to "skate" on that obligation, figuring the likelihood of ever doing another Canadian project was slim, so why join? I chose the other path and joined. Since then, the WGC has collected retransmission and other fees on my behalf from my Canadian produced project, which have easily surpassed the amount of dues I've paid them, over the years. A worthy investment, and the dual Guild membership doesn't look bad on a resume.

In Summary: Overall, the benefits of membership in the Writers Guild of America, West or East, far outweigh the disadvantages. It provides invaluable services, the result of decades of sweat and blood shed by those who came before us. It represents a major step in a screenwriters career, validates a writer to those who would employ her, and puts her among an elite, if somewhat eccentric crowd.

Producers

Producer's Son: "Hey, dad, can I have fifty dollars?"

Producer: "Forty dollars? What do you want with thirty dollars? I don't have twenty dollars!"

Here's a title that covers an awfully lot of ground. Producer credits are handed out like business cards in the entertainment industry, and that's a shame, because it doesn't do justice to those who really deserve it.

There are a number of sub-categories in the Producer job description, from Line Producer, which is totally legitimate, to Associate Producer, which is quite murky.

A true producer is an organizer, who juggles each and every aspect of a production, top-to-bottom. A producer may hire the director, participate in casting, coordinate with the studio and generally oversee the assembling of the entire crew, all while putting out fires on a daily basis. While every other job title in the production of a film or television show is unique unto itself, working within its own little realm of responsibility, the producer has to deal with them all. It takes a special kind of personality to do it well.

An Executive Producer has more narrowly defined responsibilities, generally doing his work behind the scenes, handling accounting and legal issues connected to the project. Often times, particularly in the independent film arena, the Executive Producer secures the financing that makes the dream a reality.

Line Producers, on the other hand, are on the set daily, overseeing the day-to-day functions of the shoot. The line producer is on board early in the game, with responsibilities which include below-the-line budget estimates for all crew positions, equipment rental, location costs and other expenses as they arise. It's a true hands-on position, and requires knowledge of every crew member's job.

The Associate Producer title is where it starts to get tricky. Since this is a title which is not regulated by the Producer's Guild, it is often handed out, sometimes in lieu of money, for some minor involvement in the film. Maybe a friend of the producer or director handled some minor function. Maybe the star's personal assistant ran a few errands during the shoot. Maybe, the director has a girlfriend who...well, you get the idea.

In Summary: Screenwriters and producers meet face-to-face quite often in the early phases of pre-production, and the producer is the entity to whom the screenwriter answers, until all rewrites, tweaks and punch-ups have been accomplished. When the script is deemed "finished," the writer will probably never hear from said producer again, unless they are teamed on another project.

Studio Executives

Question: How many studio executives does it take to screw in a light bulb?

Answer: No one knows. Light bulbs last longer than studio executives.

Primarily, I'm referring to Story Executives, because those are likely the only kind you'll encounter in any business proceedings. This is mostly a middle-man position, and the qualifications for holding it are widely diverse.

As I've mentioned, when a screenplay is accepted for consideration by a studio, it must run a gauntlet of executives before it reaches the top and is either accepted or passed on. This is the executive who starts that process.

The Story Executive is charged with the responsibility of finding material worthy of consideration and more-or-less vetting the writer to make sure he isn't:

a) difficult to work with

b) unable to handle the development process or

c) totally insane.

Once those pitfalls have been ruled out, the Story Executive will then become the screenwriter's proxy in all dealings with the studio, until such time as the screenplay has been purchased or rejected. She will also coordinate meetings, hash out some preliminary contract issues and exchange information with the writer's agent.

In Summary: Known within the entertainment community as "the suits," Studio Executives represent the corporate interests of the industry. Story Executives constitute the point at which the business and creative sides of a writer's journey must mesh. As the first level of the studio hierarchy for a writer, your relationship with these executives is a valued one.

Attorneys

"My daddy is a movie actor and sometimes he plays the good guy and sometimes he plays the lawyer." - Harrison Ford's son

Entertainment attorneys do pretty much what every attorney does: they handle legal and contract issues. They simply have their specific area of expertise, and it just happens to be in the field in which you want to work. While agents may negotiate the basics of a screenwriter's deal with a studio or producer, every agent will tell you that they do not delve into the minute financial issues of a contract. That's where Entertainment Attorney's come in.

In the Hollywood system, most of the legal details of a writers agreement are covered in standard, boiler-plate contracts, particularly if the writer is a member of the Writers Guild, where most of those details are predetermined. There may be cases, however, when a writer will need the services of a good Entertainment Attorney.

In such a case, it isn't wise to feel that any attorney will do. The entertainment industry has its own set of quirks, and only an attorney trained to read between the lines and decipher the lingo will be capable of interpreting the fine points of a contract.

This reflects back to my "you have to be there" creed. Hollywood is lousy with entertainment attorneys, but try finding one in Des Moines.

In Summary: It should be obvious, by now, that, to paraphrase, no screenwriter is an island in Hollywood. We are part of a very large, well-oiled machine, and must learn to mesh, in order to succeed.

CHAPTER 8

Form and Format

Form

A screenplay is no less unique in its makeup than any other form of literary expression. Just as there are structural constants which make a poem a poem, a novel a novel, a song a song or a play a play, there are certain components within the makeup of a screenplay that make it uniquely a screenplay. Yet, all of these forms have one shared goal:

To tell a story.

That means, there is a specific set of structural components which exist in all of them; the basic structure which makes a story a story.

That is the simplicity from which every nuanced philosophy on screenwriting has sprung and evolved, as motion pictures and their audiences have grown more sophisticated. Yet, the only hard and fast rules which exist in structuring a screenplay are the simple, basic rules of telling a story: Beginning, middle, end. Set-up, complications, climax.

We like to call that Act One, Act Two and Act Three. There are contemporary disagreements on the number of acts, and we'll get into that later, but at the heart of it, there are only three.

A certain acceptable length of time is allotted for each of those acts, and each act has a job to do; a mission to accomplish. That mission is different for each act, and therefore each act has its own specific needs in terms of storytelling tools. Combine those acts and we have a story, and the purpose of a story is to evoke emotion.

I'm going to repeat that last statement.

The purpose of a story is to evoke emotion.

Hold tightly to that thought. If you tell a story that makes your audience feel something; if you can move them, emotionally, you've succeeded. That's the bottom line.

I've encountered many perfectly formatted scripts, with all of the right elements in all the right places, the acts laid out nicely and the story tracking logically. It wasn't that they didn't make sense. The trouble was, I felt nothing from them.

I call these "left brain scripts." The writers understood the technical requirements of screenplay; the nuts and bolts of constructing a story, but the stories were flat and lifeless. We must make our audience feel something. Hopefully, something other than disgust.

The screenplay is, of course, a close evolutionary child of the stage play, which was already quite refined by the time moving pictures entered the scene. The earliest films were little more than plays performed in front of a camera, but nascent filmmakers were quick to utilize the portability of the camera to expand their horizons. This, even though the cameras weren't all that portable in the beginning. At any rate, at even a rudimentary level, they allowed the story to move in ways never before imagined, and the innovations triggered by that still come at an astonishing rate.

Where screenplay sets itself apart from other writing forms is in its reliance on visualization. While stage plays also employ visualization, they do so in a much more confined fashion. Actors and sets provide visuals, but plays rely primarily on dialogue to get the message across. The scope of film, with its unlimited possibilities for locations, dwarfs that of a stage play, where locations are basically implied, rather than literal.

In Summary: In films, seeing is believing, and therefore, physical action must drive the story. The "show, don't tell" axiom applies almost exclusively to film making. The rules which are unique to the screenwriting form are built around this one constant. Though dialogue is necessary, even critical, in order to take full advantage of the form, the visuals must carry the bulk of the load. Once you have found that ever-important emotional thread, you must present your story in the proper format, or it won't even be considered.

Format

As film making became more refined, so, too did the screenplays that fed the mill. They developed into a unique format, which is also still evolving, by the way, and which is distinctly distant from its stage-play lineage.

When I say "format," think "presentation," and that's what we're going to look at; the boring, left-brain details of how the words are arranged on the page.

In these wondrous days of screenwriting programs, a lot of formatting has become a mindless task, and that's a real blessing, particularly for a beginning screenwriter. Programs like Final Draft and Movie Magic do the lion's share of the formatting work for us, but they're also expensive, and my blue-collar mentality tells me that a lot of beginning writers out there might not be able to handle the cost, at least at the outset. That means, they will be relegated to a basic word processing program.

If you're in that boat, let me offer a couple of handy alternatives. A fiction writer named Richard Salsbury developed a little program called "Roughdraft," which includes a template for screenplay format, and he has posted it on his website: http://www.salsbury.f2s.com/ for anyone to download.

The program is donationware, which means you can get it and

never pay a dime, if you have no conscience or no money, but I strongly recommend that you kick a few dollars his way, if you can, to reward him for his generosity. The program is well worth it. It doesn't have the bells and whistles of the major screenwriting programs, but it packs a pretty good wallop, and provides an affordable option.

A more sophisticated, and quite popular program, Celtx (https://www.celtx.com/index.html) is freeware, and will work well for you. The freeware program is ad-supported, but fully functional. There is also a paid version available for $14.99, with no ads and a few more capabilities.

Another nice program, nominally priced at $40.00 is Scrivener, (http://www.literatureandlatte.com/) a multi-functional writing program with a nice screenwriting capability.

Understand that the current standards in Hollywood are Final Draft and Movie Magic. In these times of sending files of our screenplays over the internet, rather than printed hard copies, not all file formats will be acceptable. Most programs will create a PDF, which is pretty generic and generally accepted, but again, many entities are likely to ask for a Final Draft or Movie Magic file, at some point.

You should also bear in mind that a screenplay written in other programs may change in length, when transposed to Final Draft or Movie Magic. For instance, a screenplay written in a standard word processing program, in a Rich Text (.rtf) file, will come out shorter, by several pages, when converted by Final Draft.

Aside from the fact that the major screenwriting programs do much of the formatting for us, there are still some issues pertaining to the format of a screenplay which are not provided by these expensive programs, and should be examined and understood.

When I discuss the rules and choices available in writing a screenplay, and stress how flexible so many of these rules are, I'm referring to the development and writing of the story. The rules of format; what that story looks like on the page, are more rigid, and even the high-tech screenwriting programs can't keep you from screwing up, if you don't understand them.

That's not to say there isn't some flexibility here, as well. Read ten produced screenplays and you probably won't find two which are formatted exactly the same. Yet, the basic, etched-in-stone format elements are there, within each of them, properly used and clearly understood by the writer and understandable by the reader.

You may stylize the format to a minor extent to fit your personal style, but not to any great degree. Adhering to those formatting rules is important, because your screenplay format is the first thing the readers see; the first impression they have of your screenwriting ability. They're already judging you, at a glance. At this stage, it only has to pass one simple litmus test:

Does it look like a screenplay?

It may not sound like a major issue, on the surface, but it certainly can be, because, if it doesn't look like a screenplay, it may never be read. You've already shown them that you don't really "get it." You've entered a cake in a pie-baking contest. Why should they waste their time?

In Summary: Struggling with proper formatting is probably as much responsible for screenplays being abandoned as writer's block. Like learning to play a musical instrument, it requires practice; repetition, for it to become second nature.

Now, let's take a look at some specific formatting issues you will need to understand, beginning with:

The Title Page

While a finished screenplay, if there really is such a thing, begins with a TITLE PAGE, that's usually the last thing that I generate, after the script has been completed. However, it's going to be the first page a reader opens to, and therefore, the reader's first opportunity to determine whether the script that follows will be professionally formatted.

First, don't confuse the Title Page with the Cover Page. Cover pages are generated to protect the contents of the script, and while many of them bear some script information on them, they do not qualify as a Title Page, which is actually part of the script.

Some writers try to get "artsy" with their cover pages, with fancy bond paper, exotic fonts and sometimes graphics or eye-catching colors. Please, don't. It won't help your cause one whit. It only tells the reader he's dealing with a novice.

The Title Page only requires a limited amount of information, but there are some minor variations on what that information can be.

First on the Title Page comes the name of the script. That should appear about one-third of the way down the page.

Double-spaced and centered below the title come the authorship credits. In this arena, a script is broken down into two basic categories: story credit and writing credit, as defined by the Writers Guild of America.

Credits

The story credit will appear first, if it is warranted, and it is only warranted if the story credit is assigned to someone other that the writer who actually writes the script.

Therefore, "Written by" will indicate that the writer credited with penning the screenplay is also solely responsible for creating the story. In that case, no separate story credit will appear.

Following is a list of defined screenwriting credits:

A SCREENPLAY

Written by I.M. Writer

("Written By" indicates that the writer is credited with creating the STORY and writing the SCREENPLAY)

***

OUR SCREENPLAY

Written by:

I.M. Writer & Sammy Scribe

(An ampersand, "&" indicates that the STORY and SCREENPLAY were written by a WRITING TEAM.)

***

OUR SCREENPLAY

Written by:

I.M. Writer and Sammy Scribe

("and" indicates that the STORY and SCREENPLAY were written by INDIVIDUAL WRITERS, working independently. This generally indicates that one writer was re-written by another writer, and each attained equal credit.)

***

The "Screenplay by" credit replaces the "Written by" credit when another entity is responsible, or partly responsible for creating the story, as in:

YOUR SCREENPLAY

Story by I.M. Writer

Screenplay by Sammy Scribe

(SEPARATED CREDITS indicate that one writer developed the story, and another writer wrote the screenplay. Generally, this suggests that the writer of the screenplay was ASSIGNED to the story, as a work-for-hire.)

***

THE SCREENPLAY

Screen Story by M. Goode Writer

(This tells us that the screenplay was written based on another source, but is substantially different from the source material.)

***

BEST SCREENPLAY

Screenplay by M. Goode Writer

Narration Written by Sammy Scribe

(The "Narration Written by" credit, rarely seen, refers to a writer whose major contribution to the story consists of narration, alone. The WGA terms "narration" as material, typically off-camera, to explain or relate sequence or action (excluding promos or trailers.)

***

NEW SCREENPLAY

Adaptation by S.P. Writer

(This is an odd duck, where writing credits are concerned. It means that the writer didn't construct the screenplay in a manner to substantially differentiate it from the source material, and therefore could not qualify for a "Screenplay By" credit. The Adaptation credit can only come as a result of arbitration.)

***

SOME SCREENPLAY

Screenplay by Leary Writer

Based on Characters Created by Joy Writer

(This can reference a couple of situations. The first is when a writer is entitled to separated rights for a movie or television sequel, separated rights being the writer's individual rights to the creation of a story, on which a sequel is based.

The second accepted use of this credit comes when the story is based on source material, and the screenwriter has not substantially altered the story on which the screenplay is based. In this case, the author of the source material will receive a "Based on Characters Created by" credit.)

That's pretty much it, as far as WGA sanctioned credits are concerned. I say "pretty much," because there is an option to lobby the Guild for a waiver to include other forms of credit. Such waivers are not often handed out.

If the story you're telling is inspired by an outside source, like a song, poem or true life experience which you, hopefully, have the right to exploit, it's fine to indicate that below the credits, i.e., "Inspired by the song "Anything Goes," by Cole Porter" or "Based on a true story."

As noted, however, these are not writing credits, in Hollywood screenwriting terms. They are an indication of source material which is either in public domain or has been acquired through legal channels by the writer of the screenplay.

For more details on screenwriting credits, check out the Screen Credits Manual on the WGAw website (http://www.wga.org/). The Credits Manual is a free PDF download.

Contact Information

Now, on our Title Page, we drop down to the bottom of the page. At the bottom left, it is common practice to place your contact information, which can consist of any or all of the following:

Name, address, phone number and e-mail address.

Be aware that if your screenplay is going to be shopped by an agent, the agency will not want your contact information on the title page. The contact is the agency, and everyone will know it. In fact, if they're sending out hard copies, they will probably put a cover page on the script that bears the logo of the agency.

If you are personally sending out your screenplay to prospective buyers or agents, your contact info is a must. Screenplays drift around out there in the industry ozones all the time, passed from one hand to another. It isn't unusual for a script to wind up in the hands of someone who is far-removed from the person you actually sent it to. If they read it and like it, you certainly want them to know how to reach you.

Registration/Copyright

Below the contact info, still at the bottom left of the title page, comes this important little bit of info:

Registered, WGAw

Because, you are going to register your script with the Writers Guild registration service, aren't you?

Now, you may prefer to copyright your script, and that's fine. But, my suggestion is to do it along with a WGA registration, and not instead of. The Writers Guild Registration Service has become the most commonly accepted form of protection for screenplays, and everyone in the industry really likes to see it on the title page, before they consider reading. It's a bargain at $20.00 for non-members and $10.00 for members, and the entire process can be done in no time online at the WGA Registry (http://www.wgawregistry.org/webrss/).

Some authors also like to put the registration number right on the page:

REGISTERED, WGAw #XXXXXXX.

For me, that's overkill. Just knowing the script is registered should be enough. I seriously doubt anyone is going to check, just because they have the number. If you prefer to include the registration number, go right ahead. There's no particular taboo attached to it.

Should you prefer to copyright along with, or instead of acquiring a WGA registration, then your standard copyright info should be placed in the same location as the registration info.

Now, we zip over to the right side of the page, across from your Registered, WGAw notice. Here, we write:

FIRST DRAFT

This is a cute little fact of screenwriting life. Let's say, you send out your first draft and someone gives you rewrite notes. So, you do a rewrite. Does that mean you should put SECOND DRAFT on your cover page? Absolutely NOT! It may be a second draft to you, but when you send it back out, it's going to be, guess what?

FIRST DRAFT

It doesn't matter how many times you've gone back through the script and made changes. As far as the marketplace is concerned, it's a first draft. After someone buys it for production, the subsequent rewrites will then be numbered, First, Second, Third or Twenty-Seventh Draft. But, when you're shopping it, it's always FIRST DRAFT.

And, that's it. That's the title page. The only exception comes, as mentioned previously, when an additional notation crediting source material, i.e., "From the Novel," "Based on the song," "Inspired by a true incident," etc. is appropriate. That notation can appear anywhere between the writing credits and the bottom of the page.

When completed, your title page should look like the following example:

Title Page Example

My Screenplay

Story by Sammy Scribe and I.M. Writer

Screenplay by Sammy Scribe

Based on a true story

Address
Phone Number
Email

Registered, WGAw   FIRST DRAFT

Page One

With our title page set, we now, turn to page 1 of your screenplay. The title appears, again, at the top of the page, then a few spaces down (how many is pretty much optional, from my research) left-justified, in CAPS are the words:

FADE IN:

Always. No exceptions.

It's like starting a fairy tale with "Once upon a time." There are some screenwriting programs which place the FADE IN: on the right side of the page, and that's acceptable, but I favor the old fashioned method: left-justified.

The Scene Heading

You're now ready for your opening scene. That requires a SCENE HEADING, which contains three, occasionally four vital bits of information; usually there will only be three, which will tell the reader, at a glance:

- Are we inside or outside?
- Where, exactly, are we?
- Is it day or night?

This information is important for every reader of your script, at every level of production. It isn't there simply to inform the industry reader who is judging your script for a possible sale. Once a sale has, God willing, been made, this information will become the outline in the breakdown of your screenplay for principal production.

The director uses the scene headings in making up his shot list and shooting schedule. The lighting department needs to know how many day scenes and how many night scenes are in the script. The location manager needs to know which locations to look for. Producers and production coordinators use the information to determine the number of shooting days and cost.

Everybody counts on the scene headings. And, they are simple, which is why I'm constantly puzzled by writers who use them incorrectly, and I see it a lot.

So, let's answer those three initial questions. Are we inside or outside? That gives us the first element in our scene heading. It's either INT. for "interior" or EXT. for "exterior." Can't get much more basic than that.

Next, where are we, exactly?

The specific scene location is what we're looking for, here. Keep it brief and to the point. Don't tell them more than they need to know. It's INT. COUNTRY BAR, for instance, not INT. COUNTRY BAR IN A REMOTE SUBURB ON THE OUTSKIRTS OF DALLAS, TEXAS.

That added information may be relevant to the story, but the Scene Heading is not the place to put it. If it is a new location, requiring some specific descriptive detail, put that information into the ACTION BLOCK that follows the SCENE HEADING, rather than the scene heading, itself.

Once the COUNTRY BAR location has been chosen, or possibly built on a sound stage, the darn thing can be on the moon, for all they care. They may actually shoot this COUNTRY BAR IN A REMOTE SUBURB ON THE OUTSKIRTS OF DALLAS, TEXAS in a warehouse in Detroit.

Just the facts, ma'am. COUNTRY BAR should suffice.

In the case of generic locations, such as CITY STREET or SUBURBAN NEIGHBORHOOD, again, put the detailed description into the action block that follows, but make sure you differentiate between like generic locations.

You may have two or three different city street locations, so they can't all be called CITY STREET. You must give each location a label that distinguishes it from all the others, otherwise, it's going to confuse your reader.

DOWNTOWN CITY STREET can be one city street location,

while DECAYING CITY STREET might be another and BUSTLING CITY STREET yet another.

The last bit of info in your SCENE HEADING is one that I see most often abused.

Is it day or night?

That's it, my friends. Day or night? Not dawn, not dusk, not early evening, not the wee hours of the morning, not high-noon. As far as your SCENE HEADING is concerned, it's either DAY or NIGHT, period. So, your country bar scene should read like this:

INT. COUNTRY BAR – NIGHT

or

EXT. COUNTRY BAR – DAY

The detailed description of the time of day, if it's appropriate, can be included in the ACTION BLOCK that follows, i.e.:

INT. COUNTRY BAR – DAY

The reddish haze of an approaching sunset streams through the windows.

The "approaching sunset" tells us that it's dusk, and that adjustment can then be made, if it's appropriate, but if it isn't dark yet, it's still "day."

At the beginning of this subject, I mentioned three or four types of information for your scene headings. The majority of the time, you will only need the three I've just noted, but occasionally, one of three relevant bits of information is required. The first of those is ESTABLISHING.

If this is a shot designed to establish a location where the action takes place, and that's all it's designed to do, then you've created an ESTABLISHING SHOT.

In a screenplay, every Scene Heading denotes a scene. A quick, establishing shot of a building before cutting to the action inside that building is still a scene.

We've all seen establishing shots for ages, and they provide a wonderful tool for introducing a location. They also "trick" our brains into accepting the location that follows.

For instance, if we see a simple stock-shot of the Empire State Building, then cut to an office scene, we're going to assume that this is an office in the Empire State Building. More likely, it's a set on a sound stage, or in some other office building, altogether. Or, maybe in that warehouse in Detroit.

A more important distinction occurs on the technical side of the process, when a screenplay destined for production is broken down, piece by piece, by those who will turn that screenplay into a film. Every location must be accounted for, even a two-second establishing shot.

Any change of locations is a new scene. The only variation to this that I know of is a change of locations within a montage, which doesn't have to, and doesn't often employ scene headings, although it can. We'll cover the montage structure later in this section.

Let's assume that we're cutting to a scene which will take place inside our COUNTRY BAR IN A REMOTE SUBURB ON THE OUTSKIRTS OF DALLAS, TEXAS. We've not yet been to this location in the story, so we want to establish where this little country bar is, before we go inside. Our scene heading will look something like this:

EXT. COUNTRY BAR - NIGHT – ESTABLISHING

A run-down tavern in a remote suburb, on the outskirts of Dallas, Texas.

(Then, we'll cut to:)

INT. COUNTRY BAR – NIGHT

It's a shabby little place; old, with creaky wooden floors, a couple of booths and a few tables. Dimly lit, and that's a blessing. You can almost smell the stale beer and cigarette smoke...etc.

You only need to use ESTABLISHING in your scene heading the

first time we see the location. If we cut back to the EXT. COUNTRY BAR location at a later time, there is no longer a reason to establish it. Since we've been here before, we already know where we are.

Another element which may appear in your SCENE HEADING pertains to movement, usually from within a vehicle. That element is described as either MOVING or TRAVELING. So, if we're in a squad car, being driven to the police station, the heading might read:

INT. SQUAD CAR - DAY – TRAVELING

Again, this is an important piece of information when determining the requirements of physical production.

Some writers also add CONTINUOUS to this short list of SCENE HEADING elements. Let's say, two characters are having a conversation as their car pulls into the driveway of a house. They get out of the car, still talking, and we CUT TO a new scene inside the house, while the dialogue goes uninterrupted. This can also apply when characters move from one room to another. You might, then, want to indicate that by writing:

INT. HOUSE - DAY – CONTINUOUS

It's an approach I don't personally favor, because I feel like the action should tell us when dialogue is continuous, and it shouldn't need to be pointed out. Some feel that using CONTINUOUS can add clarity to the tracking of the sequence, and since it won't scare away any industry readers, I leave it as a matter of personal choice.

The order of the informational elements in a SCENE HEADING are pretty much a lock, as well. That means, HOUSE - DAY - INT. or DAY - INT. - HOUSE or any variation of INT. HOUSE - DAY can get you in trouble, just like grammar or spelling errors on your resume.

The Action Block

Okay, we've decided on our location and time of day. The SCENE HEADING is written. Now, we drop two lines below the scene heading and begin our ACTION BLOCK. This describes what we're seeing on the screen. The action within this ACTION BLOCK is always written in present tense. *Always.*

This is a particularly tough one for novelists to deal with, when they decide to turn their great American novel into a screenplay. It's a hard habit to break, changing your mind set from "John handed the gun to Kyle" to "John hands the gun to Kyle," but there's no wiggle room on this one. It has to be done.

Remember, we're the audience, watching the action unfold on the screen. We're seeing it as it happens, and therefore it must be written as it happens. All writers can get past this little hiccup with practice. Just don't let a script with action written in past tense go out into the market. It's instant death.

Another common foible in writing action is the tendency to tell the reader things we aren't going to see or hear on the screen. This is another novel writer's handicap, but it isn't restricted to those poor souls. A lot of beginning screenwriters do it.

If you're going to tell me, as a reader, that "Charlie grew up in Chicago, an abused child of alcoholic parents, and as a result, he trusts no one," well, then, you'd darn well better find a way for me to see or hear that information somewhere in the story.

It's nice, informative info for the reader, but it won't do much for the audience, who isn't privy to it. They'll just scratch their heads, wondering why it is that Charlie doesn't trust anyone.

Keep it Concise

One of the most common issues I run across, when reading scripts from new writers, is the length of the Action Blocks. There is block after block of description; blocks nine, ten, twelve lines long, often followed by another Action Block just as long. My God, it's like reading a novel!

That's not the experience your readers are looking for, from a screenplay. Your Action Blocks should be brief; succinct and yet colorful and clearly descriptive. No problem, right? It's a challenge, but one we must meet, if we expect to compete with seasoned masters of the craft.

One good "cheat" when you have a lot of description that needs to take up some space is to break a long Action Block into two or more short ones. Find a logical place for the break, like an implied shot change from one character to another, or one object to another, and break the big block into little blocks.

That's only an occasional option, however. As previously stated, in general, keep the Action Blocks brief, moving and interesting to read. Otherwise, your reader's eyes will glaze over.

After attending a script-reading workshop presented by the Writers Guild some years ago, one producer actually remarked that when he read a script, he only read the dialogue, and glossed over the action blocks. Imagine if the story had relied on numerous long action blocks to make its point! This guy would have read the script in about fifteen minutes!

As previously noted, professional script readers make instant judgments based on an "at a glance" evaluation. Incorrect formatting and sloppy spelling or grammar mistakes can kill an opportunity to have a script read.

This same evaluation technique applies to Action Blocks. In this case, what they're looking for is "white space" on the page. Lengthy, overbearing Action Blocks limit white space, revealing what will likely be a cumbersome and detailed read, and therefore a story pace which drags.

DON'T SHOUT!

Another bad habit I see in action blocks is the tendency to capitalize a lot of words. I'm intimately familiar with this faux pas, because I was guilty of it, myself, in my early writing.

It's okay to put a key word in the action block in caps, in some instances. There are times when emphasis is needed. A lot of readers do skim the action blocks, especially long ones, and may miss an important bit of information.

So, let's say you have action like this:

Kyle and Detective Morgan slip into the apartment and scan the room. Detective Morgan sifts through some papers on a desk. Junk mail, bills, a local newspaper and some flyers. Something on the floor catches Kyle's eye. It's a BUSINESS CARD. Unseen by Detective Morgan, Kyle quickly picks up the card and stuffs it into his pocket.

There's the block. In this instance, the business card is an important clue, and the fact that Kyle doesn't let the Detective see him take it is significant.

If the reader misses that little item in the action block, it can be create confusion, so we put it in caps, to draw attention to it. But, like a lot of writers I see today, I went "cap-crazy," so an action block like the one above would come out looking like this:

Kyle and Detective Morgan SLIP into the APARTMENT and SCAN the room. Detective Morgan SIFTS through some PAPERS on a DESK. JUNK MAIL, BILLS, a local NEWPAPER and some FLYERS. Something on the floor CATCHES KYLE'S EYE. It's a BUSINESS CARD. UNSEEN by Detective Morgan, Kyle quickly PICKS UP the card and STUFFS it into his pocket.

You can tell at a glance that it's overkill. Not only that, but the business card, the thing we're most concerned about being overlooked, is now lost in the shuffle of towering letters.

The first real indication I had that this was a problem came from a director, who asked me why I capitalized so much. *"It feels like you're shouting at me,"* was his complaint, and I realized it was a valid one. Now, I exercise more restraint in the CAPS department.

Keep Them on the Hook

As if these demands don't create enough challenges to writing good action blocks, there is one major requirement remaining.

They must be entertaining.

This is where a writer's personal style comes into play, but here's a short list of suggestions to help you accomplish this:

1. Use active verbs as much as possible. For instance, your character shouldn't always just ENTER a scene. Give it some color, where you can. He bursts in, charges in, strides in, sweeps in, parachutes in, or what ever the hell you can think of to create interesting action. Also, make certain that you write in present-tense, i.e., gives, not gave, walks, not walked, sees, not saw, etc.

2. Keep your sentences brief and descriptive. You're aiming for a fast read through these blocks of action, so don't bog them down with a lot of tedious detail, and don't repeat information we've heard before. I see a lot of redundant description in scripts I read, as though the writer is afraid we won't get it in a single pass.

3. Make your physical descriptions conceptual, to create a tone and a relatable visual image. So, rather than:

It's a large, three-story southern-style mansion in disrepair, with peeling paint and decaying walls.

Instead, it's "every spooky house you've ever seen in a horror movie."

And, if Joe is a "tall, handsome man, mid-thirties, physically fit and clean cut."

Rather, you might write, "He looks like the college quarterback, ten years later."

It's a matter of developing a descriptive, visual style.

4. Be specific. It's not a car, it's a Chevy. It's not an automatic rifle, it's an AK-47. She's not eating breakfast, she's eating oatmeal and toast. It not only creates a clear visual, but these specific choices add little nuances to your character. Oatmeal and toast says something significantly different about a character than does a jelly donut.

5. Create action where it doesn't exist. If you have a scene with two characters delivering dialogue, avoid making it "talking heads" by giving the characters some action to perform.

The common term for this is "business," and it simply means having your characters do something while they interact. Usually, when we create business for a character, it's unrelated to the forward movement of the plot. The story doesn't need it, necessarily, but it can certainly benefit the development of a character. Here's an example:

In the movie "A Few Good Men," there is a scene, early on, where Demi Moore's Joanne confronts Tom Cruise's Danny Kaffee over a legal issue, all while Danny participates in softball practice. The action is relevant to the character, but not necessarily to the plot.

This scene could easily have taken place in Danny's or Joanne's office, and the story wouldn't have suffered. However, the visual experience would have. The business created for the characters at softball practice gave us interesting action to look at; another dimension of our lead character, while the on-story dialogue was being delivered.

In Summary: Beyond these little shortcuts to good scene description, it still comes back to personal style. Perhaps, you have a well-defined style, going in, but if not, reading screenplays and seeing how other successful writers do it is a terrific education, and will help you find your voice. You may want to borrow a stylistic choice here-and-there, or the experience might just open your eyes to a new approach of your own. More than anything, it should be comfortable to you, and your words should flow naturally; rhythmically onto the page.

The Dialogue Block

Once we've mastered the intricacies of the Action Block, we're faced with the Dialogue Block. Since there is a section of this book devoted to dialogue, I won't go into the details of how to approach writing it, just what it looks like on the page.

The formatting requirements of the Dialogue Block are basic, yet again, it's an area I see frequently abused. Final Draft, the industry's current standard for screenwriting programs, allots 35 spaces to a line of dialogue. Anywhere within a space or two of that will work fine, but what I often see in scripts written on basic word processing programs are lines of dialogue stretched out far beyond those margins.

It's an obvious formatting flaw, and it tells a reader two things: you don't understand formatting and your script is probably significantly longer than your page count indicates.

The Character Heading

Before dialogue can be spoken, we must have a Character Heading; the name of the character who is speaking. This is centered on the page, in capital letters.

There are a couple of elements which can follow the character's name in the heading, in parenthesis, and they both are indicators of the location from which the speaker is delivering his dialogue. One of these is (O.C.) which indicates the character speaks from Off Camera. A substitute for (O.C.) is (O.S.), meaning Off Screen, also acceptable.

(V.O.) indicates Voice Over narrative; a character speaking from outside of the scene.

Character Direction

Directly below the Character Heading, in parenthesis, comes CHARACTER DIRECTION, if there is any.

This is another often misused element. It's an area where the less-is-more approach really applies. If you don't absolutely have to write in character direction, don't. Part of our job is to create characters with personality traits and characteristics which will allow an actor and director to interpret a speech with the right attitude and inflection. The bulk of the time, we should know if Mary is angry, without having to write:

>MARY
>(angry)
>How could you say that?

If you've written your action blocks with clarity and developed your character thoroughly, it just shouldn't be necessary to add a character direction to indicate a simple direction like that. If Mary is angry when she delivers the line, we should already know it.

The second common mistake in character direction is a tendency for some writers to write action that belongs in the Action Block into Character Direction, instead. It winds up looking like this:

>JOHN
>(Goes to the front door,
>then goes back to couch
>and sits)

Even though it's action specific to that particular character, this kind of stuff still doesn't go into Character Direction. That's Action Block material.

The rule for deciding just what does qualify as necessary Character Direction is about as basic as any can be.

Does it clarify?

If the reader, actor and director don't have this direction as a guide, will it confuse them? Can the intent of the line be misinterpreted? Most of the time, you'll find that the character direction doesn't need to be there.

Sometimes, it's necessary to insert an action within a character's speech. Again, most of the time, this is Action Block material.

You'll just need to break up the speech. So, rather than this:

          JOHN
I knew you were going to come.
          (he turns his back on
          her, walks to the counter
          and sits down on a stool)
You can come in, if you want to.

It will appear like this:

          JOHN
I knew you were going to come.

He turns his back on her, walks to the counter and sits down on a stool.

          JOHN (cont'd)
You can come in, if you want to.

The benefit of limiting character direction is two-fold. First, it saves valuable space, and second, less character direction enhances the flow of the dialogue.

You want to develop a rhythm to each character's speech pattern, and reading a flat, literal direction, especially in the middle of a speech, detracts from that. Not to any critical degree, maybe, but small details add up.

Dialogue

Centered below the Character Direction, should that be required, comes the Dialogue. The same rule which applies to large, cumbersome action blocks applies here. Short and sweet, with few exceptions.

Any time you employ a long-winded speech, it should be significant; a character's moment to shine; a Shakespearean soliloquy.

In courtroom dramas, the trial summation is an ideal example of a story beat which almost demands a long speech. Jimmy Stewart, filibustering on the floor of the senate in "Mr. Smith Goes to

Washington" deserved a long speech.

We got a beauty from George C. Scott, right at the top of "Patton," and Jack Nicholson's "You can't handle the truth" speech is another great example. The entire outcome of the story hinged on that one speech.

It's not a matter of do-or-don't, it's a matter of when-and-where. If you have a script loaded with long speeches, however, that's trouble.

If a specific character has two speeches, separated by action, it's acceptable to put a (cont'd) following the character's name in the next Character Heading.

This is a format choice I prefer to forgo, in most cases. I figure if JOHN has two speeches in a row, then JOHN is clearly indicated as the guy speaking both times, so it's understood that he's continuing, right?

I think, a reader can figure that out without being told. But, that's my little quirk. If it feels better to you to add a (cont'd), by all means, do so, as I did in the example above.

Slightly off-topic, but the same applies to placing a (CONTINUED) at the bottom of a page and/or the top of the page that follows. It's an option in most screenwriting programs, and one that I see little point to.

If I'm reading page 10, and the next page is page 11, that's pretty much continued already, any way you look at it. But, again, it's an option, and acceptable if you choose to use it.

Transitions

Transitions are the tools we use to get us from one place to another in our story.

There are two types of transitions: those which occur between scenes and those which occur within scenes. We'll start with an old, reliable one which has, in recent years, fallen from grace.

CUT TO

Previously, correct format was to place a CUT TO transition between most scenes, unless what I term "dramatic intent" was warranted. In other words, if the transition was a simple cut from one scene to the next, CUT TO was always employed. All it did, basically, was tell the reader when a scene was over and the location was changing, like this:

EXT. HOSPITAL - DAY – ESTABLISHING

                                        CUT TO:

INT. HOSPITAL – DAY

The thinking nowadays is that these simple cuts are not needed. If we write:

EXT. HOSPITAL - DAY – ESTABLISHING

INT. HOSPITAL – DAY

The cut is implied, isn't it? So, why write it? Eliminating it removes clutter and saves space; the very reasons I favor getting rid of (CONTINUED) at the bottom of the page and eliminating extraneous character direction.

Personally, I'm reluctant to give up my CUT TO transition, probably just because I've just grown used to it, over the years. I like the way it reads, with the cuts in it. But, the logic of removing it is undeniable.

The trend toward this came to my attention a couple of years ago, when a writing student was given a note after submitting a script to a contest. The reader downgraded the writer's score for the inclusion of CUT TO's in the script formatting.

To this reader, it was just flat wrong. I wanted to see the evidence of that, so I jumped on the internet and cruised over to Drew's Script-O-Rama and downloaded some screenplays, all written by industry pros, all produced.

What I discovered was a pretty even split. About the same number used CUT TO's between scenes as those who didn't.

But, I discovered another category, as well, and this category served as a consolation to my concerns over the loss of the CUT TO scene transitions.

This formatting category consists of eliminating CUT TO's, but retaining some of the specialized scene transitions, like DISSOLVE TO and MATCH CUT. This is the formatting choice I prefer and use.

This is an important distinction, because specialized transitions like these have a dramatic intent. They aren't simple cuts, but are designed to evoke emotion. Take a look at a few, and you'll see what I mean.

DISSOLVE TO

This one is used frequently. Almost every script has at least one. A slow dissolve creates a much different tone than a simple, quick cut. Its intent is to take us gently out of one scene and ease us into the next, and it usually comes out of a subdued, dramatic moment, where a quick cut would be too abrupt.

SMASH CUT

Just the opposite in tone to a DISSOLVE, a SMASH CUT's job is to startle us. It's an in-your-face moment that rocks us back on our heels; an assault on our senses.

A sudden explosion is a popular choice, or dropping into the middle of high-intensity action, like a race car blasting toward us, a group of motorcycles barreling down the highway, police sirens and flashing lights, a screaming train whistle, anything that's splashy and loud.

MATCH CUT

Also used a lot, the MATCH CUT is a handy little device that provides a nice, seamless transition, using irony to connect two radically different settings.

For example, let's say a character is in his game room, playing with his model train set, and we zoom in on the toy train engine as it circles the track. Then, we MATCH CUT to a real train, chugging down a real track. It's good imagery and creates a seamless segue.

It should be noted that there are actually two kinds of MATCH CUTs, the visual and the audio.

Sometimes, it isn't the images that match, between scenes, but the sounds. There's a beauty of an audio MATCH CUT in "A Few Good Men." Lt Col Markinson is about to commit suicide. He sticks a pistol in his mouth, and as he pulls the trigger, we MATCH CUT to the courtroom location, just as a clap of thunder from a storm outside rocks the room, reflecting the gunshot. The gunshot matched with the thunder clap created a stirring transition.

INTERCUT

This is a handy little transition that cures a couple of ills. It allows you to cut back-and-forth between two or more locations without having to constantly re-establish the locations with new scene headings.

The INTERCUT, also known as a CROSSCUT, does this with a minimum of hassle. I find it particularly useful when writing a phone call, wherein I want to see both parties during the call. Once you've established both locations, an INTERCUT can do the rest. It goes like this:

INT. JOHN'S APARTMENT – NIGHT

John picks up his phone and punches in a number.

INT. JAN'S HOUSE – NIGHT

The phone rings, and Jan picks up.

>   JAN
>   Hello?

INTERCUT: Phone call between John's apartment and Jan's house.

>   JOHN
>   Hi, Jan. It's me, John.
>
>   JAN
>   Hi, John. How nice to hear from you.

And, so on. Once you've established the two locations, you can carry on this phone call for as long as you like, without the need to constantly write scene headings for the same two locations. As long as we stay in the locations we've set up, the INTERCUT does the rest.

(Flip To)

No doubt, you've noticed the parens around the heading. That's because I'm fudging a bit on this one. This transition isn't in use any more, and hasn't been for years, at least, not in a literal sense, meaning you won't actually write it, but you do need to understand it.

The last remnants of the FLIP TO probably appeared in some films and TV shows of the early 60's. Yet, it still exists, in unspoken terms.

The FLIP TO is an ironic reversal from one scene into the next. It was designed to accommodate comedies, primarily, and while we never see a literal FLIP TO typed on any script page, it is still in use, and it still works.

Let's propose that our two characters, Mike and Steve, need desperately to get into some place where only women are allowed. Mike offers up a plan: they'll dress up like women and sneak in.

Steve is horrified, and vehemently objects.

INT. STEVE'S HOUSE – DAY

Steve looks at Mike in horror.

> STEVE
> Dress like a woman? No way! Not gonna happen! Forget it!

FLIP TO:

INT. STEVE'S HOUSE – DAY

An hour later, Steve stands in front of a full-length mirror in a slinky, black evening gown, admiring himself.

> STEVE
> Does this dress make me look fat?

There you have it. The FLIP transition delivers the ironic punch line.

As I've emphasized, you won't write it. It will be treated like a plain, old, CUT TO transition, but unspoken, unwritten or not, it is a valid transition.

WIPE TO

Another type of transition you may see in a film, which is never written in a screenplay is the WIPE. We've all seen it. The picture is wiped from the screen, usually, but not necessarily, in a horizontal direction, and as one scene wipes off, the next scene wipes on.

That's purely a director and/or editor's choice, not a screenwriters, so just, you know, forget I mentioned it.

These are the transitions within a screenplay that we use to separate scenes.

Just as important to understand are those which are employed within a scene: Internal scene transitions.

Internal Transitions

Transitions which occur within a scene are FLASHBACK, MONTAGE, SERIES OF SHOTS, DREAM SEQUENCE and INSERT.

Flashback

FLASHBACK is pretty self-explanatory. We're going into a new scene-within-a-scene to give us backstory information. At the end of our Flashback, we may return to the original real-time scene during which the Flashback occurred, or it can serve to transition us into a new scene.

There are a number of logical reasons to use a Flashback. It allows us to go back in time as far as we want to, without having to account for all of the time that passed between then and now.

It can be a tool to enhance mystery around a character, taking us deep into the story before we reveal the source of the character's motivation through a flashback.

In any case, the Flashback requires its own motivation. Since it most often occurs within a character's mind, it must be triggered by a real-time story event which justifies traveling back in time.

Haphazardly jumping from real-time to Flashback without the proper segue creates a disjointed effect, which will detract from the rhythm of the story's tracking.

At the end of our Flashback, common, acceptable "out" transitions are OUT OF FLASHBACK, END OF FLASHBACK, END FLASHBACK or BACK TO SCENE. They all work just fine.

As previously pointed out, a Flashback is actually used to provide setup information. It reveals motivation for a character's actions in the real-time story, or it delivers exposition to clarify a real-time story point.

Montage

In the case of MONTAGE, we have pretty much the same in-and-out structure used in our Flashback. We come in with MONTAGE and go out with OUT OF MONTAGE. The options for the "out" transition cited above for Flashbacks also work here.

The structure of the Montage, itself, is one of the more flexible format rules available to us. It's one I've seen written in several different ways, and most all of them work. The key will be clarity. Will they get it, or be confused by it?

The shots in the Montage will not be treated like actual scenes, as written. In other words, every shot will not require its own scene heading, though some writers choose to use them. It's perfectly acceptable to present them in this manner:

MONTAGE:

a) John and Mary frolic in a FIELD of flowers.

b) John and Mary frolic at the BEACH.

c) In a public PARK, John and Mary frolic with the kids on the playground.

You can see how the actual locations of the shots are in caps. It's only one shot, in a field, at a beach or at a park, and they can be anywhere. There won't be any dialogue, unless it's extraneous background, so it doesn't require the kind of physical setup as a regular scene, and often is filmed by a second unit camera crew.

As mentioned, some writers prefer to be more specific, and use scene headings for each shot, like so:

a) EXT. FIELD – DAY
John and Mary frolic among the flowers.

b) EXT. BEACH – DAY
John and Mary frolic in the surf.

c) EXT. PARK – DAY
John and Mary frolic with kids on a playground.

A little more rigid, but also fine. Some writers also prefer to use numbers rather than letters to label the shots. The result is 1) instead of a), on down the line.

Also acceptable is the double-dash preface; a simple -- in front of the action, rather than 1) or a).

Any of those, or combination of those will fly. You may even tweak the format for yourself. As long as the information and location are clear, you have nothing to fear.

Series of Shots

There is some confusion, among beginning writers, regarding the difference between a MONTAGE and a SERIES OF SHOTS. The distinction is actually clear and simple. A MONTAGE is a sequence of shots which can span a period of time over several locations, and is designed to evoke a mood or emotion, or give backstory

A SERIES OF SHOTS is a sequence of shots which condense events occurring in real time, in a common location.

A MONTAGE might show images of John and Mary's blossoming love affair, as in the example above, in a field, on the beach, at the park, and over several days, weeks or even years.

A SERIES OF SHOTS might show, as in "Rocky," a sequence in a boxing match, the rounds flashing by, condensing ten or eleven rounds into a thirty-second sequence.

A SERIES OF SHOTS can be formatted in any of the acceptable MONTAGE formats demonstrated previously.

Dream Sequence

DREAM SEQUENCE is also pretty self-explanatory. Structurally, it works exactly the same way as the Flashback, except it's a dream. It can be a dream which reveals a memory, exactly as the Flashback does, or it can be a dream of pure fantasy, as most dreams are.

Dream Sequences are employed to tell the audience what's going on inside a character's head. They are visual interpretations of internal emotions.

Hallucinations also qualify in the Dream Sequence category, with one caveat. Hallucinations are driven by entirely different catalysts. Since they are artificially induced, rather than a reveal of a character's true emotions, they are a distortion of a character's emotions, generally in a negative fashion.

Insert

The INSERT isn't technically a transition, so much as a specified shot, but it is used frequently within scenes, and is worthy of mention.

An INSERT is exactly what it says it is: the insertion of a shot of something we want the audience to get a clear look at, like a letter, a newspaper headline, or a map.

Here's the part you need to be aware of. An insert has to be filmed outside of the scene, all by itself, and inserted into the scene during editing. It requires its own specific camera and lighting setup, so stopping in the middle of shooting a scene to get it makes little sense. Use it judiciously, and don't overuse it.

On the page, the INSERT the will look like something like this:

John picks up a note from the table and reads it.

> JOHN
> Oh, no! Pete, look at this!

He hands the note to Pete.

INSERT: Note - Pete, I'm leaving and I'm not coming back! Angela.

BACK TO SCENE

Pete is stunned.

Using the INSERT allows us to see the information from our

character's point-of-view, in the moment; a more emotionally potent choice than having that information related to us in an expositional line of dialogue.

In Summary: It's important to understanding transitions and their proper use, since they indicate movement between locations within your story. The use of the "Cut To" transition has largely been abandoned in today's screenwriting climate. However, specialized transitions, designed to evoke a specific emotion, are still valuable tools.

Camera Direction

Now, we come to what is a formatting issue for a legion of screenwriters, and that is Camera Direction, or other technical direction like sound effects.

While I encourage you, the writer, to see the movie in your head, I do not endorse directing the movie in your head.

The temptation to direct the screenplay seems to be too great for some. They insist on loading it up with "DOLLY SHOT," "CRANE SHOT," "ECU," "PAN" and the rest.

DON'T!

Especially with really specific shots. That's a director's job, and if you try to do it for him, not only will he hate you, but everyone who reads your script will, as well.

I know there are times when it really feels like some sort of direction would add clarity, and there are some very generic directions you can get away with, if you really feel the need to draw attention to something.

Some examples in this category are ANGLE ON to shift our point-of-view, or FOLLOWING, to indicate we're moving with someone in the scene.

We're also allowed, without impunity, to use the technical direction SUPERIMPOSE, if written narrative needs to appear on the screen, i.e.:

SUPERIMPOSE: "Chicago, 1940"

I've seen the direction written in several ways. Aside from SUPERIMPOSE:, there is TITLE OVER:, ON SCREEN: or just SUPER: They all work and they're all acceptable.

Beyond some simple, basic directions like these, however, leave the directing to the director. Aside from being an affront to the director, it hinders the reading experience, so why do it?

Really, you don't have to say:

CU: John's worried face.

All you have to say in your Action Block is:

John looks worried.

And, instead of...

SFX: GUNSHOT

..it's just as easy to write in your Action Block:

There is a GUNSHOT!

They'll get it. Honest, they will. Trust me on this.

The Credit Roll

One more little foible I encounter, from time-to-time is a tendency for the writer to tell us when the credits are going to come and go, with ROLL OPENING CREDITS or ROLL END CREDITS.

There are rare instances where a scene or montage may appear during a credit roll that actually applies to the story; enhances the story or visual experience in some way.

The use of out takes from a film during closing credits is one example, and many films have employed this device.

For the most part, however, choosing where the credits will appear is just another waste of time and space.

Not only will it hinder the reading experience, but the best response you're likely to get from the director and editor is a hearty laugh. Just, tell the story. That's your job.

When all of the script elements have been formatted properly, you're screenplay page should approximate the example on the following page:

Form and Format

Script Page Example

```
                    MY SCREENPLAY
FADE IN:

EXT. SCENE HEADING - DAY

The ACTION BLOCK follows the Scene Heading.

                    PROTAGONIST
               (Character Direction)
          Dialogue - No more than 35 spaces
          per line
Action

                    ANTAGONIST
               Dialogue
Action

                                        TRANSITION

INT. SCENE HEADING - NIGHT

ACTION BLOCK

                    PROTAGONIST
          Dialogue
               (Character Direction
                within a speech)
          More Dialogue

INTERNAL TRANSITION (i.e. FLASHBACK:, MONTAGE:, ETC.)


INT. SCENE HEADING - DAY

INTERNAL TRANSITION ACTION BLOCK

OUT OF INTERNAL TRANSITION (i.e. END FLASHBACK, OUT OF
MONTAGE, ETC.)
                    PROTAGONIST
               Dialogue

                    ANTAGONIST
               (Character Direction)
          Dialogue

                                        FADE OUT:
```

Note the significant amount of "white space" on the page. This is your goal. It is what readers like to see, because it indicates a tight script and a fast, smooth read. To this end, you can understand why long passages of dialogue and/or action and unnecessary camera direction can work against you.

In Summary: Screenplay formatting is a struggle for a beginning writer, and understandably so. It's left-brain orientation, and gets in the way of your creative flow, because you're constantly forced to think about it.

Don't despair! That struggle will dissipate, the more you write. Formatting will become second nature, so don't let it stop you, in the early going. Just, be patient and know that it's all a part of the learning process.

PART TWO

CHAPTER 9

The Elements of Screenplay

Now, we get into the "meat" of screenplay writing, with the essentials of actually telling a story. To make this a bit more palatable, I've grouped the primary elements which make up a screenplay into three categories:

- Theme
- Story
- Character

While they all must work in harmony, there are tools and devices which are specific to each category, as will be demonstrated.

Theme

There are varying thoughts on what theme is, and in some camps, whether it is even worthy of consideration when writing a screenplay. For me, it is..and then some.

I put a lot of stock in theme. It determines story, character and overall tone. Everything relies on it.

First, don't make the mistake of confusing theme with genre.

They are completely different animals. Western, Action Film, Courtroom Drama and Romantic Comedy are genres, but within those genres can be found many variations on theme, as you will see demonstrated in the Genres chapter. But, for now, we start with theme.

I break the theme category into three sub-categories:

- Master Theme
- Active Theme
- Character's Take on the Theme

The Master Theme

As simply as I can state it, the Master Theme is what your story is about.

Yet, when I ask a new writing student what his story is about, this is generally how the reply starts:

"Well, it's about this guy...."

Gotta stop ya!

No, it isn't! It's about a value. It's about love, revenge, redemption, greed, power, honesty, fear, sacrifice, bigotry, fame, faith, hope, depression, addiction...and the list goes on.

It is about a quality which is pertinent to the human condition. "This guy" is simply the character responsible for carrying out that theme.

"Rocky," for example, is not about boxing, it is about redemption.

"Saving Private Ryan" is not about war, it is about sacrifice.

"Gone With The Wind" is not about the Civil War, it is a love story.

Most disaster films are about survival, although "Titanic" is a disaster film which is actually a love story at its core. The disaster threatens the relationship, as the Civil War was an obstacle for

Rhett and Scarlett.

Most courtroom dramas are, by their nature, about justice. "Twelve Angry Men," "Judgement at Nuremberg," "Inherit The Wind," "And Justice for All" and "A Few Good Men" are all classic examples. Yet, "The Verdict" was a courtroom drama which was actually about redemption, and "To Kill A Mockingbird" was a courtroom drama with a Master Theme of bigotry.

Now, I know, we've been relating stories by starting with "It's about this guy..." for centuries, but that's telling me the story, not telling me what it's about.

From a writer's perspective, I need to know where the emotion is coming from. I need to know what's at stake. I need to know why I should care. And, I need to know it without hearing someone recount the entire story in a thirty-minute dissertation and letting me figure it out for myself.

There is a simple exercise I learned in my early days in the craft, and it's particularly helpful in finding the Master Theme of your story. It goes like this:

Tell me your story in a page.
Now, tell me your story in a paragraph.
Now, tell me your story in a sentence.
Now, tell me your story in a word.

Once you've narrowed it down to that one word, you've found your Master Theme. That's what your story is about.

At this point, you might be asking yourself, *"Do I really need to know this, before I write?"*

The answer is, you probably already know it, instinctively. When you formulate a story in your head, your Master Theme is inherent to the story; built in.

When we get hit with that flash of inspiration, it's never, *"I know! I'll tell a story about love!"*

I get that. It starts with a concept, a character, a situation, a bit of action, or the visualization of a great scene that reaches out and grabs you from the recesses of your brain.

What I am advocating is that there is value in identifying the Master Theme, and in keeping it at the forefront of your mind, as you develop your story. Why? I've already told you.

Everything in your story relates to the Master Theme.

When that inspirational moment that triggers your story drives you to the computer, that's when you have to sit down and fill in the blanks. One flash of inspiration does not a story make. You now must start constructing beginning, middle and end; setups, complications and climax, characters, plot and subplots.

You need a common thread to guide you, something that links all of the elements of a story together, and that is the Master Theme.

For me, it's my security blanket, when I'm developing a story. It's the theme that determines the message, and the message that determines the ending. All it really takes is to be aware of your theme and apply it to your story elements. It just makes things easier.

Now, on to the next step in the theme trilogy.

The Active Theme

Once you've determined your Master Theme, the human value that will be explored, you now must decide what your story will say about that value.

What is your story's position on "love," for instance? Love is blind? Love conquers all? Love makes the world go 'round?

Simple stuff, but it can go much deeper. There is physical love, dysfunctional love, obsessive love, family love, destructive love, love of self, love of home, love of country, love of ideals, and on and on. So many ways to go. And, any of those variations can provide your Active Theme.

Let's take a common genre that does double-duty as a Master Theme: War.

Now, you might not consider War to be a value, since it also doubles as a genre, but there is a human value inherent to it, and that is conflict. Since the act of war is the highest level of human conflict, it is rife with thematic possibilities.

Within the War theme can be many common Active Themes. As we've seen in the examples of "Gone With The Wind" and "Saving Private Ryan," Active Themes within the Master Theme of War can be as varied as love and sacrifice.

Let's look at some classic war films, and the thematic choices made by the writers and filmmakers.

Most war movies made in the 40's and 50's were basically propaganda films. John Wayne, Audie Murphy and stars of that ilk were always the "good guys" while the enemy, be they Nazis, Japanese or whoever were not only "bad guys," but they were portrayed as less than human. Evil for evil's sake. Beyond redemption. Unfortunately, this level of blatant bias reflected the morals and politics of the time.

Our leads, the "good guys," were always heroic, righteous and victorious in a just cause. The message they sent was that War is noble. War brings honor.

War makes heroes of men.

Now, enter the 70's, when attitudes began to change, thanks in large part to that nasty Vietnam conflict. Movies like "Apocalypse Now," "Platoon," and later "Full Metal Jacket" delivered just the opposite message of the earlier rah-rah war stories. They showed us the "dirty" side of war, and what it does to those immersed in the conflict; how it hardens them and brings out the worst in human nature. They told us that...

War makes monsters of men.

Same Master Theme, but completely different Active Themes.

Here's yet another take. "Catch 22" and "MASH" told us that war is ironic, even laughable; worthy of ridicule. Insanity forced upon the average man against his will. In other words...

War is absurd.

Some genres have obvious Master Themes, and a good example is Romantic Comedy. In this genre, "love" is always the Master Theme, otherwise, it isn't a romantic comedy. It isn't a romantic anything. The Active Theme, however, is more flexible.

In "The Graduate," the story faithfully hit all of the required Rom Com beats: Boy meets girl, boy loses girl, boy gets girl back. The ending, however, was a far cry from the warm, fuzzy, "happily-ever-after" endings we had grown used to in the earlier films of the genre, from the 40's and 50's.

The ending of "The Graduate," in fact the entire film, was bittersweet; a struggle, emotionally, physically and morally for our leads. The ending didn't tell us that Ben and Elaine would live happily ever after in wedded bliss. It told us they were taking a huge chance, throwing caution to the wind. Don't believe it? Watch the film and look at the uncertainty creep over their faces as they ride away on that bus.

Love is risky.

It was risky throughout the entire story, and it was still risky at the end.

Now, take a look at "There's Something About Mary." Everyone loved Mary in some warped, dysfunctional way. Not your mother's romantic comedy. The Active Theme, here, was...

Love is obsessive.

But, the Master Theme is still love.

"Slasher" films also embrace simple, basic Master Themes. In a slasher film, it's either about survival or revenge, depending on who we're rooting for; the killer or his victims. Therefore, the Active Theme isn't likely to vary much in this genre, either.

Perhaps a character learns that only by enlisting the help of others can she defeat a crazed killer, telling us that...

Survival is achieved through unity.

Another approach might have our hero fighting back to stay alive, concluding that...

Survival is achieved through conflict.

The messages remain pretty simplistic and familiar in slasher films, but there is always a message.

Hollywood studio pioneer Samuel Goldwyn once quipped:

"If you want to send a message, call Western Union."

I suppose, today, it would be "send a tweet." With all due respect to Mr. Goldwyn, every story has a message, whether we intend it to, or not. It's part of the package. Even Jerry Seinfeld's "show about nothing" was always about something. The Active Theme, what your story has to say about your Master Theme, is your message.

There is usually more than one Active Theme being played out, within a story. "Rocky," while primarily a story of redemption, also contained a Love theme in the subplot between Rocky and Adrian.

"The Wrestler" explored the same two themes, Redemption and Love, except as a tragedy. In both films, our central protagonist was attempting to overcome long odds to make a comeback, and in both films, love was a sub-theme. In "Rocky," our hero succeeded in achieving redemption and winning love. In "The Wrestler," Randy "The Ram" failed at both.

Believe it or not, the same two themes were explored in the classic 40's noir film "Casablanca." In this case, Love was the dominant theme, while Redemption the sub-theme. In "Casablanca," Rick won redemption, but lost at love. Once you start playing with those combinations, you unlock a Rubik's Cube of possibilities.

Now, on to my last piece of the Theme puzzle:

The Character's Take on the Theme

Once your theme has been established, it must be reflected in every possible manner within your story. How do the characters relate to the theme?

I'm talking about every character, because they all must have an opinion; a point-of-view on the theme being explored. That's one significant way to add dimension and nuance to your story. It also creates areas of conflict between characters, and conflict is everything in a story, especially a story designed for the screen.

I'll use the same examples I use in my screenwriting class, from the terrific courtroom drama "A Few Good Men."

As a classic courtroom drama, the Master Theme of the story is Justice. First, for those who aren't familiar with this movie, here's the setup.

Two young Marines, Lance Corporal Harold Dawson and PFC. Louden Downey, are accused of murder while performing an illegal disciplinary action against a third Marine, PFC. William Santiago. We soon learn that this illegal action was ordered by their Commanding Officer, Col Nathan Jessup. Jessup's Executive Officer, Lt Col Matthew Markinson and Platoon Leader Lt Jonathan Kendrick are a part of the conspiracy to cover up Jessup's involvement, Markinson reluctantly, Kendrick willingly. It's up to our heroes, Lt Danny Kaffee, Lt Sam Weinberg and Lt Cdr Joanne Galloway to defend the accused Marines. Capt Jack Ross, a friend of Danny Kaffee, is the prosecutor.

A veritable bevy of characters, no? But, each one has a "take" on our justice theme, and each take is slightly, if not significantly different.

Let's start with Lt Danny Kaffee, our Central Protagonist, played by Tom Cruise.

Kaffee initially believes his clients' best defense is to attempt to plea bargain their murder charge to a lesser charge. In his mind, they are clearly guilty, and chances of acquittal are virtually nil.

His take on justice changes, as the case progresses. Eventually, he will come to believe his clients should be acquitted. A change in goals is not unusual for a central protagonist, since we want to see them grow.

So, at first, Kaffee tries to plea bargain the case, meaning Justice would be a reduced sentence for his clients. When new information comes to light that they were ordered to perform the action that led to Santiago's death, he decides that Justice means setting his clients free, except he's not the attorney for the job. He's never tried a case in court, and has serious doubts about his ability to win the case at trial. On top of that, losing could destroy his career. So, justice is clear for Danny, but the risks of failure are enormous.

Sam Weinberg, played by Kevin Pollack, is Kaffee's friend and co-counsel. Yet, even though he's defending Dawson and Downey, and even though he knows Jessup ordered them to discipline Santiago, Sam still believes the two young Marines should be punished.

This is pointed out clearly, when Danny Kaffee suggests that Sam doesn't believe their clients' story, and thinks they should go to prison for the rest of their lives. Sam's reply is that he believes every word of their story...and thinks they should go to prison for the rest of their lives.

In Sam's view, all his clients did was "beat up on a weakling." That's his take on the theme. Yes, they were ordered, but that still doesn't justify the act they committed. They performed their duty, but in doing so, sacrificed their integrity and humanity. They need to be punished. That's justice, and a source of internal conflict within Sam.

Now we come to Joanne Galloway, portrayed by Demi Moore.

Joanne has an idealistic take on the theme. These are two noble young men serving their country. They "stand on a wall" to protect the rest of us. They followed orders, like good Marines. They deserve their day in court, and they deserve to go free, plain and simple.

Our prosecutor, Jack Ross, played by Kevin Bacon, has a dispassionate point-of-view on the subject. He represents the government, and he has a case. No conflict within him, in that respect. The outcome is of no personal concern to him.

What does concern him, and where his internal conflict exists, is the fate of his friend and courtroom rival, Danny Kaffee, who Jack feels is sacrificing his career in a lost cause by defending these two Marines.

And, what about those two Marines? Do they, also, have a "take" on what Justice is? Of course.

LCpl Dawson, played by Wolfgang Bodison, is so convinced of his innocence, he literally forces Kaffee to take the case to trial, not because he's afraid of going to prison, but because his honor is at stake. That is his take on the theme. Justice is maintaining his honor.

Likewise, his cohort, PFC. Downey, portrayed by James Marshall, wants only to remain a Marine. Marines follow orders. He followed orders. Therefore, he's innocent. For him, it's black-and-white.

Now, let's look at our bad guys, starting with Col Nathan Jessup; portrayed by superstar Jack Nicholson. Naturally, being on the other side of the issue, he has a completely different take on what justice means. In his view, ordering Dawson and Downey to discipline Santiago was designed to make Santiago a better marine.

That's Jessup's job: to train marines to defend their country. Doing otherwise would put Santiago's fellow marines, and the nation, at risk. He didn't set out to have Santiago killed, only to train him. Santiago's death was a sacrifice that had to be made for the greater good, and Dawson and Downey likewise. Justice is flawed, because he, Jessup, answers to a higher calling. That was the "truth" we couldn't handle.

Lt Col Markinson, portrayed by the late, great J.T. Walsh, gave us one of the more interesting takes on the Justice theme. Markinson's character was so torn between duty and conscience that he ultimately turned to suicide. For him, justice clashed with duty, and there was no way to reconcile the two. He finally decided that the only real course was to reveal the truth, so that others may sort it out.

At one point, Markinson states to Kaffee that he's not proud of his complicity in the events of this case, but neither is he proud of informing on his long-time friend and Commanding Officer. He is a tragic character, so internally conflicted as to be unable to live with the consequences of his actions.

Keifer Sutherland's Lt Jonathan Kendrick gave us one of the quirkiest, almost humorous takes on this Justice theme. In his view, Santiago was an inferior marine. All Kendrick did was assist in trying to make him a better one. He, too, followed orders, but it goes beyond that. The victim, Santiago, violated a sacred code and sacrificed his honor, and therefore was doomed to die by a higher power. *"God was watching,"* he tells us. How's that for a take on the justice theme? God killed Santiago!

Theme in Review

The Master Theme, which reflects a human value, is the first flicker of guiding light in building our story. The Master Theme is to a story what the subject of a sentence is to a sentence. It's what it's all about.

The Active Theme makes a statement on the Master Theme. What does our story have to say about that Master Theme? That's the message our story will deliver on a subject which reflects a human value.

The Character's Take on the Theme provides us with the vehicles to deliver the message of the Active Theme. All characters, not just the Central Protagonists and Antagonists. The more diverse the points-of-view presented by the characters, the more complex the story.

In Summary: The three aspects of Theme: Master Theme, Active Theme and Character's Take on the Theme create the basic building-blocks of a story. A clear understanding of theme allows us to add depth, dimension and conflict to our story and define our characters' personalities.

All aspects of Theme exist in every film, and once we identify and understand them, we will have a solid framework on which to build our story.

And, story is what we'll attack next.

CHAPTER 10

Story

I once had a director tell me, *"The audience doesn't care about the story."* It horrified me to think that might be true. We were discussing an action film; a genre in which story and character often draw the short straw.

In his belief system, my director was right. In an action film, the audience wants action, and they're much more willing to overlook insignificant little things like gaps in story logic, implausible plot points and one-dimensional characters. Since he was a highly successful director, with far more credits in his craft than I had in mine, how could he be wrong?

Here's how:

Action isn't diminished by a compelling story and multi-dimensional characters, it is enhanced by them. Of course, the action must be the focus of an action film, but that hardly means that character and story structure don't matter. It only means that we, as writers, have less time to spend; fewer pages to devote to building that structure and creating well-rounded characters.

The stories in "First Blood," "Raiders of the Lost Ark," "Star Wars," "The Terminator" and "Lethal Weapon" were masterfully crafted, and the characters rich and well-developed. It made those heart-stopping action sequences much more exciting, and created memorable (and profitable) characters, who would live on in sequels.

Without a well-crafted storyline, we risk falling into the "been-there-seen-that" mold; just another average story. Without a cohesive story structure and some emotional investment in our characters by the audience, all aspects of the story are diminished. It is one thing to write thrilling action scenes. It is another to write thrilling action scenes that matter, and make sense.

That it puts a greater demand on us, the writers, is a good thing, because it can potentially bring more out of us and make us better at what we do.

Keeping it Real

The plot of a story, as the term is used in the Poetics, is not the sequence of events so much as the logical relationships that exist between events.

The emphasis in the statement above is on "logical." If you want to immerse the audience in the world of your imagination, you must create a world they can believe, and then you must keep them there. If you don't, you risk losing them completely. I've known this since a very early age, from a time long before I ever considered writing for the screen.

When I was a kid, I went to the theater to watch a grade "B" Western. The cowboys were fighting the Apaches in a big field, with mountains in the background. It was one of those climactic battles, where probably most of the production budget had been spent, and they pulled out all the stops. With dozens of extras, lots of horses, blood, guts and gunfire, it had me at the edge of my seat.

Then, something caught my eye; a movement in the mountains in the background that seemed out of place. I quickly focused on it, drawn from the drama of the shootout, and realized...it was a school bus!

I watched in surprise as the bus wound its way around a curve on the mountain. It was tiny, mind you, being some distance away, but it was clearly identifiable in all of its bright yellow glory. Then, it disappeared behind the trees.

To say the moment was lost would be an understatement. I had been drawn into that world. I had accepted the characters, their predicaments and their environment. I was there. The last thing I needed was to have my suspension of disbelief shattered by, of all things, a school bus!

Certainly, no one in the film's crew had any inkling that a school bus was going to pop up in the background, in the middle of shooting their action finale. The time and expense of re-shooting the scene was likely prohibitive, and maybe they figured no one would notice. I did, and I'm sure I'm not the only one.

The school bus example is an extreme one, of course, initiated by a continuity problem, rather than a writing flaw. Yet, it serves to point out the importance of keeping your audience firmly rooted in your world.

Moments such as this can often be traced to a poor creative choice by a writer, director or editor. To me, it signals one of two things: someone was too lazy to do it right, or someone underestimated the intelligence of their audience.

In Summary: Too often we are subjected to that "the audience doesn't care about the story" attitude. The audience does, indeed care about the story, down to the minutest of details. When we violate their trust by taking them out of the reality of the world we've created, they feel insulted, and they have a right to. Our job, from screenwriter to producer to director to editor, is to keep the world of our story credible. Little things count, from the writing, right down the line.

Story Logic

On the structural front, you want to make sure you haven't left any holes in logic. But, story logic is not the same as real-life logic. What flies in a movie does not often reflect the logic of reality.

In film, artistic license, for the sake of entertainment, takes precedent. Story logic means "acceptable." Will they, the audience, "buy" it? I'll give you an example.

In Alfred Hitchcock's classic "North by Northwest," there exists a rather famous scene wherein Cary Grant, playing our hero, Roger Thornhill, is directed to take a bus to a remote location on a dirt road, surrounded by farmland. He stands there, waiting for the mysterious Mr. Kaplan, who is to meet him there.

Soon, a car approaches, then passes. Another car arrives, and a farmer gets out and stands on the other side of the road. Cary Grant approaches him and asks if he's Kaplan. He isn't.

An old biplane; a crop duster flies overhead. The farmer's bus arrives, and as he boards, he remarks that it's odd that the crop duster is dusting *"where there ain't no crops."* Then, the bus departs, leaving our hero alone, once more.

That's when the crop duster descends on Cary Grant and there begins a mad chase through a nearby field, as the airplane pursues him, spewing gunfire from the cockpit. Cary Grant evades the airplane and eventually runs to the highway, where a large tanker truck approaches.

Ultimately, the airplane crashes into the tanker truck in a humongous explosion!

It's a very exciting scene, but in examining it later, I found myself asking:

"Why a crop duster?"

Really, he was standing there, on the side of the road, way out in the boonies, all alone. All our bad guys had to do was drive up, roll down the window and shoot him dead.

That's the way it probably would have happened, in real life. I mean, that's the way I'd do it, were I prone to do such a thing. But, that wouldn't have been nearly as exciting or visual as an airplane chasing a man through a field, and then crashing into a tanker truck, leading to a fiery explosion. And, this is not real life, this is a motion picture. Thus, story logic prevailed.

Mr. Hitchcock termed these moments "icebox scenes," meaning that these minor flaws in logic surface after one gets home from the theater, opens his "ice box" for a snack and suddenly says to himself:

"Wait...that didn't make sense!"

Of course, by now, it's too late. We've already seen and enjoyed the movie.

Had the realization of that flaw hit us while watching the movie, that might have been a problem. But, the scene was too exciting, keeping us on the edge of our seats, for us to think about something trivial like logic.

However, Story Logic has its limits. If we push things too far, we may cross the line of acceptable logic and lose our audience, or, at the least, offend them. Mr. Hitchcock's "ice box" moment may hit us then and there, and not wait for us to get home and reach for a snack.

In Summary: While the scene I've just described from "North by Northwest" may defy real-world logic, it is still believable. It could happen, and that is what makes it acceptable. That is story logic.

Story Devices

When crafting your unique story, it's often helpful to rely on the familiar as a starting point. There are many tried-and-true Story Devices to lean on, to accomplish this.

These are plot moments and situations which have withstood the test of time. They work in movies today as well as they did for Hemingway in his novels. They provide a context, in which to inject our singular, personal point-of-view.

I've picked out a few Story Devices to illustrate.

The Ticking Clock

This is a device which will "turn the screws" on our hero, and add suspense to any aspect of our story. It is designed to put our Protagonist in a position where he is under the pressure of time constraints to achieve a goal.

Sometimes, the Ticking Clock provides the very premise of the story, as we've seen in "Speed," "Unstoppable" and "Crank," and consider the classic Western "High Noon," where our Ticking Clock device was a literal ticking clock, counting down the minutes before the bad guys come to town to kill our hero, Gary Cooper.

The Ticking Clock is a flexible device which can be used, not only as the premise of a film, but in a sequence within a film, or even in just a scene. Some James Bond films, along with many suspense films, rely on the Ticking Clock to turn up the heat for a sequence within the story, rather than as a premise for the story, itself.

It can be a matter of getting to the bomb to diffuse it, before it explodes, or rescuing a victim who is buried alive, before he suffocates. Every kidnapping sequence relies on the Ticking Clock, forcing our hero to come up with the ransom, or a plan, in time to save the kidnap victim.

The issue doesn't even have to be life-or-death for the Ticking Clock to work. It can be a stop-the-wedding sequence in a Romantic Comedy, for instance, or a character trying to reach a destination by a certain time in order to make a job interview, or make it home by Christmas, or make it to her child's school play.

Anything that puts a time limit on our character to achieve her goal qualifies. The Ticking Clock is a wonderful tool for creating tension and suspense, and it nearly always works.

Irony

There's an age-old axiom that came out of the newspaper business: Dog bites man is not a story. Man bites dog, however, is.

Why?

Because, it's ironic.

Irony is a wonderful tool which applies equally well to story and character, comedy and drama. It is used countless times, with great effect, to complete a character's story arc, and serves particularly well to finish off a villain, as in a "bad-guy-gets-his-just-due" scenario. Irony can be found in most films made, and can be thematic in nature, or character oriented.

When the Titanic, a ship hailed as unsinkable, hits an iceberg and sinks on her maiden voyage...

That's irony.

In the film "Jaws," Robert Shaw's character of Quint is a shark hunter. Already, there is some irony here, when we reflect on the story he tells about being aboard the U.S.S. Indianapolis, which is sunk by a German submarine, leaving the crew stranded in the ocean for days, at the mercy of sharks. No doubt, that was the character's motivation for becoming a shark hunter to begin with: to elicit some sort of revenge. In the climax of the story, Quint, the shark hunter, is eaten by a shark on his own boat.

That's irony.

Luke Skywalker engages in a one-on-one battle with Darth Vader, then discovers, at a critical moment, that "Luke, I am your father!"

That's irony.

Irony plays a major part in the creation of the next device on my list: the "twist."

The Twist

I think it's more than just the surprise factor at work, here. We all like for a story to surprise us, as long as the surprise is honest, and not superficial or contrived. But, I think there's another aspect to the popularity of The Twist device, and that is its ability to involve the audience in an intimate fashion.

Mysteries always include a twist as part of their makeup, and the attraction for the viewer is the brain-teasing exercise of figuring out who the guilty party is, before it is revealed.

The Twist keeps that reveal hidden, by withholding, until the right moment, that critical piece of information needed to solve the mystery.

To repeat my premise that audiences have grown more sophisticated, it isn't as easy to surprise them as it used to be. A good twist that really works is a thing of beauty. "The Sixth Sense," and its reveal of Bruce Willis as a ghost was quite effective, and when Jay Davidson's character, Dil, dropped her...that is, his dress in "The Crying Game," well, who saw that coming?

We think most often of twists coming at the end of our story, but the twist can be used just about anywhere. It's such a powerful story tool, with such impact on the overall story, that it's usually best employed as a major story point. It is quite effective as an Act Break, as well as a mid-story turn.

In terms of our old friend Irony's contribution to the twist device, it's pretty much a requirement. The irony creates the element of surprise.

In the 70's produced Western "The Professionals," which starred Lee Marvin, Burt Lancaster and Robert Ryan, a wealthy rancher, played by Ralph Bellamy, hires a group of men to find and return his wife, played by Claudia Cardinale, who has been kidnapped by a Mexican outlaw and his gang.

At the mid-point of the story, our protagonists do, indeed find the damsel in distress, inside the outlaws camp. However, the rescuers quickly discover that the woman wasn't kidnapped at all, but went willingly with the outlaw; her lover!

Now, it's our good guys who must do the kidnapping, and return her to her husband in order for them to get paid. A nice, ironic twist that brings a whole new perspective to the story.

"The Usual Suspects" also relied on an ironic twist. Kevin Spacey's "Verbal" Kint, the physically handicapped, low-level pawn of the crime gang, is grilled for hours by police who are trying to uncover the identity of the mysterious criminal mastermind, Keyser Soze. On Verbal's release by the police, we learn that not only is he not physically handicapped, but he is Soze, and has been making up his story all along.

The twist is a flexible little Story Device. We can utilize it in Story and Character, drama, comedy or action, and it can be verbal or visual. A handy tool for a writer's toolbox.

The Maguffin

A Maguffin is an object, any object, which drives the story. It is the thing everyone involved in our story wants. It keeps things really simple, in terms of story structure, because it provides us with a tangible goal which motivates every character, hero or villain.

"The Maltese Falcon" is a clear example, or the original "Pink Panther," which gave us a diamond as our prize. In espionage films, especially the early versions, the Maguffin was often a microfilm of some important, top secret document.

The Ark of the Covenant in "Raiders of the Lost Ark" is another classic Maguffin. Historical artifacts work nicely, since they allow us to endow our Central Protagonist with a positive motivation, that of preserving the artifact for posterity, while our Central Antagonist can be motivated by the negative qualities of greed, or power.

The Cliffhanger

The Cliffhanger doesn't only leave your character twisting in the wind, it leaves your audience there, as well. In its most literal form, we see it pop up in most Action and Adventure films, wherein our character is left in imminent physical jeopardy, while we cut away to some other action.

It serves two purposes. It's an adrenaline-evoking device, designed to leave us with our hearts in our throats, and it's a tool to make darn sure the audience doesn't go anywhere. Even if the character hanging from the cliff is our hero, and we know he isn't really going to die, we can't wait to see how he gets out of the fix he's in.

The term "Cliffhanger" creates a pretty stark, in-your-face image, but it can be utilized in a more subtle fashion in other forms and genres. Emotional cliffhangers are frequent in Character-oriented films, such as Romantic Comedies or Character Studies, as in:

"She just saw her fiance with another woman, making nice. What will she do? Tune in next week!"

And, that brings up the most prolific use of the Cliffhanger: Episodic Television. In fact, it isn't just used in long-form TV, it is a major element of its structure.

The need arises from purely commercial requisites. There are more commercials in the show than there are acts in a story. So, at least half of those times when we take a commercial break in "CSI" or "Law and Order," we're using Cliffhangers, rather than Act Breaks, to get us out.

In episodic detective shows of days gone by, I swear, the good guy was getting conked on the head almost every week, usually while snooping around looking for clues. As he sagged to the floor, unconscious, we went to a commercial. Episodic television shows still use this device, though generally not in such a blatant fashion.

Symbols

I feel that most of the time, any symbolism should spring naturally from the story. It will be there, subliminally, in your mind and you will create a visual symbol to express a thought, emotion or thematic point.

Symbolism is a fine tool, but sometimes tricky and can be dangerous. It must be judiciously placed so as to appeal, most often, to the subconscious, rather than conscious mind.

If the audience recognizes a symbol as such, it often has the same effect as a continuity error in a film. It leaps out from the screen and says, *"Look at me! I'm a symbol!"* as if to imply that you just won't get it unless it's jammed in your face. It becomes a distraction, and reminds the audience that they are being manipulated.

In earlier times, when nudity and any form of explicit sex was verboten in cinema (check out the history of the uproar when Clark Gable simply uttered the word "damn" in "Gone With The Wind") symbolism was the tool which told that part of the story, along with dialogue subtext.

Symbols told our imagination how to fill in the blanks. The tired old cliche of the train, going into a tunnel to symbolize the sex act is a good example. As George Carlin once aptly remarked of this filmic device:

"You don't have to be Fellini to figure that one out."

Symbolism can be attached to almost anything, even when what it's attached to isn't really intended to symbolize anything. Someone will always find a hidden meaning behind every bush.

Symbols are often used as a sub-theme; a general emotion-evoking tool, such as employing vast expanses of desert to express loneliness, or a sense of insignificance. Water has been utilized to evoke an emotional reaction in countless films.

Color is another symbolic device to tweak us, emotionally. Remember the little girl's red dress in "Schindler's List," the only item of color in a black-and-white film? This was obviously not a subliminal symbol, but a pretty blatant one. It worked, because that little red dress told a story all its own. A story which was in complete concert with the theme being played out in the main storyline.

In the classic Western "High Noon," there is a shot of Gary Cooper standing in the street, in the middle of town. It's the story moment when he has exhausted every effort to enlist support from the town's citizens in facing the villains, and failed.

There he stands, in the center of a dusty street. We get a camera angle from above him, and the camera pulls back, and back, and back, until we can see the entire town, below, spread out before us. Alone, in the middle of the street, stands this tiny spec of a man. That's some powerful symbolism.

In fact, there was so much symbolism read into this film, that it actually drew fire from the McCarthy, red-scare crowd, who believed the film's story was an allegory for the plight of blacklisted screenwriters. This probably stemmed from the fact that Carl Foreman, the screenwriter, was suspected of having Communist ties, and was eventually blacklisted.

There were others who found symbolism in "High Noon" which they interpreted as a protest against the Korean War. Like I said, you can read your own symbolism into almost anything, but, as Freud once reminded us, *"sometimes a cigar is just a cigar."*

For our purposes, the symbol, like every story tool, should fit neatly into our story and serve the theme. Think about the immortal "Rosebud" in Citizen Kane; the little sled that meant nothing to anyone but him. It defined his character, yet remained a mystery throughout the story.

In "Butch Cassidy and the Sundance Kid" there comes the moment when Butch, Sundance and Etta are about to depart on their journey to Bolivia. Butch picks up the bicycle, the symbol of progress (our Master Theme, by the way) and unceremoniously rolls it down the hill, where it topples into a ditch, as Butch derisively spouts...

"The future's all yours, ya lousy bicycle."

As they ride away in their carriage, in the background, the spinning wheel of the upturned bicycle holds the foreground. Butch is running away from the future in a moment symbolic of Butch's rejection of progress, which, like the wheel, keeps on moving. A symbolic omen of the tragic ending to come. At least, that's what it said to me.

How, where or even if you use symbols is strictly a personal choice. Chances are, someone will find symbolism in your story that you didn't even design, and weren't aware of. Just understand that a symbol can be a useful device, since it is another tool which can provide that all important shorthand we need to squeeze a rich, full story into the limited space of a screenplay. However, if used improperly, it can inflict serious damage to the story's credibility.

In Summary: These are just a few examples of Story Devices. Keep in mind that every genre has its own conventions, which qualify as story devices specific to the genre. The chapter on Genres will delve more deeply into this.

Conflict and Complications

All good stories have one major element in common to create an emotional experience, and that is conflict. It is one crucial factor which cannot be overlooked, and the more ways we can weave it into every level of our story, the stronger our story will be.

Conflict needs to exist, not only in the central storyline, but in subplots, within relationships between characters and within the characters, themselves. Sub-plots, backstory and well-developed supporting characters, each with his own storyline, provide fertile ground for conflict.

In order to have conflict, we must have an opposing force, be it internal or external. There must exist some form of antagonism. In truth, there should be many forms of antagonism played out in a good story, but just as there is a Central Protagonist, the "hero," there must be a Central Antagonist, the "villain," who provides our Central Force of Antagonism.

The Forces of Antagonism

There are four basic forces of antagonism, as I understand them, and they are:

Man vs Man

As I've pointed out, "Rocky" is a story of redemption. The force of antagonism keeping Rocky from his redemption is Apollo Creed. Therefore, this is a Man vs. Man Central Force of Antagonism. Apollo was the obstacle between Rocky and his redemption.

"The Fugitive" pitted our hero, Dr. Richard Kimble (Harrison Ford in the most recent incarnation) against Sam Gerard, (Tommy Lee Jones,) the cop determined to capture him. Again, Man vs. Man. It is common in most every Western ever made, and most War films, as well.

Nearly every super hero story depends on a Man vs Man force of conflict. "Superman," "Batman," "Spiderman" and every member of "The Avengers" team must contend with their own super villain to emerge victorious. Often, these villains will be supported by organizations; systems, but primarily, once the Central Antagonist has been defeated, the battle has been won.

Man vs the Elements

Here, we're most frequently dealing with Disaster films. "Armageddon," "Earthquake," "Volcano," "Airport," "The Impossible" and "The Perfect Storm" all pit our protagonists against the forces of nature.

Movies dealing with survival in the wilderness, such as "Cast Away," "Into The Wild," "Jeremiah Johnson" and "127 Hours" also fall into the Man vs. The Elements category, as do the "animal villains" in "Jaws," "Cujo" and "Snakes on a Plane."

I'll take it one step further. I think this also encompasses Monster movies and Sci Fi films with alien beings to contend with, since these creatures are forces of nature which we can't control.

So Man vs. Creature, such as "Alien" or "Frankenstein," becomes a sub-category, if you will, of Man vs. The Elements.

With this in mind, when we encounter a super hero in the form of an "Iron Man," we deal with a protagonist battling forces of nature: an army of robots. A similar Man vs The Elements conflict appeared in "War of the Worlds," "Invasion of the Body Snatchers" and countless other instances of alien invasions.

Man vs the System

Any system. It was there in both "MASH" and "Catch 22," where the military system provided the opposition. Politics is also an easy target, as we've seen in "Dave," "All The President's Men," "Wag the Dog," "The Candidate" and "Mr. Smith Goes To Washington," to name a few.

This force of antagonism provides us with intrinsic underdog style heroes, since systems are inevitably much more powerful than our protagonist.

In "The Insider," the system was the tobacco industry. In "Philadelphia" it was society in general, and how it dealt with AIDS victims. In "The Verdict," it was the Catholic Church. In "Absence of Malice," it was the press.

The James Bond series always sported a colorful villain, but these were not Man vs. Man central conflicts. Each master villain had a system; one which needed to be brought down to save the world. Bond destroys the system, but sometimes, our villain escapes to fight another day.

Man vs Himself

This takes in stories of addiction, such as "Leaving Las Vegas," "Days of Wine and Roses," "Bright Lights, Big City" and "The Man With the Golden Arm," wherein our hero's conflict is internal.

An unquenchable thirst for power, as in "Citizen Kane" or "The Last King of Scotland" or "The Man Who Would Be King" qualifies. The same goes for characters unable to deal with fame, as in "The Rose," "A Star is Born" or "The Doors."

In "Apocalypse Now," Robert Duval's Lt Col Kilgore was addicted to the adrenaline of war, as Jeremy Renner's Sgt James in "The Hurt Locker" was addicted to the adrenaline of bomb disposal. Any time our hero's biggest obstacle and greatest conflict is internal, we have a Man vs. Himself Force of Antagonism.

Now, we'll play mix-and-match again, because as you'll discover, more than one source of conflict can and should be utilized to drive your story and motivate your characters.

In "Butch Cassidy and the Sundance Kid," Progress was the Master Theme, and it was also the Central Force of Antagonism. Progress threatened to do away with Butch and Sundance.

The Super Posse, then, became the personification of progress. They just kept coming. Our heroes couldn't stop them and they couldn't outrun them, but there was also a Man vs The System conflict playing out, as there always is when outlaws are pitted against law enforcement. We also saw Man vs Man conflicts in every gunfight, and in the relationship between Butch and Sundance.

In "The Verdict," a redemption story, the central force of antagonism was Man vs The System; a down-and-out lawyer doing battle in court against the mighty Catholic Church, but there was a very strong Man vs Himself element, as well, as there must be in redemption themes.

When Paul Newman's character chooses to take his case to court rather than settle, he is set upon by both his friend, played by Jack Warden, and the victim's family, creating a Man vs Man conflict.

In Summary: Pick most any well made film and you'll certainly find more than one form of conflict demonstrated in the storytelling.

Just like Theme, conflict can take many forms, but also just like theme, only one can be the Central Force of Antagonism. One easily identifiable main villain must be overcome for the goal to be achieved.

Complications

Directly related to the conflict created by our forces of antagonism are conflicts created by Complications. Complications are the obstacles which make the task more difficult for our protagonist. They can be physical, emotional or psychological, as long as they provide roadblocks for our protagonist in pursuit of his goal.

We want many complications in our story, but that doesn't mean we want our story to be complicated. What we want our story to be is complex, and that is achieved by adding layers of sub-structure to our basic story structure.

Once we have our basic storyline established, it's time to add the nuances which give it depth. Creating more or stronger conflicts and complications is the most constructive way to accomplish that.

I liken it to building a new house. I've laid the foundation and created a structure. As it stands, it's a house. But, it's not my house, until I make it so. What color should I paint it? What kind of carpet? How will I decorate? What style of furniture?

I'm adding complexity to the basic structure of my new house and putting my personal stamp on it.

The same applies to a story. We lay out the basic story structure, then look deeper within that structure for ways to add complexity to every moment, every character and every action, always using conflict as a guide.

Any time our hero makes a choice to take an action, that's our cue to create a roadblock to that action. If he needs to reach the other side of the river, create a flood to wash out the bridge. If she makes a promise to do something, make her break it. If he's in a hurry, slow him down.

In Summary: Complications, large and small, are tools to make our hero's struggle more difficult. The harder the struggle, the sweeter the victory, and the more worthy our hero.

Subplots

Subplots, by their nature, add complexity and depth to a story.

In "Rocky" there is a famous scene built around a subplot; the relationship between Rocky and Adrian's brother, Paulie, played by Burt Young. Paulie works for a meat packing company and the scene takes place in a meat locker.

If you've seen this film, you already know which scene I'm talking about. It's the one where Rocky and Paulie argue, and Rocky gets so angry, he slams his fist into a side of hanging beef. Then, he repeats it, again and again, until Paulie pleads:

"You're breakin' the ribs!"

The ritual catches on as a training tool, Paulie exploits it and Rocky is interviewed for television demonstrating it. When the fight comes, Rocky wears a robe into the ring with the logo of the meat locker on the back. Paulie gets three-grand for the advertising. Rocky gets to keep the robe.

This subplot gives us an interaction between two characters which not only tells us more about them, but creates its own little dramatic story arc; setup, conflict, resolution. The story of Rocky and Paulie. A story within a story.

Any time we put two characters in a relationship, we have a subplot. Yet, the main storyline, that of Rocky's redemption, does not hinge on this subplot. The writer, Sylvester Stallone, could have created an entirely different subplot storyline to serve the relationship between Rocky and Paulie, and the main storyline would still have worked.

Maybe, Paulie could have become Rocky's cut man. Maybe, Paulie could bet everything he owns on Apollo Creed, and Rocky finds out.

The field is wide open, and having the comfort factor of already having our main storyline developed leaves us with tremendous flexibility. As long as our subplot serves the theme in some manner, it will suffice.

Each subplot should add further heat to our hero's primary task. It should add a layer of conflict to all of the other conflicts, making the odds greater against our hero, and therefore the resolution of the story more satisfying.

The Rocky-Paulie subplot did serve the main theme and storyline. When Rocky's training technique in the meat locker shows up as a story on a local news program, Apollo's corner man sees it, and becomes concerned. It's our first indication that Apollo may be underestimating Rocky's worthiness as an opponent.

The corner man suggests to Apollo that he should take a look at this guy he's going to fight, but Apollo is too wrapped up in his marketing strategy to pay attention. Another character moment, revealing Apollo's fatal flaw of over confidence, reflected in this subplot.

In Summary: We're going to have subplots in our stories, and that is just a fact. We can't write a story without them. Don't sell them short. Well-developed subplots enrich any story in a variety of ways. Whether they are employed to heighten the drama, create more obstacles for our beleaguered hero or provide comic relief, they can broaden the scope of any story, and should never be approached haphazardly. Because they are critical in adding complexity to our stories, we must get the most from them.

CHAPTER 11

Character

We have very little time, in a screenplay, to create clearly defined characters. As screenwriters, we don't have the luxury of long passages of narration to establish our characters, as does a novelist. Yet, we must create the same depth of experience and personality into our characters, and we must reflect it visually and verbally for the screen.

It's hard to separate character from story, since they feed off of one another. Just as a story must be constructed so as to deliver a message on a theme, a character must be developed to do exactly the same thing. They must have personal storylines which serve the central storyline and theme.

However, while the construction of a story is largely a matter of left-brain thought, that of placing events in the proper order and tracking those events to a logical conclusion, the development of a character is all about emotion.

Before I go any further, it should be noted that when I speak of a "character," I'm not always talking about a person. There's a wonderful line that has been attributed to George Burns, who was an Executive Producer of the classic sitcom "Mr. Ed," about a talking horse. One of the writers had written a line for Mr. Ed, and tried it out on Mr. Burns. His response?

"The horse wouldn't say that."

Whether the quote is actually true or not, I can't say, but it makes a good point. We've seen all manner of animals and inanimate objects humanized in films. Mr. Ed, himself, was inspired by the "Francis, the Talking Mule" series of films, seven in all, which were very popular in the 1950's.

By now, we've seen dogs, cats, pigs, cars, toys, trees, dragons, robots, you name it, all given life. And, we believe them, because the writers gave them the same consideration they give any character; attitudes and aspirations, conflicts and weaknesses, personalities, flaws and character traits.

A character is a character, and if we bring our characters to life properly, the audience will be more than happy to accept them and become emotionally invested in them. You probably have little in common, on the surface, with a character like Shrek, a big, green glob of an ogre, but Shrek was in love, and we can all identify with that.

"Likeable" is a word that gets kicked around a lot as a prerequisite for our lead character, but that isn't always the case. Clint Eastwood's man-with-no-name wasn't a likeable guy. Watch the classic film "Hud" some time and see how likeable Paul Newman's character was in that. Kevin Spacey's character Lester Burnham in "American Beauty" was no angel, yet the role won him an Academy Award. And, who did you like among the unsavory characters in "Who's Afraid of Virginia Woolf."

Okay, how about "identifiable;" possessing common traits we all share? Again, not necessarily. I certainly didn't identify with Sean Penn in "Milk," or Michael Douglas in "Wall Street," or Mickey Rourke in "The Wrestler." I could empathize, but not relate.

That is part of the beauty of characters of this type. They aren't "every man," and therefore give us characters with unique qualities which make a character-study film worth watching. What we're looking for is *interesting*. Compelling. When people watch reality shows, it's as much to see characters they don't like as it is to see characters they like.

The rule is a bit more rigid in television, because they want us to come back week-after-week, but even there, we have fluctuations. Hugh Laurie's character in "House" is pretty much of a jerk. Same can be said of Larry David in "Curb Your Enthusiasm."

Ted Danson in "Becker" was vain, irritating and self-serving, but a wonderful curmudgeon. Archie Bunker was a narrow-minded bigot, and the entire family in "Married With Children" was comically flawed. It was part, if not all of their charm. And, they are all interesting. Even if we just tune in to see them get their comeuppance every week, we want to see them.

They all have some redeeming qualities, of course, but these are characters defined by their flaws. Despite their glaring negatives, we hold out hope for them.

So, we don't necessarily have to like them, or even identify with them. They can be totally strange personalities to us. We just have to be interested in them, enough to follow them through the story and have an emotional stake in the outcome.

This is where a well-developed backstory becomes critical. Backstory fills in the blanks for our audience, by providing relevant information which occurred before our story began. It establishes our characters, by creating the very basis for their the inner desires and conflicts.

If we have developed a comprehensive life-experience for each character, we will know how that character will act or react in a particular situation, and understand the choices he makes.

Backstory

Backstory info is tricky to get into a screenplay, without slowing things down, simply because, as the word implies, we're no longer moving forward in the story.

Therefore, backstory must be judiciously inserted into the story, in a manner which informs us of valuable facts we need to know about a character and at the same time entertains us, without dramatically stalling the forward progress of the story. Backstory can be delivered in any of three ways:

- Through dialogue
- Through a flash-forward - opening hook
- Through a flashback

Backstory Through Dialogue

This is the most frequent method, when we learn about a character's background history by simply being told, either by the character, himself, or by another character who is privy to the information. This is handy, since the backstory can be meted out in bits-and-pieces, as the story progresses, or it can be delivered in one significant speech.

One method is the straight-ahead, blatant exposition from the character, himself. First-person exposition of backstory means the character is openly telling another character something about his past. Having a character talk about himself can be effective, but it can also make a character seem self-serving, if that expositional moment isn't properly justified.

If the backstory info is tragic, your character comes off sounding like a whiner. Poor me. If the backstory is complimentary to the character, he may be perceived as a braggart.

It's often safer to have the backstory information delivered by a character other than the character who's backstory is being revealed.

Having a character state, *"I was an Olympic Gold Medalist in track"* sounds boastful. Having another character say, *"He was an Olympic Gold Medalist in track"* is informative. This also allows the backstory information to be delivered without the knowledge of the character who is the subject of the backstory, which can sometimes prove more effective.

Backstory Through a Flash-Forward

The Flash-Forward, which is actually just an opening hook, is a device which is quite common. Action occurs in the opening of our story which sets up the character, and possibly his goals and motivations. Then, we dissolve into a future time, when our story actually begins.

The story is now prefaced by backstory, which adds important information for the real-time story. You can witness this device in both "A Few Good Men" and "The Usual Suspects," where it was used effectively.

Backstory Through a Flashback

Flashbacks are, in reality, setups. If we flash back to a dramatic event which occurred between two of our characters, we're delivering setup information which we need for the real-time story we're watching.

In Summary: Backstory through dialogue, probably the most common method, is more effective when provided by a character other than the character who's backstory is being revealed. Remember, however, that talking is not showing, so this method should be employed with discretion.

Flash-forwards, which are actually opening hooks, can introduce backstory and serve as an opening hook for the real-time story to follow.

Flashbacks can work nicely to deliver backstory, when not overdone. They provide setup information designed to deepen our understanding of a character and his motivations. Use them too much, however, and the result is a stutter-start pace that only slows down the progression of the story. Constantly jumping back-and-forth through time can be distracting.

Physical Proxies

Once you have established your characters' backstory, you must now find ways to reflect that backstory in a character's actions and words. If you want to reveal a character's inner-workings visually, then you must do so with, guess what? Action.

The internal thought or emotion you want to reveal must be delivered in a manner which is visual, and allows the actor and director to interpret it. For my own edification, I've termed these actions "Physical Proxies."

There's really no mystery to it, or anything new. It's simply a reflection of the old "show, don't tell" rule. The first thing I try to incorporate into my screenwriting process, and I know many screenwriters do this, is an ability to watch the movie as I'm writing it.

When I have emotional information I want to convey; the kind which would be delivered through narrative in a novel, I picture the scene, the characters and the interaction going on and ask myself how each character would translate their internal emotions through an action, a reaction, a look, or other body language.

Physical Proxies can be supported by dialogue to achieve their greatest impact, but if I'm going to support that emotion with dialogue, then I'm looking for subtext. I don't want a literal translation of emotion into words, I want to say it in subtext which is unique to that character's attitude; subtext which mirrors the emotion conveyed by the action portrayed.

"Rocky" Again

Let's utilize a scene from "Rocky" to examine some physical proxies. We'll take another look at this scene later, in an example of scene length.

Early in the story, Rocky has been offered the fight with Apollo Creed, for the championship. Mickey, the boxing trainer, wants to be Rocky's manager.

The trouble is, the men had an earlier run-in, when Mickey took away Rocky's locker at the gym and gave it to another fighter, whom he deemed a "contender." Rocky, however, was a "tomato," who fought like an ape, and should retire.

Now, here's Mickey, showing up at the door of Rocky's shabby little apartment, hat-in-hand.

Once inside, Mickey follows Rocky around the apartment, making his case. He talks about his experiences and shows Rocky pictures of young Mickey as a boxer.

And, what does Rocky do? He keeps moving away from Mickey. He throws darts at a dart board. He gets a beer from the refrigerator. He walks to his bedroom. Finally, when all else fails, Rocky goes into the bathroom and closes the door.

These are the physical proxies Rocky employs to express what he's feeling. Here's a big, tough, heavyweight fighter, and what is he doing? Avoiding confrontation! He can go toe-to-toe with brutes in the ring, but emotional confrontation makes him uncomfortable.

This scene is just such an emotional confrontation. The more Mickey persists, the more uncomfortable Rocky grows. He's squirming, before our eyes. That's a reveal of a characteristic which is demonstrated throughout the story, not just in this scene.

Rocky keeps telling Mickey that the fight is set, and he doesn't need a manager. That's the text, but we know what's really going on. Mickey gave up on him. Mickey told him to quit. Mickey hurt his feelings. You could see it, churning around inside him. You knew the reason he was saying "no." Nobody had to tell us, because Rocky showed us.

The only time it was really addressed verbally was when Rocky, still trying to avoid the subject, steps into the doorway of his bedroom. Mickey follows him in and sees a poster of the heavyweight legend Rocky Marciano on the wall. Mickey remarks that Rocky reminds him of Marciano. He moves like the champ. He's got heart. Rocky's deadpan reply:

"Yeah, I got heart. But, I ain't got no locker, do I, Mick?"

There it is, in glorious subtext. It's personal.

Now, let's look at the scene from Mickey's point-of-view, and the action he takes to convince Rocky. He brings a picture of himself as a young fighter to show Rocky, who just remarks that he hasn't taken very good care of it.

Mickey relates exploits of some of his tough fights. He insists that Rocky needs him.

Nobody has to tell us Mickey is desperate for this. We can see it in his demeanor; the growing frustration as he continues to press, with more and more urgency in his tone. When Rocky finally goes into the bathroom and shuts the door in Mickey's face, we can see the fight go out of Mickey; the defeat in his mannerisms. His body slumps. He wearily rests his forehead against the bathroom door and mumbles:

"I'm 76 years old."

More delicious subtext for "this is my last chance." From confident hope to desperation to defeat to utter resignation, all shown through his actions, reactions, subtext, facial expressions and body language.

Another fine example can be found in "Forrest Gump." In this scene, Forrest and Jenny, the girl he loves, have returned to the house where Jenny grew up, which is now abandoned. Jenny, venting her anger, begins to throw rocks at the house, one after another, with a growing fervor, until she sinks to the ground, weeping.

Forrest moves to her and sits beside her. Then, in Voice Over narration, we hear Forrest say:

"Sometimes, I guess, there just aren't enough rocks."

While it was never stated verbally in this scene, is there any doubt that Jenny was abused in that house? We can only imagine what indignities she suffered, but we certainly know that bad things happened to her, there.

That information, that backstory, was expressed through action.

The throwing of rocks became the Physical Proxy to express the anger Jenny was feeling. Talking about it could never have had the same impact as this action.

Think of it as mime, if you like. Think of it in terms of a silent film. Ask yourself:

"What if there is no sound? How can I show what my character is feeling?"

If your character is well developed; well rounded, the right action for that character to express his inner feelings will be there. Rocky was a brute with a soft spot. Tough and crude, yet also sensitive and vulnerable.

Those conflicting traits going on inside him caused him to react to a given situation in his own unique, personal way. When he could no longer control his anger and frustration, he struck out physically, but always at inanimate objects. Never at people, unless he was in the ring. He struggled to conceal his inner feelings, fearing that expressing them would show weakness.

Rocky's Physical Proxies were his, alone. The better developed your characters, the more mannerisms and characteristics you can create to visually express their feelings.

In Summary: Employing Physical Proxies in your Action Block is one very effective way to reveal the inner workings, thoughts and emotions of your characters. It does so in a manner that both works for the reader and translates visually to the screen.

External and Internal Conflicts

External conflicts are pretty easy to grab from the story we're telling. By definition, external conflicts are physical, and therefore, played out before our eyes. The gunfights, car chases, courtroom standoffs, political posturing and natural disasters come organically from the story.

Internal conflicts rely on a character's inner-workings. Attitudes and personalities are formed by environment and past experiences.

Those characteristics do not come organically from the story. They rely on us to create them and fit them to the character, the story and the theme.

Internal conflicts arise when we force our character to do something she doesn't want to do; face something she wants to avoid.

If she can't commit to the one she loves, because of anger and bitterness from a previous relationship, she must be faced with losing "Mr. Right" forever, unless she overcomes it.

If he doesn't rise to a challenge, because he's afraid to fail, then we must force him to meet that challenge head-on.

Our characters must confront the things they fear the most. It's how they grow.

The failing comes when we create an attitude for "Jack," then have Jack play that single note, throughout the story, without fluctuating, and that can get pretty monotonous. No dimension to Jack. No growth for Jack.

Jack's attitude must be challenged and countered and questioned within his personal storyline. It requires going deeper into Jack's character to create those moral and emotional stumbling blocks for Jack to confront and overcome.

In "A Few Good Men," as one example, the character of Lt Sam Weinberg had to defend two young Marines who he felt should go to jail, because, in his view, *"They beat up on a weakling. That's all they did."*

This situation created an internal conflict for Sam, which was then reflected in his attitude toward his clients and his case.

The actor, Kevin Pollack, completely sold that attitude. Physically, he's not particularly imposing. He's not tall or muscular, he's slightly balding, visually "soft" in most respects. When he delivered that "they beat up on a weakling" line, I said to myself, *"This is a guy who was probably bullied at some point in his life."*

I don't know if Kevin Pollack was ever bullied, but I was dead certain that Sam Weinberg had been, even if he never articulated it. The internal conflict which arose from it was honest and emotional.

In "Avatar," Sam Worthington's character of Jake Sully suffered an internal conflict which provided the catalyst for the crisis of the film, itself. After living with the natives of Pandora and falling in love with one of them, Jake's loyalties completely reversed, setting the course for an external conflict with the corporation he worked for.

Sylvester Stallone's John Rambo suffered an internal conflict which served as the impetus for the first film in that series. Already feeling that he and those he served with had been abandoned by the country he fought to defend, he was now being brutalized and humiliated by a small-town Sheriff and his deputies.

It was the catalyst that drove Rambo over the edge. Without that internal conflict, his actions would not have been justified.

All of these examples serve to demonstrate how our characters' internal conflicts must serve the central storyline, and the theme.

"A Few Good Men" was about justice, and Sam's conflicted feelings about his clients played directly into that theme. Jake Sully's internal conflict placed him in direct opposition to the "greed" theme of "Avatar," and John Rambo's conflict created the "retribution" theme for the first "Rambo" film.

Internal Conflicts can also be viewed as a moral gauge for our characters. A character's morality is reflected in the manner in which he deals with his personal demons. Either, he rises above them, or he is destroyed, or at least defeated by them. They go a long way in creating depth and dimension within our characters.

In Summary: As you can see, internal conflicts shouldn't just be haphazardly dropped into a character's personality, just because you feel it might be an interesting conflict for that character. For it to matter, it must serve a higher purpose, and be true to the storyline. Internal Conflicts lead to External Conflicts, those visual actions our characters take. Internal Conflicts also affect the choices our characters make, both good and bad.

Archetypes

As pointed out in Joseph Campbell's book "The Hero's Journey," each character within a story has a specific function to perform. The Mentors, Allies, Shadows and Shape Shifters of Campbell's Mono Myth theory appear, if not literally, then metaphorically, in every form of storytelling.

The archetypes of the screen have been with us from the time we first began watching movies, and because of that, the characters, and their roles in the story, have become inherently familiar to us. That is both the good news and the bad news.

On the positive side, that familiarity helps us to connect with the story being told, and that's comforting to us as viewers, and convenient for us as writers.

On the down side, harken back to the old axiom, "familiarity breeds contempt." Archetypes are helpful in categorizing characters, in terms of their function within the story, but they also harbor a hidden danger, in that archetypes give way to stereotypes.

When we go no further than the obvious "type" choices, we wind up with cliches. The characters, no matter how small their role, must be personalized and individualized. They must be given depth and dimension, so that, while they perform an archetypal function we've all seen before, they bring to it qualities which make it unique.

Johnny Depp's Captain Jack Sparrow was played completely against type. Yes, the roguish, cocky attitude we associate with "lovable" pirate types was there, but it was countered by a playful wit, and wispish mannerisms and vocal patterns; a dichotomy which made the character distinct and all-the-more fascinating.

We simply can't have a compelling, emotional story with characters who are flat and one-dimensional. Even heavy action films, which tend to be less character-development oriented, must have characters that shine in order to work to their fullest.

"Battlefield Earth," "Speed Racer," "The Adventures of Pluto Nash," "Hudson Hawk," "Waterworld" and "The Postman" were all action films which featured name actors and studio backing, and all failed, at least relative to their budgets. But "Raiders of the Lost Ark," "Die Hard" and "Lethal Weapon" were hugely successful. The difference was largely in character development.

Once we have established a character's backstory, we have a much more definitive vision of who our character is. Now, we must reflect that characters personality to the audience.

This is accomplished in two ways: through Characteristics and Character Traits, delivered through dialogue and action, ultimately resulting in a distinctive attitude.

In Summary: Archetypes provide us with a template in creating characters necessary to support our story. However, leaning too heavily on the common traits attributed to those Archetypes can lead to stereotypes.

The writer should lean more on an Archetype's function within the story than on cliched personalities, and strive to create characters with unique qualities.

Characteristics

Characteristics are the internal qualities within a character which shape the character's personality and view of the world. Integrity and lack of same, honesty and larceny, patience and impatience, trust and suspicion, bravery and cowardice, are all characteristics.

The characteristics we create for our characters define and motivate them. The words they speak, their actions and reactions, will all be driven by those characteristics.

The Verbal Kint character, as portrayed by Kevin Spacey in "The Usual Suspects" had the characteristic of deceit. He was a devious liar, in Joseph Campbell's terms, a "shape shifter," pretending to be a low-level pawn, when he was, in fact, the mastermind and villain, Kaiser Soze. He employed this talent throughout the story, to deflect and diffuse moments of physical conflict.

If we want well-rounded, complex characters, and fodder for internal conflict, then we must "mix and match" our character's characteristic qualities. Simply put, the good guys can't be all good, and the bad guys can't be all bad.

Even if our character has only one positive characteristic, offset by many negative ones, he can still be a hero, because he possesses a redemptive quality. The Man With No Name is a good example of that, and Charles Bronson's "Death Wish" character is another.

Butch Cassidy, the outlaw, was just, darn it, a likeable guy. He was non-violent, fair-minded and generous with the money he stole, but he was still a thief, and that's not a very positive characteristic, is it? But, Butch was our hero.

"I never met a man more affable than you, Butch..." quotes Sheriff Bledsoe in the film.

We've all heard the old "write what you know" axiom, but you don't have to be a cowboy or a soldier or a jock or a Wall Street Wizard to write those characters.

There is a more important internal aspect to the write-what-you-know philosophy. We all share universal experiences of fear, elation, anxiety and the like. We've all been lied to or manipulated, angry with, in love with or suspicious of someone, at some point.

These are the wells we go to, when we create a character. They are characteristics common to us all.

Turning to our old friend, the downtrodden Rocky Balboa, we find an interesting characteristic within him which not only helps to define him in a positive light, but creates a nice internal conflict for him.

To revisit an example I pointed out previously, when Rocky got really angry, he struck out, but never at *people*, unless he was in the ring. He took out his frustration and bursts of anger on inanimate objects, as when he breaks open his locker.

At the meat-locker where Paulie works, the same kind of moment occurs. Rocky gets angry at Paulie, but instead of hitting Paulie, he hammers his fist into a side of hanging beef.

Rocky doesn't really want to hurt anyone, but his frustration dictates that he must vent, physically, on *something*. Nice characteristic, and one we all recognize, perhaps even experienced in our own lives.

In another example, we had Jack Nicholson as Col Nathan Jessup, who had a characteristic of arrogance. That characteristic was reflected in every action he took and every line of dialogue he spoke.

His arrogance made him feel like he was above the law, and it was his arrogance that became the Achilles Heel that led to his downfall.

When Danny had Jessup on the stand, he was able to browbeat him into a confession for only one reason: Jessup was so sure of himself as to believe he was untouchable.

He was a powerful man, a leader and commander, and here he was, being interrogated by some smarmy, punk kid. His ego just couldn't stand it. Without that attitude instilled in Nathan Jessup, the ending would never have worked.

However, Jessup's negative characteristic of arrogance was countered by other positive characteristics, which gave him more depth, and humanized him.

Yes, Jessup was arrogant, but he was also dedicated, patriotic, highly professional, intelligent and, at times, even charming. He even presented a logical, reasonable case for his actions. He almost made us willing to accept and excuse his arrogance and forgive him.

What Jessup demonstrated was the value of Opposing Characteristics within his character.

Opposing Characteristics

One of the most effective methods of developing a unique, well-rounded character is to give that character *opposing characteristics*.

As I've stated repeatedly, conflict is what drives a story, and opposing characteristics provide great internal conflict. Some opposing characteristics are already familiar to us.

The "hooker with a heart of gold," for instance, as in "Trading Places" and "Pretty Woman," or the politician who must choose between personal integrity and political expediency, as in "Mr. Smith Goes to Washington;" the honest cop who must bend the rules to achieve justice, like "Dirty Harry;" or the previously mentioned Lt Col Markinson in "A Few Good Men," who was driven to suicide by an internal conflict between his opposing characteristics.

I saw "Hud" in the theater, when it first came out. The film was directed by Martin Ritt and written by Irving Ravetch and Harriet Frank Jr. from Larry McMurtry's novel, and if you haven't seen it, put it at the top of your watch list.

I was already a Paul Newman fan, thanks to a compelling performance in "The Hustler," but this film defied every logic I had encountered in my movie-going experience, regarding heroes. Paul Newman was the star, and wasn't the star supposed to be a "good guy?"

Not Hud!

Hud was a real jerk, in every sense of the word. In the film was a line of dialogue that struck a chord with me. I didn't know why, at the time.

It wasn't one of those cool, unforgettable lines like *"Go ahead, make my day,"* or *"I'm mad as hell, and I'm not going to take this anymore,"* but I never forgot it. It's a simple line, delivered by Paul Newman's Hud character.

Here's the setup:

Hud is an insensitive hedonist; a rowdy, hard drinking, selfish lout, who hates his upstanding, conservative rancher-father Homer, who pretty much hates him, right back. All they do is bicker with each other, and can't agree on anything.

It is discovered that Homer's cattle have hoof-and-mouth disease, and a government man comes out to oversee the slaughter of the entire herd. The men stand above the pit with rifles and shoot every head of cattle below, in a gut-wrenching scene, until the animals are all dead.

But, the government official spots a small herd of longhorn steers, corralled nearby. The longhorns are special to Homer, who started his ranch from scratch with longhorns. When Homer assures the official that he'll take care of the longhorns, himself. The official asks:

"How do I know you'll do it?"

And, then comes the line from Hud, who glares at the man and angrily growls:

"He just said he would."

Hud stuck up for the old man! It was the only time in the entire film when Newman's character showed a flash of a redemptive quality. Oh, Hud had his charm. He was witty and rebellious and free-spirited, but beneath it lay a seething, mean-spirited underbelly.

Any way you looked at it, this guy was no hero. I kept waiting for him to show me something positive, and he just kept being an ass, until the moment he delivered that line.

It was only a moment, mind you, but it was significant for me. The reason it stuck with me is because it delivered an opposing characteristic; a brief flash of a redemptive quality I had not yet seen in Hud. Somewhere, deep inside of him, was a grudging respect for the man he professed to despise. He was telling us:

"Hey, I can hate my old man, but don't you dare call him a liar!"

It signaled the existence of conflicting emotions within the character, and that added dimension.

Opposing characteristics not only create wonderful conflict, but make our characters more real and believable.

It's also noteworthy to remember that each new characteristic we present for our character is a DEFINING MOMENT for that character.

Once our character displays that characteristic for the first time, we have revealed an aspect of the internal workings of that character, and now, we're stuck with it. To remain consistent, we must now stay true to that characteristic.

If we reveal a moment of greed in our character, then we have established that the quality of greed lives within that character. If our character is deceptive at some point, the audience will question that character's motives and actions from that moment forward. We must make certain that's what we want, before we establish it.

In Summary: Characteristics reflect the moral and psychological aspects of a character's personality. They are qualities instilled within our character based on that character's backstory; his past environment and experiences, and which are revealed by his attitude, particularly as pertains to our story and its theme.

Character Traits

Related to characteristics are CHARACTER TRAITS; the physical reflection of characteristics through visual and verbal expression. Does he have a nervous tic, like tugging at his ear when he thinks, or does she avert her eyes when she's caught in a lie? Is he a chain smoker, or an obsessive gum-chewer? Does he have a signature phrase that he frequently uses?

In "A Few Good Men," Danny Kaffee was a baseball fan, who always carried his baseball bat around his apartment, because it helped him think. James Bond took his vodka martini "shaken, not stirred." Henry Winkler's Fonzie from the sitcom "Happy Days" expressed a myriad of feelings with his trademark

"Aaayyyy."

The actor Barry Pepper played the part of a sniper in "Saving Private Ryan," who had a quirky and unique character trait. As he sighted in on his target, he prayed to God to make his aim straight, in order to vanquish his enemy.

Take a look at Quint in "Jaws," a character portrayed by the late, great Robert Shaw. Now, Quint, unlike Johnny Depp's Captain Jack Sparrow, was the epitome of a pirate, except Quint existed in the 20th Century, making his character somewhat out of context. He had, as a character trait, a little seafaring song he liked to sing that went like this:

"Farewell and adieu to you fair Spanish ladies,
Farewell and adieu, you ladies of Spain,
for we've received orders for to sail back to Boston,
and so, never more will we see you again."

A quaint little ditty, but it wasn't thrown in arbitrarily. It was firmly entrenched in the character's personality and used to great effect. Quint sings his little song three times in the film, and each time it is delivered in a different context.

The first time is when Matt Hooper, Richard Dreyfuss is bringing his shark cage aboard the Orca. Quint stops him.

"What have you got there?"

Hooper replies, *"A shark cage."*

Quint gives him a bemused look. *"Shark cage? You go in the cage?"*

Hooper nods.

Quint: *"Cage goes in the water?"*

Again, Hooper nods.

Quint: *"Shark's in the water? Our shark?"*

Once more, Hooper nods.

With an impish little smile, Quint begins to sing, *"Farewell and adieu to you, fair Spanish ladies..."*

In this case, Quint's character trait is employed as a reflection of his attitude, and as subtext:

"You're going to die, you fool!"

The next time we hear the song, the three men, Quint, Hooper and Sheriff Brody are sharing a bottle of peach brandy below deck, getting a bit tipsy as Quint and Hooper boisterously exchange shark-attack stories.

Then, the mood gets somber as Quint relates the story of the U.S.S. Indianapolis, on which he served; the ship that went down with all hands, wasn't found for days, and left the survivors set upon and terrorized by sharks. Grim stuff, and the jovial mood has dampened.

There is a lull when the story ends, and Quint begins to sing, soft and low...

"Farewell and adieu to you, fair Spanish ladies..."

Now, the song is used as a hymn to his lost comrades; a tribute.

The last time the song is used, the men have hooked the huge shark, but the boat struggles to keep it in tow. The beast fights hard, pulling them backward. The Orca's engines strain and groan. Smoke pours from the engine room. The stern of the boat dips nearly into the water. Quint stands at the wheel and in a course, loud voice through gritted teeth, belts out...

"Farewell and adieu to you fair Spanish ladies...!"

This time, though, it comes out like a fight song; a war chant. A challenge.

So, there's a character trait given to Quint that not only enhances his character, but works into the story on three separate levels. That's the kind of character trait we want to create for our character. One that is distinctive, unique and effective in defining the character.

In Summary: Character traits are repetitive physical behaviors instilled in our characters, which reveal aspects of a character's internal workings through actions we actually see on the screen.

Character Goals and Conflicts

Beyond Characteristics and Character Traits, our characters, most pointedly our Central Protagonist, must have internal goals and external goals, as well as internal and external conflicts. It isn't enough to simply have them strive for the brass ring. The failure to achieve the goal should have long lasting personal consequences for our hero.

As pointed out, Frank Galvin's story in "The Verdict" was one of redemption. Settling his case would have achieved his external goal of a nice, fat fee, but would have done little to reward him with the redemption he sought and needed.

Rocky Balboa was also handed an opportunity for redemption, but his greatest internal goal was to simply not be embarrassed, to not have what little pride he had left dashed. He was risking his self-respect. When he is first offered the fight with Apollo Creed, he declines. He considers himself a ham-and-egger, while Apollo is the best.

"It wouldn't be a very good fight."

Similarly, in "A Few Good Men," Danny Kaffee is plagued by the memory and reputation of his father, a highly respected Judge Advocate General. Internally, he has a need to meet up to those high standards. He does so by trying and winning a case his father would never have taken on.

And, it goes deeper. He also has a desire to prove himself as a Naval Officer, a challenge leveled at him by Harold Dawson, his Marine client. When Danny urges Dawson to plea bargain for a lower sentence, Dawson contemptuously snaps:

"You're such a coward. I can't believe they let you wear a uniform."

He then refuses to salute Danny. But, in the resolve, after Danny has fought his heart out for Dawson in court, Dawson does salute him, with the line:

"Ten-hut! There's an officer on deck!"

These were two internal goals and conflicts which were tied up neatly in the end, in our resolve.

Internal Goals and Internal Conflicts go hand-in-hand. Throughout your story, complications should arise which challenge not only the external story goal, but challenge our hero on a personal level. Losing must come at a grievously high price.

When you hear the much abused term "character arc," that is what they're talking about, although many who use it aren't entirely aware of that. I have nothing against the term, mind you. I think it's quite definitive. It's just important that you truly understand what it means. It signals growth; evolution in a character.

Danny Kaffee losing one case in court would not be a tragedy. Losing his freedom, his reputation and his future, along with failing to live up to his father's standards, would be.

In Summary: Through his struggle to attain the external story goal, our hero must resolve issues within himself, so that by the end of the story, if he wins, he has gained wisdom, maturity, often salvation through the struggle. And, if he loses, he has lost all that is of greatest importance to his personal growth.

The Villain

"The Villain is the hero of his story."

I don't know who first coined this phrase, or I would certainly credit them, but I find it tremendously enlightening.

Too often, villains in films are given short shrift. The fact is, the hero is only as worthy as his opponent. We want our heroes to face tremendous odds, and therefore, the opposition needs to hold all the cards; have much greater power for our hero to overcome.

In action films, our villains are often driven by a desire for greed or power. But, even then, we can bolster their characters by giving them positive qualities.

If the villain is the hero of his story, then he must have a legitimate and logical point of view. He must also have internal and external goals, and internal and external conflicts. He must have something within him that we can relate to, even if we disagree with it.

He must have his own story.

Jack Nicholson's Col Jessup had this in "A Few Good Men". When he made his "You can't handle the truth" speech, he made many valid points that were hard to dispute.

"Santiago's death, while tragic, probably saved lives."

and:

"You want me on that wall. You need me on that wall!"

This point-of-view made his character a much stronger opposition. Even though we, the audience, knew he was wrong, we could understand how he felt the way he did. We could actually elicit some sympathy for him.

It's a device that has been used effectively in many, many films. The Frankenstein monster and King Kong are a couple of clear examples. When they met their demise, we actually felt sorry for them.

In "Apocalypse Now", Marlon Brando's Col Kurtz has some stellar qualities, and an impeccable military record, causing his assassin, Martin Sheen's Capt. Willard, when looking over the Colonel's record, to comment:

"I couldn't believe they wanted this guy dead."

The trouble was, Col Kurtz had gone mad. He was now an insane warrior with his own personal army, but just because he was crazy didn't mean he wasn't still smart. Smart and crazy makes for a great villain. He also had, even in his madness, some logic to his philosophy and actions. He thought he had a better idea for how to fight a war, and had the track record to support it.

Intelligence is a characteristic we like in our villain. One doesn't gain many karma points for defeating a stupid bad guy. "Clown" villains work fine in light or slapstick comedies, but even then, they must present a formidable obstacle to overcome.

Odds are, if our villains are dumb, our heroes are also not the brightest bulbs on the tree. Harold and Kumar, for instance, or Cheech and Chong, or pick any of several Jim Carrey characters. Just remember, audiences have a natural tendency to root for the underdog. We want our hero, not our villain, to be that underdog.

In Summary: Our villains should be developed with as much care and consideration as our heroes. Villains should be endowed with negative and positive qualities, opposing characteristics and internal and external goals and conflicts.

We must never limit the dynamics of our hero's opposition, for it is the strength of that opposition which determines the quality of our hero's achievement.

Supporting Characters

Okay, we've developed a Central Protagonist; our hero, and our Central Antagonist, the villain. Now, we need Supporting Characters. And supporting characters are there to support our leads, right? Well, yes, but just as importantly, they are there to support the story, and so doing, serve the theme.

Protagonist supporting characters will assist our hero in attaining his goal, and antagonist supporting characters will assist in opposing him, but they cannot do so without staying *on story*. They have a function to serve in moving the story forward, aside from helping our hero. And, as pointed out, they must also have a relationship to the theme, a "take."

The amount of story time a supporting character gets is relative to the importance of that character to the story. If we really like a character we've created, and want to keep him around, then we'd better give him something to do; some responsibility which is significant; a personal goal to achieve.

Just as I've pointed out for our villain, each supporting character also has a story. If a character has an "arc," that means story, however limited in terms of scope.

Even the smallest of roles demand our attention. The more we can do to make them unique in some respect; the more we can humanize them, even in the tiniest of ways, the more believable they will become.

An actor brought this point home to me, when he asked if I would give his character a name in a sitcom script I wrote with Danny Morris for "Safe at Home." He had one of those "Cop #1" type, non-speaking rolls.

My initial thought was, *"It's a bit part, with no lines. What difference does it make?"* but when I asked him why, he explained that "Officer Johnson" looked a lot better on his resume than "Cop #1." It looked like a real part.

Remember what I said about perception in the industry? His point was made, and I gladly conceded. It helped me realize the value of paying attention to the little details when creating a character, at any level, not just for the actor's sake, but for the sake of making the script more believable.

There are no police officers cruising the city streets with "Cop #1" on their name tags. That may not matter on the screen, but it can matter in the script...and on an actor's resume.

Of course, there are going to be characters who don't warrant a name; tiny parts, largely insignificant, and very brief on the screen. But, if they're in any way prominent in the story, particularly if they have a line or two, they're worthy of a moniker.

In Summary: When we give our supporting characters the same benefit of depth and dimension that we apply to our leads, even though at a lesser degree, it will strengthen our story immeasurably, and it will serve to strengthen our lead characters, in addition.

Protagonist as Antagonist

In any well-designed story, there will be at least one Supporting Protagonist, sometimes more, who will oppose the choice our hero has made, at some point.

There are some specific terms for this moment in a story, but I simply call it "Protagonist as Antagonist." It is designed to reflect the raising stakes.

We expect our hero to be opposed by the villain(s), but when it comes from one of the "good guys," it has a much greater impact. It emphasizes the level of risk our hero is taking.

For example, let's go back to "The Verdict," wherein Paul Newman's character, Attorney Frank Galvin, has been handed a medical malpractice case by his close friend Mickey Morrissey, played by Jack Warden. Mickey expects the case to settle. So do the clients, and indeed, the defendants have offered a juicy settlement.

But, in a crisis-of-conscience moment, Frank decides, on his own, to take the case to trial. Mickey corners him and verbally bashes him with a "What are you, nuts?" speech. The clients are outraged, and threaten Frank with repercussions. Now, if Frank fails, he has more to lose than ever. The stakes have gone up.

You can often find the mirror of this moment among our Antagonist Support. In other words, Antagonist as Protagonist.

This is clearly demonstrated in the character of Kevin Bacon's Jack Ross in "A Few Good Men." Jack was Danny Kaffee's opposing counsel in the trial, but interestingly, they were good friends.

At various points in the story, Jack makes specific attempts to save Danny from himself. He urges Danny not to go to trial, not because Jack is afraid of losing, but because he's concerned about the damage it will do to his friend.

While Jack Ross is technically an antagonist, for story purposes, he is a protagonist in his subplot arc: his relationship with Danny Kaffee.

This serves two purposes. As pointed out, this action by Jack emphasizes the increasing risk that Danny is taking; a warning that too much is on the line. In addition to that, it creates a nice internal conflict for the character of Jack Ross. He's here to win a case, and Danny is his opposing counsel. But, Danny is also his friend, and Jack fears for him. He's conflicted. A double-whammy of a story point.

In Summary: Building characters through the combination of characteristics, opposing characteristics, internal and external goals and conflicts, character traits and backstory, we have made those characters whole. We've created human beings.

CHAPTER 12

The Acts

Among screenwriting camps; philosophies, there is some disagreement on the number of acts in a screenplay. I've heard about the five-act structure, the nine-act structure and the twelve...yes, twelve act structure. This conclusion is usually arrived at by those who, wrongly, I believe, classify certain story beats as acts.

There are major story beats; important plot points, such as the opening hook, inciting incident and mid-point story turn, but I see those as story beats necessary to specific acts, rather than as traditional acts, themselves. It's a matter of perception. Pick your poison. I deal with the three-act structure, so that's what I'll talk about.

An Act, in literal terms, is a sequence of scenes which make up a portion of a story. Each act has a unique and specific duty to perform. Our first act sets up the story, our second act puts the story into motion and complicates it, and our third act brings all prior story events to a climax and resolves the story.

Each act break may be viewed as a bookmark, of sorts. It marks the location of a significant, critical plot point in the story, and signifies a SHIFT in the story; the story going in a new direction. There are two act breaks within a story written for the screen: The Act One break and the Act Two break, and they are radically different in design.

There is another major story shift at the mid-story turning point, which I like to call "Page 60." This is viewed by many as an act break, as well, but I do not, because it doesn't meet the requirements to qualify. Rather, I consider this moment of story-shift to be an element of the second act.

The end of the third act is, of course, the end of the story, so I don't categorize that as an act break, either.

Therefore, when Act One has successfully performed its duty of grabbing our interest and setting up the story, we, the audience, must have a clear grasp of who our Central Protagonist is, what he wants and what he's up against. That's the RESOLVE for Act One.

We also need to know what our protagonist intends to do about the issue which has been presented to him in the first act, driven by the Story Trigger. What is his next move? That's the MOTIVATING FACTOR that propels us into Act Two.

The second act provides the obstacles our protagonist must overcome, raises the stakes and ends with its own RESOLVE and its own form of motivation into Act Three.

The resolve and motivating factors of Act Two are much more flexible than those of Act One, as will be explained, but they must be there, and they must be clear.

Act Three, then, provides the climactic win-or-lose conflict of the story as its MOTIVATING FACTOR, and the result of that conflict gives us the RESOLVE of not only the act, but of the story, itself.

When broken down into its basic plot points, the Three Act Structure of a screenplay will lay out in this manner:

The Three Act Structure

ACT ONE - SETUP – Establish:

Theme - Master and Active

Central Protagonist

Central Force of Antagonism

Value at Stake

Story Trigger

Act One Break (Up or Down)

ACT TWO - OBSTACLES AND COMPLICATIONS

Heighten Forces of Antagonism

Develop Subplots and Supporting Characters

Increase Threat to the Value at Stake

MIDPOINT - The False Ending/Point-of-no-return

Act Two Crisis

Act Two Break (Up or Down)

ACT THREE - CRISIS/CLIMAX/RESOLVE

Crisis/Ultimate Threat to the Value at Stake

Climax/Moment-of-truth Confrontation

Resolve of Plot

Resolve of Subplots

THE END - (Up or Down)

Now, let's take a closer look at each act, its function, and some of the structural elements employed.

Act One - The Setup

The basic function of Act One is to introduce our hero and his world, create the impetus for the story and send our hero in pursuit of a goal. This is where we meet our Central Protagonists and Antagonists; the "good guys" and the "bad guys."

However, the task of the setup doesn't end with the central storyline or characters. Subplots, supporting characters, internal issues, relationships and many elements of potential future conflict must be addressed, as well.

It is commonly accepted in screenwriting that when we encounter story problems in later acts, it can usually be attributed to the lack of a first act setup.

Make that plural: Setups, because everything that follows in our story relies on what happens in the first act. Story arc, character arcs and potential complications all begin here. As leery as I tend to be of etched-in-stone, hard-and-fast rules, here comes one that I swear by:

If you set it up, you must pay it off!

I know that sounds simplistic. Pure logic, right? Still, it's surprising how often I see it violated. I all too frequently see setups without payoffs and payoffs without setups.

It's a cheat for the audience, because they're savvy enough to know, right up front, when something or someone of significance to the story is being introduced to them. They recognize setups as setups. They'll be waiting for a payoff, and we'd better give it to them.

If a woman protagonist has an antagonistic boss who berates her in Act One, then we're tasked with the responsibility of having her turn the tables on him, somewhere down the road. We've set up a conflict. We must pay off that conflict.

If we create a character who appears to have significance to the story, then disappears, we've created unfinished business, and the audience, be it of the theater or reader variety, will not be amused. Moreover, that conflict must reflect a characteristic in our protagonist, and play into her personal story. It's part-and-parcel of establishing the character.

It works in reverse, as well. It's easy, when we're into the third act, to forget about our first act. It's so far behind us. Yet, if we create a big moment that hasn't been justified; hasn't been set up,

The Acts

we risk leaving the audience members baffled, wondering where the hell that came from.

If our hero in the Act Three climax wins the day by creating a bomb from ingredients found in his mother's kitchen, we'd better have some indication that he knows how to do such things.

Perhaps, Johnny was a chemistry-nerd in high school, or maybe he wrote a dissertation about terrorist tactics, and picked up the info there.

A setup can be expressed through a single line of dialogue. It can be related through a visual; a poster on the wall, a trophy on a shelf, a book in his library. It just has to be there, in the first act.

It isn't at all unusual to repeatedly jump back to the first act to insert a setup for a wonderful payoff which has just occurred to us, many pages into the story.

Wonderful moments of creativity come, during the process, which beg to be written. That's great. Just, don't forget to go back to Act One and set it up.

Along with our initial setups in Act One, we will have an event; an inciting incident, which I like to call the Story Trigger, to set the story into motion, by challenging our hero and forcing him to make a difficult choice. That is the MOTIVATING FACTOR necessary to create our first story-shift.

This Story Trigger can be created in two basic fashions: either our Protagonist chooses to take action, or the action is forced upon our Protagonist. Act One will RESOLVE with the action our Central Protagonist's takes.

At the end of this act, we should have a sense of who our main characters are, what they want and what they're up against. The audience will know the Master and Active themes, i.e., what the story is about and what message it plans to deliver.

The way I view it, there are five major story points which must be addressed in the first act. These are the "bare bones" requirements of Act One. These elements create a basic Beat Sheet for the first act that looks like this:

Act One Beat Sheet

1. The Hook - How do we grab the reader and pull him into the story?
2. Introductions - Who is the Central Protagonist, and what is her world like? Who is the Central Antagonist, or what is the Central Force of Antagonism? Who are our supporting characters, and how do they relate to our Central Protagonist or Central Antagonist?
3. The Story Trigger - What event occurs which creates the need for the Central Protagonist to take action? Without this event, there is no story.
4. The Goal - What does the Central Protagonist want to achieve, by taking action?
5. The Resolve - What action does the character choose to take?

These five basic story points are the "must haves" for the first act.

Now, let's break down the major elements and story points of Act One in detail, starting with the first scene.

The Opening Scene

There is a train of thought that our first scene should be a microcosm of our entire story. I researched this the way I research most rules I've run across, by watching well-made, successful films and applying the rule to each of them, to see if it sticks. It doesn't always, which tells me that this rule isn't really a rule. It's an option; a choice, and it's a good one, but some fine films have been made without doing it. Here's one example.

The film "Rocky" opens with Rocky in a fight with a boxer aptly named Spider Savitch. The fight is awkward and brutal, and after some dirty tactics by Spider, Rocky prevails. That's the opening scene, but it certainly isn't a microcosm of the film.

The scene is about boxing. The story is about redemption. That scene comes next, when Rocky comes home to an empty apartment, and we see bits and pieces of his life, and how far down his life has taken him.

The opener is a great hook. It gets us right into the film, establishes the "world" of our story, and even gives us insight into our hero, Rocky. But, it says nothing about the redemption theme and little about the character. Certainly, it's not enough to be considered a microcosm of the movie.

Now, let me show you how this bendable microcosm rule works, when it works.

Let's take the first scene of "Butch Cassidy and the Sundance Kid," an Academy Award winning screenplay by William Goldman, and one of my personal favorites.

As we fade in, Butch, played by Paul Newman, comes out of a building on one side of the street and walks to a bank, on the other side. This is all done in sepia tones, everything bathed in reddish-brown, held over from the newsreel opening. The entire opening sequence; the introduction of Butch and that of Robert Redford's Sundance character are filmed this way.

Butch walks into the bank. It's closing time, and we get a series of shots; quick flashes of a safe door locking, window shutters slamming down, latches turning, doors being closed and locked, as the employees file out past an armed guard.

Butch watches all of this with chagrin, and as he walks out, remarks to the guard:

"What happened to the old bank? It was beautiful!"

The guard replies, *"People kept robbing it."*

Butch's response?

"Small price to pay for beauty."

Butch exits and the scene ends.

This scene truly is a microcosm of the movie, because it gives us both the Master Theme and our lead character's Take On The Theme. The theme, once more, is "progress." The Active Theme, we will learn later, is "Times change, and if you can't change with them, you are doomed."

The bank has upgraded. Times are changing. That point is driven into us numerous times, in different ways, throughout the film. Watch it, some time and you'll see. Just a few examples:

Butch says to his gang, *"It's harder now! You've gotta plan more, you've gotta prepare more."*

When Butch and Sundance, on the run, look up their friend, Sheriff Bledsoe, played by veteran character actor Jeff Corey, for help, he scoffs at them, *"It's over, don't you get that? Your times is over, and you're gonna die bloody..."*

When Butch contemptuously wheels his bicycle (*"The future mode of transportation..."* according to the salesman) down the hill, where it topples into the mud, he spouts, *"The future's all yours, ya lousy bicycle!"*

The Progress theme is established right off the top, in Act One, Scene One with an opening scene which is a true microcosm of the movie. Once established, the "progress" theme recurs numerous times in the story. This is an important consideration, because staying "on theme" keeps the story focused. Remember that all story and character beats should relate to the Master and Active Themes.

As for this first scene's relation to the Character's Take On The Theme, we get it from Butch's line:

"Small price to pay for beauty!"

He obviously resists these changing times. He evolves, throughout the story, from denying it to fighting it to trying to escape it. In the end, his unwillingness, or inability to change with the times; to adjust to progress, leads to his downfall.

This is an example of a character whose Take on the Theme does not change as the story progresses. We want our heroes to grow, remember?

In most cases, that growth is demonstrated by a changing Take on the Theme. That generally provides us with an "up," or "happy" ending. Only, Butch didn't grow. His Take didn't change, and because it didn't, the story could only end tragically.

In Summary: Whether your opening scene is a microcosm of the movie or not, the beginning of your story, within the first ten pages, must grab the reader, or it will never have a chance to grab an audience.

That's something you must always remain cognizant of. A screenplay is first and foremost a reading experience. You may be able to visualize a wonderful scene in your head, but if the reader doesn't see it just as clearly, you're in trouble. So, those first ten pages must hook our reader solidly, compelling him to keep reading.

That said, let's examine the Hook.

The Hook

As the old joke goes, "first you gotta get their attention," and that's what hooks are for. In these days of ubiquitous media and short attention spans, a good hook is a must.

There is a school of thought I've encountered which teaches that the Story Trigger, i.e., inciting incident, and the Hook are one-and-the-same. Although the Story Trigger can be utilized as a hook, as I will explain, they are still two distinctly different story devices.

The single responsibility of a hook is to do just as it implies: hook the reader of the screenplay, and later the viewer of the movie, in a manner which entices him to read on, or continue watching.

That's it. It does not, by its definition, set the story into motion, as the Story Trigger does.

There are many great, tried-and-true hooks to choose from, and

I've chosen a few of the more common ones as examples.

The Action Hook

The Action Hook is quite popular, of course. Opening with action is nearly always a safe choice. If it's opening an Action film, then it's almost a requirement.

Action films frequently use Action Hooks in the form of off-story action prologues. By this, I mean, we'll lead into our story with the climactic sequence of a prior event, which really has little to do with the story we're about to see, other than to set the tone.

"Raiders of the Lost Ark" employed the Action Hook in this manner, with Indy recovering an ancient artifact from a cave, nimbly avoiding a series of booby traps, only to encounter his arch rival, Belloq, before ultimately making his escape. Again, it had nothing to do with the storyline of recovering the Lost Ark, although it did nicely set up our hero and villain.

Barring that simple prologue device, action of pretty much any type will hook a viewer, because the stakes of that action are nearly always life-and-death, and the outcome is of immediate importance. Opening with the jarring urgency of a chase or fight sequence is sure to engage the viewer.

The Curiosity Hook

The Curiosity Hook is another staple. Any kind of story can open with a Curiosity Hook, since its only requirement is to create a question in the viewer's mind; a question which must be answered, before they consider getting up out of their seats.

Take the opening scene of "Sunset Boulevard," which finds our Central Protagonist, Joe Gillis, floating face-down in a swimming pool, drowned, as he narrates from the great beyond in Voice Over. Don't we just have to know how he got here?

And, look back some years to screenwriter Peter Stone's memorable "Charade," a film which opens with a man's dead body being thrown from a train.

A more subtle Curiosity Hook was used in "Saving Private Ryan," when an aging veteran approaches a very special gravestone at Arlington Cemetery. Is the man in the grave Private Ryan, or is he the man visiting the grave? We won't know, until the story comes to a climax.

These types of curiosity hooks are ideal, because the questions they ask will not be answered until the end of the story.

That requires the audience to take the full journey, if they want the answer. Whether they care enough to hang around depends on what we, the writers, do in between the question and the answer.

The Suspense Hook

The Suspense Hook is one we see frequently at the top of Suspense films, Mysteries and Crime Dramas. We might open with a woman walking down a deserted street, late at night, while a figure lurks in the shadows of an alley, ahead.

A murder, or attempt at one, is a common device. The beauty of this type of hook is that it serves more than one purpose, as it also frequently provides us with the Story Trigger, right up front.

Suspense is a wonderful tool to utilize at any point in a story, of course, but it is particularly effective in setting the tone of our story at the outset, and that is an important factor.

The Misdirection Hook

The Misdirection Hook is one which uses surprise as its main attraction. It delivers a twist, by leading the audience in one direction, then suddenly changing course. We've all seen stories which open with some tense, dramatic action, like a murder, then hear "Cut!" from an off screen director and pull back to reveal that we're actually the set of a movie or TV show, and the murder is fictitious.

The James Bond film "Never Say Never Again" also employed the Misdirection hook, actually combining it with an Action Hook. Sean Connery's James is seen overcoming a series of obstacles and taking out several bad guys in order to rescue a damsel in distress, who then unceremoniously stabs him in the stomach with a knife. The misdirection is revealed immediately thereafter, when we discover that this opening sequence has all been nothing but a training exercise.

The Suspense Hook often provides a good premise for the Misdirection Hook, as well.

Take the example from the Suspense Hook definition above; a woman walking down a deserted street, while a man lurks in the shadows ahead.

A suspenseful scenario. But, when she gets there, the guy jumps out from the shadows and yells "Surprise!" and we find out he's her boyfriend. The suspense, in this case, is a red herring event which leads us into the misdirection.

The Misdirection Hook is sometimes used in comedies, in which case, it will not only give us a reversal in the action of the scene, but in the tone, as well. It can come off like a kind of a cheap prank, if we aren't careful, to play "Ha, ha, fooled you!" with the audience, but it's effective, when executed well.

Bear in mind that each of these hooks should establish the tone of the story to come, even if it isn't a true microcosm of the story, and it must arouse a curiosity in the reader; a thirst which can only be quenched by reading on.

In Summary: A solid hook has become more important than ever, in recent years. It is our first opportunity to engage the reader, and therefore the audience. A weak hook, or lack of a hook at all in our story means that few readers, beyond friends or family, will ever make it into the second act.

Remember, though, just because we've hooked them doesn't mean we can't still lose them. We've all walked out of a theater or changed the channel in the middle of a film. It isn't unusual to see a movie start with a slam-bang, in-your-face hook, then fizzle out further down the line, because the story doesn't hold up.

Act One - Introductions

Now that we have their attention, let's delve into the next phase of Act One: setting up our main characters. Possibly, we started doing that in our opening scene. If our hook also establishes our Central Protagonist, all the better. It doesn't always, though, so that's our next consideration. Throughout this act, we need to answer some questions, and the first is:

Whose story is it?

We need to know who it is we're following, here. Who are we rooting for? "A Few Good Men" is, of course, Tom Cruise's story. Yet, the movie doesn't open on him. We first get the opening hook; the assault on Santiago by Dawson and Downey. Even then, we meet Demi Moore's character, Joanne, before we meet that of Tom Cruise.

What makes this his story is that he is charged with the responsibility of carrying out the Active Theme. In this case, that theme is "Justice will prevail." He's the guy who has to make that happen. We're a few minutes into the film, before we know that, but it is still established early in the first act.

Next question:

What does our hero's normal life; the status quo, look like?

When we do meet and connect with our Central Protagonist, we want to experience his every day world. A character must grow and evolve, explore new territory and shake up his world, once the story kicks in. That means, we must have something to compare that new world to. We have to see what life is really like for him, in order to appreciate the contrast.

Take another look at "Raiders of the Lost Ark." In the opening hook, an Action Hook, Indy is attempting to liberate a gold statue from a cave in South America. He survives a harrowing array of booby-traps and gets out, only to have his prize taken from him by our villain, Belloq, played by Paul Freeman, who then tries to kill him. Of course, he escapes.

That's a microcosm of the story, a glance at the world to come, and more to the point, a great way to introduce an action hero. In this case, we actually see the new world before we see the character's old world, in order to provide the film with a high-octane opening hook.

After that opening hook, we see Indy in his University setting. We get a look at "Professor" Jones, and the world he inhabits. In his real life, he's a teacher; quite average, even a little on the frumpy, nerdy side.

Consider that if were we writing this story chronologically, this is the world we would open on, getting all of the setup and gathering information for our journey into Act Two. But, truly, that's a lot of slow-moving, mundane action and a lot of talking. We're trying to suck our audience in at the opening gun, and a sequence like this doesn't cut it. So, we get a "new world" action sequence first, to grab our attention and tease us with the promise of the exciting action to come.

This is a structural choice often employed by action films, including those of the James Bond ilk. We'll often open with an action sequence, wherein James does something exciting and heroic, barely making it out alive. This provides our "grab-em-by-the-gonads" opening hook.

Then, we'll cut to a true "setup" sequence at headquarters, with M., Moneypenny, Q and the rest. We'll hear about the mission, get backstory on the bad guy we're after and see all the new toys James will acquire for the job. That's the normal world for Bond. When the second act begins, we'll be entering an entirely different world. Usually, this will be the villain's world.

Which brings us to our next question:

What force of antagonism opposes our hero?

We must, in Act One, introduce our Central Force of Antagonism.

As previously established, that doesn't have to be a human. It can be a force of nature, a system or the hero, himself. Yet, we must know what our hero is up against before moving into Act Two.

It isn't always necessary to put our hero into direct conflict with our Central Force of Antagonism in the first act, but we must know who, or what, stands between our Central Protagonist and his goal. That Force of Antagonism should always have a position of superior strength to our protagonist.

Okay, we've created our hook and introduced our central characters. Onward to:

What event forces our hero into action?

As I've mentioned, I like to call this moment the "Story Trigger", but "Inciting Incident" is the term you're most likely to hear floating around the industry, and it's about as definitive as you can get. Call it what you like, as long as you understand it.

The Story Trigger is as much a setup for our protagonist as any form of introduction. It's our first look at how our protagonist responds to a challenge, and is deeply revealing of his nature.

To get this ball rolling, we must create an event which changes the course of our Central Protagonist's life. Let me re-emphasize that *without this event, there would not be a story.*

Being a very flexible little plot point, this incident can occur anywhere in the first act. Anywhere. It just has to happen within Act One.

One little trick which gets our story moving mui pronto is to actually use the Story Trigger as an opening hook. There are numerous instances I can cite where this occurs. The opening of "A Few Good Men" I mentioned earlier, the assault on one Marine by two others, did this. That's what created a story for our Central Protagonist.

The first shark attack in "Jaws" does the same thing: Story Trigger as Opening Hook. Likewise, the opening scene in "Star Wars," with the attack on Princess Lea's ship, triggers that story...and many sequels to follow.

In other cases, the Story Trigger comes at the very end of Act One, and doubles as an act break. Take a look at "Dave," and you'll find the story trigger employed in such a manner. At the end of the act, the real President has a stroke and falls into a coma, and Dave, the celebrity impersonator, is chosen to double for him. "The Wizard of Oz" does it, too. The tornado which sweeps Dorothy away occurs at the end of the first act. The second act opens, in color, upon Dorothy's arrival in Oz. Moving from black-and-white to color provided a stark contrast between the two worlds.

Also, witness "Saving Private Ryan," where nearly the entire first act was taken up by the D-Day invasion. It was at the act break, however, the reveal of the death of the third of four Ryan brothers, which served as the Story Trigger.

These are handy story choices, in that they cover two major story points in one fell swoop: Story Trigger as Opening Hook or Story Trigger as First Act Break. But, as pointed out, our Story Trigger can occur at any point in the first act.

Okay, we're on a roll. We've hooked the reader, set up our main characters and created a story trigger. What's next?

What does our hero want?

Our hero has made a choice to take action, thanks to the Story Trigger we've created. But, what will be the preferred outcome of that action, for our hero? What is the goal which will bring this story to a successful conclusion? What is it that's worth the struggle? Because it will be a struggle. It has to be.

Here comes another one of those flexible rules. You'll hear from some sources that the hero's goal must change at certain points in the story. Well, yes and no...sometimes, but not always.

For instance, Rocky Balboa's goal changed twice, by my count. When we first met him, he was simply an aging fighter trying to get by, and not doing it very well. When he accepted the challenge to fight Apollo Creed, his goal changed. He wanted what all boxers want, when they climb into the ring: to win.

In Act Two, Rocky's goal changed again. Convinced that he couldn't achieve victory, he just wanted to go the distance; to prove he was worthy. No one had ever gone the distance with Apollo Creed. It wasn't winning the fight, but it would salvage his pride; it would achieve his redemption, and that is the point of the story.

In "A Few Good Men," Danny Kaffee's initial goal was to plea bargain his case. He was good at that, had done it many times, and since he had never tried a case in court, it seemed the prudent thing to do. That would have been the easy way out, which is generally the course any character will take, at the outset. We never let them get away with that, of course. When he was forced into going to court, Kaffee's goal changed. He needed to win.

Remember, however, that just because there are adjustments to the goal, the Active Theme doesn't deviate. Danny Kaffee still had to obtain justice for his clients, and Rocky still had to achieve redemption.

On the flip side, the goal of Charles Bronson's character in "Death Wish" was to seek revenge for the murder of his wife and the brutal rape of his daughter, through vigilante justice. That goal never changed, either in the flagship film or the numerous sequels which followed.

Likewise, the goal in "Raiders of the Lost Ark" also remained consistent: to recover the Lost Ark and preserve it for history. The goal was compounded; the stakes raised, when the Nazis entered the fray to acquire the Ark for their own nefarious purposes, but the goal, itself, remained constant.

The course our hero chooses to achieve his goal will most certainly change, reflecting the building complications of our story and how the hero adjusts to them, but not always the goal, itself.

As you can see by these examples, changing the character's personal goal is another one of those suggestions, rather than an etched-in-stone rule. I reiterate my caution: don't try to fit your square-peg story into a round-hole rule.

Most of the rules-which-are-actually-choices are there to guide us; to give us a road map with possible stops along the way; to offer us tools and options which help us do our job. We should not allow them to restrict our creativity.

We will also establish, in this first act, supporting characters who will serve a variety of purposes. The people who surround and relate to our Central Protagonist tell us as much about him as anything. Through these supporting characters, we will gain a reflection of our hero's thoughts and motives, and have his actions supported, questioned or challenged.

The relationships between our Central Protagonist and our supporting characters automatically become subplots, each with its own arc; a story-within-the-story. By establishing strong supporting characters with complex relationships, we're creating the building blocks to add depth and dimension to our story, as it progresses.

So, here we are at the end of Act One. We've hooked our viewers, established our main characters and supporting characters, introduced our force of antagonism, set up an event which triggers the story and given our hero a goal.

The setup is over. Now, we need an Act Break.

But what, exactly, is an Act Break, and what makes an Act Break an Act Break?

Simply put, it's the end of one phase of the story and the beginning of the next, and represents a change in story direction.

The Act One Break

The end of the first act should come with a sense of resolve. All of our necessary questions should have been answered and we should now be ready to send our character into the fight, in pursuit of her goal. Anticipation should be high. The Central Protagonist has made a choice to take action, and now it's time to set that action into motion.

We're entering a new world, established by a new set of circumstances. Rocky is going to fight the champ. Butch and Sundance are relentlessly pursued by the Super Posse. Sheriff Brody has to take steps to protect the citizens of Amity from the killer shark.

In many cases, the shift into Act Two actually involves a change of location. Danny Kaffee flies to Cuba to interview Jessup and his cohorts. Dave moves into the White House to play President. Bond enters an exotic location to begin his battle with the villain. Dorothy is swept away to the land of Oz.

But, what of the aforementioned Rocky Balboa? His setting doesn't change, at least, not physically. Psychologically, however, it's a whole new ball game. He may still be living in the same ratty apartment and working out in the same gym, but now, he's training to fight the heavyweight champion of the world. Once a nobody, now he's a celebrity. For him, this is, indeed, a new world.

It's a handy little device to clearly break an act, differentiating Act One from Act Two with a change of setting for the story, but it doesn't always apply.

In any case, the shift into Act Two will signal a major change in the life of our protagonist and force him to face new challenges. If our hero is to be successful, he must grow in order to overcome the obstacles he will face. If he doesn't grow, then he will fail, leaving us with a tragic ending.

Act Two - Obstacles and Complications

This is where most of us get lost, at least in our early writing experiences. Either it's all over the place, or we keep hitting the same beat, over and over. The first act; the setup, comes flashing to us in a moment of inspiration. Gee, what would happen if...? And, the climax is usually pretty clear, or at least, easier to find. But that stuff in the middle! Ugh!

And, on top of that, it's the longest act! Twice as long as the other two, generally speaking. It's not as easy as Act One and not as much fun or action-packed as Act Three, but it's no less important.

If we've created a solid first act, we're now in the greatest danger of losing our audience. Why? Because things tend to slow down. Well, they have to, at some point. What we're trying to create is an emotional roller coaster. We can't keep the audience at one high, intense level from start to finish. The intensity loses its impact if it isn't allowed to ebb and flow. We're looking for just the right rhythm.

So, what does Act Two need to accomplish?

We have two goals to achieve in this act, one for our characters and one for our story.

1. The Goal for our Characters:

Even though we've introduced our Central Protagonist, along with some supporting characters in Act One, we now must delve more deeply into them, in order to further cement their bond with the audience. We need to add dimension to them by strengthening their internal goals and conflicts, and revealing backstory elements which will further expose their motivations, flaws and desires. This need accounts for the moments of slower pacing required in the second act.

There will be more interaction between our Central Protagonist and his Supporting Characters in this act, interaction designed to enhance character revelation. It is in these moments where we really get to the heart of who our characters are, and allow us to understand how they will react to the obstacles they must inevitably encounter in this act.

2. The Goal for our Story.

This act is designed to heighten the conflict, create complications, increase the threat to the value at stake and remove our hero's option to quit. We need complications, and if we don't have enough things to complicate, we're going to fall flat.

Act Two is full of peaks and valleys. Our hero strives to reach her goal, but that goal becomes increasingly harder to attain. One step forward, two steps back. Two steps forward, one step back. Just when she achieves some level of success, another obstacle is thrown in her path.

She struggles to overcome that obstacle and guess what? Another, even bigger obstacle arises. And, the stakes go up. At each set of complications, there is more invested in winning, more to lose by failing.

Therefore, the major questions to tackle in Act Two will be:

What action or actions increase the threat; what places the villain, or other force of antagonism, in a superior position to our hero?

Human nature dictates that people tend to seek the path of least resistance to reach a goal. Our story characters, if they are real, are no different. Therefore, the obstacles and complications which hinder our hero must be both internal and external, and they should build in intensity incrementally.

The scope of the ultimate conflict our hero will face in the climax of Act Three will be far too daunting for our hero to face at the outset. The threats and conflicts must escalate; a series of smaller struggles, victories and defeats, which allow our hero to grow into the task.

Let's go back to Danny Kaffee in "A Few Good Men" for an example. At the outset, Danny simply wants to settle this case quickly. After all, he has a big softball game coming up. Should be no problem, since he *"successfully plea bargained 44 cases in nine months,"* according to Sam, his friend and co-counsel. The stakes aren't too high, at this point, and the risk is low. Had it been otherwise, he might never have taken on the task.

What turn of events raises the stakes?

As the threat level increases for our hero, so, too must the stakes for him be raised. While the ultimate goal may remain consistent, the price of failure must go up. Therefore, the consequences of losing which our hero accepted at the outset will become much more severe. The event which drives this moment must create a crisis of conscience for our protagonist, forcing him to dig deep into his soul in order to rise to the occasion.

In Act Two of "A Few Good Men," Danny's clients take the option to plea bargain off the table, by declining a deal offered by the prosecution. Danny has to try the case, which automatically raises the stakes for Danny. Having never tried a case in court, Danny has serious doubts about his ability to win.

Page 60

This takes us through the first half of Act Two, and brings us to the next question:

What is the mid-point story turn; the first crisis moment?

Which brings us to Page 60.

Now, don't panic. It's just a term I use, not a specific page recommendation. It's a story point which comes "about" halfway into your script, and also "about" halfway into the second act.

I've heard it characterized as the "Point of No Return," or simply "Plot Point Number such-and-such," depending on whose act structure you currently subscribe to. I generally just refer to it as Page 60, using a 120 page screenplay standard, and it is incredibly important.

In fact, I'd go so far as to say it's one of those indelible, inflexible rules of screenplay structure. Although this story point can be presented in a number of different ways, it must be there.

As mentioned, some consider this a point-of-no-return moment; an event which occurs wherein our hero has no choice but to plunge ahead, no matter how sticky things get. The idea is to remove the option to quit.

I would agree that it's a major turning point, but my research has determined that it isn't always a point-of-no-return moment. Analyzing numerous films, I came to the realization that this moment is often a false ending; a point at which it appears the story could be over.

This moment comes in "A Few Good Men" when Danny Kaffee chooses to quit the case. His clients shunned the great deal Danny acquired for them, so let them get another lawyer. After a night of heavy contemplation, however, Danny changes his mind, and does go to trial.

Now, once he makes that choice, it does become a point-of-no return, but the Page 60 moment, in my view, actually occurs before that, at the point where Danny quits the case. That created a false ending; a point where the story could have been over.

The Page 60 story beat often manifests in this way. It's the moment where we've caught the killer, except it isn't really the killer. It's the moment where we've killed the monster, only the monster isn't really dead. This is the one major story shift which is not an act break.

One of my all-time favorite Page 60 beats comes in "Saving Private Ryan." Tom Hanks and his men have fought their way into a town where Private Ryan is said to be located. After a firefight, they find Ryan, and Captain Miller, Tom Hanks, breaks the sad news to him. His brothers are dead.

Ryan weeps in grief, and asks how it happened. When he's told they died in battle, he's confused. That can't be! His brothers are still in grade school.

They've found the wrong Private James Ryan!

Our midway turning point isn't always a "moment." Sometimes, it takes place through an entire sequence. In the wonderful social comedy "Dave," we get a sequence for our Page 60 beat, and it's also a Page 60 which is more subtle than we're used to seeing.

In the prior sequence, Dave, Kevin Kline, has "become" the President he's impersonating, and he's doing it better. The critical point comes when he is scheduled to spend an entire day with the First Lady, played by Sigourney Weaver, who has yet to uncover his true identity.

The event risks blowing the lid off of the plan; revealing his true identity. It's also a Page 60 that heavily utilizes the romantic subplot; the relationship which will grow between Dave and the First Lady. That Page 60 sequence comes to a head when the First Lady busts him with:

"Who are you?"

There is also a Page 60 sequence in "The Fugitive," when Richard Kimble first risks exposing his identity to help a patient in the hospital in a time of crisis, following a serious car accident. That carries on to his narrow escape from the hospital, then at the end of Act Two, he's trapped inside a dam. He is cornered by Gerard, the cop on his trail, leading to that momentous leap from the mouth of the dam into almost certain death.

Remind you of anything? Remember the famous jump from the cliff by Butch and Sundance, when they are cornered by the Super Posse? Same thing. Not only does it make us suck in our breath, because it looks like the end for our hero, it also makes a bold statement about how far our hero is willing to go to accomplish his goal.

The Act Two Break

The final Act Two question:

What brings our hero to his highest or lowest moment?

Back to Act Two, Part Two of "A Few Good Men." Danny has had his crisis of conscience and overcome it. He dives back into the task of defending his clients. And, he's holding his own. He comes across several tantalizing bits of evidence that lead him to believe he might actually have a chance at winning this thing.

And then, it all falls apart. One primary witness is lying. Another commits suicide. Evidence has been buried by Col Jessup. At the end of Act Two, it's all gone. The stakes have been raised once again. Now, it looks as if he's going to lose his case, send his clients to prison for the rest of their lives and, by pressing on, possibly destroy his career. Things are at their worst.

We've arrived at the end of Act Two.

Let's pause here for another important message. In this story, and, I would say, in the bulk of them, the end of the second act is a "down" moment. It's a time where it appears all is lost for our hero. This is the norm, but not always the case. It really depends on the type of story you're telling.

In "Saving Private Ryan," the end of Act Two comes when our hero, Captain John Miller, and his men finally find Private Ryan. This is an "up" moment. They've accomplished the first half of their mission. They've found Ryan. Now, all they have to do is bring him safely back.

Except, Ryan won't go. He is determined to stay with his unit to defend a little French town from the advancing Nazis. So, Captain Miller and his men stay to help. And, what happens?

Our hero, Captain Miller, dies!

"Up" second act ending equals "down" third act ending. It pretty much stays consistent this way. If we're "up" at the end of Act One, we're "down" at the end of Act Two, then "up" at the end of Act Three, since most stories want our hero to attain his goal.

If the second act ends on a positive note, you can almost bet we're in for a tragic ending to the story.

So, we've come to the end of Act Two, and the major story beats we've had to address gives us this five-point beat outline for the second act:

Act Two Beat Sheet

1. How is our protagonist's chosen action countered by our Central Force of Antagonism?
2. What escalating complications challenge our protagonist?
3. How are the stakes being raised?
4. What is the Page 60 story turn?

5. How are things at their worst (for an "up" story ending) or best (for a "down" story ending) at the end of Act Two?

Answering these questions will create a bare bones structure for the second act, with all of the necessary elements provided.

Act Three – Crisis, Climax and Resolve

By now, we should have built up, via a series of problems and complications through which our protagonist navigates, to the high point of our story.

Let's review the first two acts of "A Few Good Men." In Act One, Danny Kaffee was handed this case. He and everyone else expected him to plea bargain and put it behind him. Then, he interviews Col Jessup, Lt Col Markinson and Lt Kendrick, and uncovers disturbing information linking them to the crime his clients are accused of.

In Act Two, Danny's clients refuse to accept a plea bargain, and insist on having their day in court. Danny decides to quit the case, but soon changes his mind. He uncovers evidence that leads him to believe he can win. All of his evidence evaporates at the end of Act Two. It appears that all is lost.

The Crisis

Now, to our crisis in Act Three, where Danny must rise to the task, with all of the odds against him, and the stakes at their highest. That is exactly the kind of situation we want, for our protagonist.

Demi Moore's Joanne Galloway convinces Danny that his only chance is to put Col Jessup on the stand and prove he ordered the "Code Red" disciplinary action carried out by Danny's clients. He must force Jessup to confess.

However, if he fails, not only does Danny send his clients to prison, but he faces the possibility of a Court Martial for smearing the reputation of a highly decorated officer, namely Jessup. His entire career, along with his clients' lives, is now at stake.

This is clearly the crisis point of the act. Danny operates in near desperation, throwing together some pretty weak evidence with an angle designed to play on Jessup's ego to trick him into a confession. Will it work?

The climax will tell us.

The Climax

Now, I'm going to give you another of those hard-and-fast, etched-in-stone rules.

Never, but never take the climax of your story out of the hands of your Central Protagonist! Your hero must confront the Central Force of Antagonism in your third act climax. Don't allow fate, God, coincidence or another character to solve your hero's problem. If you do, the audience will feel profoundly cheated, as well they should.

It is the job of your central protagonist to fulfill the task established by the Active Theme of your movie.

So, here comes the climax for "A Few Good Men." Danny Kaffee has Col Jessup on the stand. He throws several of his best tricks at the Colonel, but Jessup holds firm. Danny is down to his last tactic, that of actually accusing Jessup of complicity in the crime.

The courtroom waits with bated breath. Everything says "don't do it," but of course, Danny does. He riles Jessup into his famous *"You can't handle the truth!"* speech, enrages the man and gets his confession. Against all odds, he has won the case.

The Resolve

The story is effectively over, at this point, but we still have to tie up all of the loose ends. We must address each and every character in our story and complete that characters' story arc.

For Aaron Sorkin, that meant telling us what happens to Danny

Kaffee and his team. What happens to Jessup and Kendrick? What happens to Danny's clients? He must neatly tie up each subplot for each character, along with the main plot, to provide the viewer with a satisfying ending.

Now, some thoughts about endings. I favor and preach qualified endings. Audiences want endings which ring true. If it's an "up" ending, they'd like it to be true to life, which means somewhat flawed, and not perfect. "Happily Ever After" doesn't really cut it, these days. A qualified resolve is more believable, because it reflects the casualties of the battle, and the price paid for victory.

If the ending is "down," meaning tragic, they'd like something positive to come out of it; a lesson learned, a spark of hope; the message that some good can come from the worst of situations.

In the case of "A Few Good Men," Danny's clients, Dawson and Downey, are cleared of murder and won't serve any jail time. However, they are convicted of "conduct unbecoming," and are dishonorably discharged from the Marines...the very thing they were most trying to avoid.

They are devastated, but they understand why the punishment is just. They realize, now, what they did wrong. Yes, they were following orders, but in doing so, they violated a moral obligation to, as Dawson put it, *"stand up for people who can't stand up for themselves. We were supposed to stand up for Willy."*

They finally get it, which results in a satisfying resolve for Sam's dilemma. Remember his feeling that even though they followed orders, they should still go to jail? He wanted to know that they understood the consequences of their actions, and now they do. Had they gotten off Scott free, with no consequences, that would have, in Sam's mind, justified their bullying. Perhaps, even sanctioned it. We couldn't have that.

So, there's our qualified "up" ending. Danny won and his clients were acquitted of murder, but they still paid a price. Jessup went to jail, along with Kendrick, so the real "bad guys" got their punishment. In a qualified ending, either up or down, the Central Protagonist gets what he deserves, not necessarily what he wants.

The goal is achieved. The End.

That, basically, is the structure we shoot for in developing a story idea. Not so rigid as to restrict our creativity, yet structured enough to give us the constants we need.

Bear in mind, there is much more involved in all of these acts than the beats I've outlined, here. There are subplots, supporting characters, relationships and character development which must be crafted, throughout. But, those elements all hang on a solid, basic structure for the story, and that's the place to start.

That said, the Act Three Beat Sheet is made up of three basic story points:

Act Three Beat Sheet

1. The crisis: What is the event which creates the highest level of risk for the hero?
2. The climax: What is the conflict which pits the hero against the villain (Central Force of Antagonism) in an all-or-nothing struggle?
3. The resolve: How does the story, and all related subplots, end?

In Summary: Understanding the basic, major story beats required for each act, and the function each act must serve in the overall story, helps a writer in developing each act to its greatest potential. Beat Sheets, both for individual acts and for the entire story, as will be illustrated in the Development section, keep the simplistic rules of storytelling at the forefront of a writer's mind, and guides the writing process.

Script Length

How long should a screenplay be? I'm going to go out on a limb, here, and say 120 pages. I'll no doubt catch some flack for it from some people out there. That's okay. This was the standard, not so many years ago, equating to two hours of screen time. But, screenplays and media in general have fallen victim to the growing the perception that the audience has a short attention span.

While in general terms, that statement may be true, it isn't really indicative of the length of a film today's audience is willing to tolerate. "Avatar," "Inglourious Basterds," "Django Unchained," "The Hurt Locker," "Cast Away," "Good Will Hunting," "Pirates of the Caribbean," "There Will Be Blood," "Titanic," "Gladiator," "A Few Good Men" and "Erin Brockovich" all logged in at over 120 minutes running time, and this is only a short list.

At the commonly accepted ratio of one minute of screen time to one page of screenplay, that's over 120 pages. Seems to me, those films did okay. And, there are many others which can be added to this list.

Sometimes a film will run long because it's a "tentpole" film; an event-movie, like "The Dark Knight Rises" or "Pirates of the Caribbean." Apparently, it's acceptable when there are flashy CGI effects and nearly non-stop action involved. The industry can handle that, because there is enough going on, in their view, to keep the audience engaged.

Reputation can also get a lengthy film accepted. No one is going to complain, or point out the error of a filmmaker's ways if that filmmaker is James Cameron or Steven Spielberg who is delivering a two-hour plus movie.

Quentin Tarantino doesn't seem to struggle with time limitations. "Pulp Fiction" came in at 168 minutes, "Inglourious Basterds" at 153 minutes and "Django Unchained" at 180 minutes, and no one squawked. Of course not, because he has a track record. He's a known commodity.

If a fledgling writer slapped a 180 page script down on the desk of a studio reader, he'd most likely be laughed out of the office.

So, it's easy to conclude from this that the only way you can deliver a film of more than two hours is when you are "somebody."

Maybe so, but that isn't the point. The point is, if "somebody" can do it...well, everybody can do it. I mean, anybody can do it. In doing it, we aren't violating the rules of storytelling. We're violating the rules of commercial viability which the medium has manufactured.

But, the perception persists, even with evidence to the contrary. The audience, they insist, has been influenced by cell phones, twitter and the World Wide Web. They're impatient, and demand immediate gratification.

Whether that's true, or whether the audience is simply accepting what we shove down their throats doesn't matter. The perception, not the reality, has determined how long a successful screenplay can be, at least, from a beginning writer.

At this writing, the perception is that a screenplay should be about 110 pages long. If you want to make it easy on yourself, that's what you should aim for. Under 110 would probably even serve you better, in the current climate, but I take a more liberal approach.

If I can get it down to 110 without sacrificing the story, I'm happy to. But, I don't want to force it there, if it doesn't want to go. I mean, is the reader going to turn to page 111 and stop reading, because it's too long? If so, then I suggest that reader should find another line of work.

It should be noted that the length of the acts don't necessarily break down in equal proportions, according to the length of the film. A long movie doesn't, even shouldn't, automatically have a long first act, by virtue of a mathematical equation. The classic movie "Gone With The Wind" runs 3 hours and 39 minutes, but the first act is only about 30 minutes long. That's when the Civil War breaks out.

Because so many industry readers have had it drilled into them exactly how long an act should be, generally as a result of subscribing to someone's particular method, they're going to judge your script on that basis.

But, who do we listen to? One guru says to end Act One on page 17. Another says page 30. That's a pretty big spread. So, I went back to the old drawing board and watched some successful movies and read some successful scripts.

That process brought me to the conclusion that a well-crafted first act usually runs between twenty-five and thirty-five pages, and therefore, about the same length of screen time, not counting opening titles and credits. However, even that standard allows for some flexibility.

Short first acts are definitely safer and more short-attention-span friendly. Readers seem to favor the brevity and "cut-to-the-chase" style of a tight, short first act. Aside from that, the story doesn't really kick into gear until Act Two, so the longer we wait, the more we risk losing our viewers.

While long first acts are rare, they do exist. "A Few Good Men," as an example, had a first act of over 40 minutes. There were a lot of characters involved; characters who needed to be set up in the first act. Aaron Sorkin, who is a master of dialogue, managed to keep up the pace and hold our interest, making that long first act work.

Just remember, our first act is the setup. The story doesn't really kick into gear until Act Two begins, and since we want to get into this story, we want to do it as soon as possible.

Act Two affords us the greatest amount of flexibility. In films which exceed two hours in total length, most of that extra time can be attributed to the second act.

Taking broad strokes, we can expect our second act to run anywhere from 40 to 60 pages. Our mid-story turn, which I've labeled "Page 60," gives us a bit of relief in sustaining the pace of that long second act by providing a story-shift which creates the same basic tonal effect as an act break, although it really isn't one.

Act Three, then, should come in at 20 to 30 pages in length. It is the busiest of our acts, since everything we've set up in Act One and complicated in Act Two will come to a head. It contains our moment of greatest threat; the crisis, and our moment of greatest conflict; the climax. Therefore, an Act Three that drags is simply a no-no.

There are also commercial reasons for restricting a film's length, aside from pinning it on the audience's attention span. It comes down to basic economics. A shorter film can be screened more times in a day than can a longer film. When they get more screenings, they make more money.

There is a positive aspect for the writer to this shorter-screenplay mentality, thank goodness. It forces writers to economize, and that is one of the key elements in successful screenwriting.

I'm not talking about simply squeezing a story into the right number of pages. I'm talking about squeezing the most out of the story in the limited time allotted. Again, nothing in a screenplay is wasted. Everything you put on the page must be important. There is simply no time to do otherwise.

It's not a matter of abbreviating and condensing things, it's a matter of getting more out of less. Dialogue and action have to pull extra duty. Dialogue must have subtext. Every action must provide narrative. Every scene must move the story forward.

If anything about screenwriting can honestly be deemed hard, it's that. That's the craft part of the deal; putting the art down in the most constructive, economical way. Once you've honed that talent, it becomes much easier to write a well-told story within the confines of page and time limitations.

I recall hearing stories of writers who, when told their script was too long, went back and extended the page margins on all sides, without changing a word of the story. Don't try it. They're onto us.

In Summary: While screenplays 90 to 100 pages in length are more acceptable in today's marketplace, the real gauge of script length should be the requirements of the story being told. If a story is engaging enough, written in an entertaining style, with a pace that flows comfortably, then page length should never be a factor for a truly discerning reader.

CHAPTER 13

Scenes and Sequences

Scenes

"What is a scene?"

Someone in an early sitcom class I conducted asked me this question, and I must admit, I was initially stumped for an answer, off the top of my head. I knew what a scene was, of course. I had written many of them, but the realization hit me that I hadn't really defined it for myself. So, I gave it some thought, and here it is:

A scene is a segment of time within a screenplay which reveals the character and moves the story forward.

Please don't think of this on too literal or superficial a level. He goes here and does this, which causes him to go there and do that. Yes, that moves the story ahead, but keep in mind all of the masters you're serving. You also need to stay true to the character's growth.

Each character has an individual storyline which parallels the central storyline. All storylines should then serve the theme. So if, within a scene, you're playing out a subplot between two characters, you're advancing the story. If your scene contains dialogue which reveals information about our character, you're advancing the story.

Just know that as you advance the story, you also want to give it dimension, and therefore, every scene must serve more than one purpose. Its primary job is to move the story forward in a logical fashion. Its secondary job is to add complexity which will enhance the story. Each scene should serve as a building block to add more dimension to the story, in the overall.

Each scene must also serve as a segue into the next scene, by creating an impetus for the scene that follows. While a scene must have its own sense of resolve, it should also create a question or issue for the viewer which can only be answered by moving further into the story. Just as connecting the dots gives us an image, connecting our scenes results in a complete story.

I'm keeping this confined to the screenplay format, because a scene in a screenplay differs from a scene in a play. As I've previously pointed out, in a screenplay, every SCENE HEADING denotes a scene.

A quick, Establishing Shot of a building before cutting to the action inside is still a scene. True, nothing happens. We're just looking at a building for two seconds before we cut away. But, it tells us where we are, which is someplace different that we just left, so in a sense, it still moves the story forward. It transitions us.

But, the more important distinction occurs on the technical side of the process. A screenplay destined for production is broken down, piece by piece, by those who will turn that screenplay into a film. So, every scene heading in the script will be categorized into day shots and night shots, interiors and exteriors and locations. Therefore, every scene heading denotes a scene.

Any change of locations is a new scene. The only variation to this that I know of is a change of locations within a montage, which doesn't have to be, and isn't often, designated by a scene heading.

You'll note in my definition that I've said "reveal the character and move the story forward." Sometimes, you'll do more of one than the other. There are pure character scenes which you will write that simply reveal important information about the character. Perhaps they will play out a subplot; a romance, a confrontation with an ally or a heart-to-heart between a father and son. Maybe, they will give us backstory which will become important to us, down the line, or set up a later conflict.

These character scenes not only give us more information about the character, they also justify the physical actions that character will take and the choices he will make, as the story progresses.

When we're ten-years-old watching an action film in the theater, these character scenes are generally the moments we choose to go out for popcorn. These scenes don't seem to move the action of the story ahead, but in truth, they do. Our characters are where the emotion is coming from, so involving us more deeply into their souls is paramount. The plot; the action doesn't matter one whit, if we have no concept of who these people are, and have nothing invested in them, emotionally.

Action scenes, on the other hand, appear to only move the plot forward and tell us nothing about the characters. High concept, tentpole action films have a lot of these. Still, within them, we should be able to expose some tiny grain of a character's internal workings.

How a character reacts in a tense or dangerous situation can be very revealing. Does she show fear? Or, the reverse, an absence of fear? Is he reactive to the moment, or proactive? Maybe, our character is a spontaneous quick-thinker, instantly creative under fire, or pulls some tricks out of thin air that smack of the repetition of experience.

Some of our favorite heroes, Indiana Jones or James Bond, for instance, respond to impending danger with dry humor. John McClain, the Bruce Willis character of the "Die Hard" franchise, always has a wisecrack for any occasion, even under fire. Many Clint Eastwood characters, like Dirty Harry or The Man With No Name, take the heat with stoic confidence and self-assurance. We can't imagine them losing, because they can't imagine losing. So, even in these action scenes, we learn more about their inner workings.

It's easy to lose sight of these character nuances when you're plotting out an extended car chase or gunfight, but those flashes of personality, attitude or hints at a character's backstory give life to those blocks of action.

The balance of action and character is dictated by the genre. If we're writing a Romantic Comedy, of course, it's going to be loaded with character scenes. An action film, just as obviously less so. Key is finding that right balance.

What every scene must have going for it, though, is conflict. Now, you're probably going to test this rule and convince yourself that you've found scenes which have no conflict. Trust me, it's there.

When I talk about conflict, I don't necessarily mean yelling and screaming or punching and kicking. A scene can add to an existing conflict, even in some subtle way. It can raise the stakes for our hero, thus elevating the conflict, or it can highlight an internal conflict.

Let me give you an example, utilizing our old friend, Rocky Balboa.

Early in the first act of "Rocky," he returns to his dingy apartment after a fight. He stands in front of a mirror and looks at his battered face. Stuck in one corner of the mirror, at the frame, is an old black-and-white school photo of Rocky, aged ten-or-eleven. He looks at it, and the contrast between the two images is stark; the fresh-faced, smiling kid and the battle-scarred, old-before-his-time warrior. Tell me that ain't conflict.

And, it's heart tugging. It immediately evokes sympathy for our Central Protagonist. Yet, it eats up only a few seconds, and there is not a word of dialogue. That's getting the most from a scene.

There is another standing rule in screenwriting, and of course, it's a rule I've seen violated, as well. So, of course, it isn't really a rule, is it? Well, in this case, at least for myself, I'd say *"yeah, it is."* The rule is to get into a scene as late as possible and get out of it as early as possible.

One of the primary arguments for this "get in late-get out early" philosophy is that scene length dictates pace, remember? If you're writing long scenes, you're probably slowing the story down. That's not always bad, but it generally is, especially in the current climate.

Long scenes are sometimes appropriate, but they must be justified. Is there enough going on? Enough story exposition? Enough conflict? If we can keep the story moving and the audience engaged, then a long scene may be acceptable; even warranted.

For an example of that, let's take another look at a nicely crafted lengthy scene that works from "Rocky." This scene takes place in a confined space; Rocky's apartment, and is more than seven minutes long. That's almost eight pages for one scene, which is lengthy by any standards. Yet, it worked.

The reason it worked is two-fold. The emotional tension was high, because of the inherent conflict involved. Secondly, the director did a brilliant job of finding ways to keep the two actors moving throughout the scene.

Mickey, played by Burgess Meredith, wants to be Rocky's manager. Rocky is still hurt over the way Mickey has treated him in the past. So, Mickey is pitching and Rocky is constantly moving away from him; to the kitchen, to the dart board on his wall, to his bedroom and finally to the bathroom. That keeps the scene active.

Not only was the conflict at a peak level, but we learned something very significant about Rocky. Although he's a heavyweight fighter who beats up on guys in the ring, he avoids emotional conflict. He doesn't let go and vent on Mick until Mick is leaving, walking down the sidewalk a half-block away.

At the end of this long scene, we've learned a lot of Mickey's backstory, a lot about their relationship, a lot about Rocky's pride and character, and we've discovered his sensitive side. The story point that came out of this scene was basic and simple: Mickey becomes Rocky's manager. Yet, we got much more important character information from it. Otherwise, it could easily have gone like this:

Mick: *"Hey, Rock. Sorry about the other day. Look, I'd really like to be your manager."*

Rocky: *"Okay, Mick."*

Exciting, huh? Yes, it moves the story ahead. In fact, it does everything our seven-minute scene does in that regard, in just a few seconds. But, it's utterly devoid of conflict or emotion. No real character revelation. A really rich, well-developed story will give us many "mini-stories" at many levels within it, through character interactions and subplots. All of these mini-stories give our central storyline greater dimension and emotional impact.

A scene is a self-contained "nugget" of our story, with its own beginning, middle and end; its own little "arc," if you will. There is a goal to achieve within it, and resistance to that goal, whether active or implied. And, there should be a sense of finality; resolve at the end of it, that leaves us with that "what happens next" question in our minds.

We need to come out of each scene feeling we've acquired information to further the story and enhance our involvement, and that some conflict has been raised, foreshadowed or dealt with, and that our character is another step deeper, more fully committed to the goal.

One lesson I learned in sitcom was to "button" a scene. In sitcom, it's pretty cut-and-dried. It's comedy, so we button a scene with a joke.

In screenplay, it isn't so rigidly defined, but it's there. That sense of, *"Okay, we've gotten everything we need from this moment. Our work here is done. Time to move on."*

Take a look at some screenplays by the top writers and see how they button their scenes. It will quickly become apparent what I'm talking about.

There is one rule out there, also not really a rule, but a good suggestion, that you should always end a scene with action, even if that action is a reaction. Mary says *"I was out with your best friend,"* let's say, and we end the scene on John's shocked expression. Or, sad expression, or angry expression, whatever is appropriate. Or Mary delivers her line and John angrily storms out the door. Always ending on an action, rather than a line of dialogue helps to add that sense of completion to your scene and a sense of movement toward the next scene.

In Summary: Scenes should always be constructed with the purpose of revealing characters and advancing the story. They should be designed in a "stand alone" fashion, with the same beginning, middle, end and overall purpose as is applied to the story in its entirety. Within our central storyline are many mini-stories; subplots and character interaction, and by creating scenes which address these mini-stories and keeping them connected, thematically, to the central storyline, we will create greater dimension, overall.

Sequences

Sequences are scenes strung together in a designed fashion to create a segment of our overall story, and contain a dramatic through-line; a beginning, middle and end. How many sequences are present in a script depends entirely on the requirements of the story, and don't let anyone tell you otherwise.

I find that a clear understanding of sequences makes writing the story much easier. No longer am I writing "FADE IN:" and looking at a hundred-plus blank pages ahead of me. Instead, I'm able to focus on the opening sequence.

An opening sequence may be as simple as:

WE MEET THE PRESIDENT AND FIRST LADY.

That's the opening sequence in the movie "Dave," where Kevin Kline plays the good guy and look alike of Kevin Kline, the President. The President's helicopter lands on the White House grounds. The President and First Lady smile for the cameras and exit to the White House. Once inside, the President and First

Lady quickly go their separate ways, and it's evident there is tension between them. The President meets with staff, and reveals himself to be a nasty, corrupt guy. That's the end of the opening sequence.

The second sequence, then, is:

WE MEET DAVE, AND SEE HIS WORLD.

We see him as a celebrity look alike of the President, opening a shopping center. We see him at work, at his employment agency, and at the accounting office of his best friend, trying to get a job for one of his clients. *"It's Monday! Everybody works on Monday!"* We see him peddling home on his bicycle, belting out the title tune from "Oklahoma." We see him at his apartment, where he is confronted by two Secret Service Agents, who inform him he's been chosen to fill in for the President at a function. End of the WE MEET DAVE sequence.

In creating a sequence of scenes, you must be cognizant of the through-line you're serving. It's a "chunk" of the story, and as stated, has its own beginning, middle and end; its own arc of conflict. I will go into more detail regarding sequences in the next section, as we examine a sequence breakdown of the film "Saving Private Ryan."

Within a sequence will be one scene which represents the point of the sequence, somewhat like the subject of a sentence. This is the story moment at the center of that sequence of scenes, which I designate the Anchor Scene.

The other element I look for is the Resolve of the sequence.

What resolves this sequence of scenes that further propels the story and complicates the plot for our protagonist?

Now, here's a small caveat. Sometimes, a single scene will achieve the same results as a sequence. So, you may have a rhythm that goes: Opening Sequence, 2nd Sequence, SCENE, 3rd Sequence, etc.

Within a group of scenes will sometimes fall one single scene which deals with its own subject matter, and doesn't require a sequence to make its point. In my own definition, this is simply a one-scene sequence. There's an obvious one in "A Few Good Men."

Stuck between two sequences of scenes in the first act is a quick scene of our two defendants, Dawson and Downey, arriving at the military prison in Washington D.C. As they are removed from the car, Downey asks Dawson, *"Hal, is this Washington D.C.?"* The guard then tells them to move along. That's it. It's just intended to show us these guys arriving from Guantanamo Bay. It doesn't require a sequence of scenes to make its point.

In order for a sequence of scenes to qualify as a true act, it must provide a MOTIVATING FACTOR and end with a RESOLVE.

Motivating Factor

A Motivating Factor refers to the event which occurs within the sequence which further motivates the forward movement of the story. Motivating Factors differ in design, depending on the act in which the occur.

An Act One Motivating Factor can occur as a story beat in the set-up sequence, by demonstrating the qualities our hero possesses which give him the necessary tools to accomplish the task he will be faced with.

Our Story Trigger, or inciting incident, also provides a Motivating Factor within an Act One sequence, as it provides the catalyst for the Central Protagonist to take the action which propels the story into the second act.

A Motivating Factor in an Act Two sequence can be any obstacle which our hero has encountered and overcome, or it can be a valuable piece of information or clue our hero has obtained, which leads him to the next encounter.

A Motivating Factor in Act Three may appear in a sequence which occurs prior to the final climactic conflict, wherein our Central Protagonist plots a strategy, or obtains an object or information which will give our hero an "edge" in the coming conflict. The Resolve sequence of Act Three is motivated by the need to wrap up the plot and subplots which have been established for the story.

Sequence Resolve

A Resolve to a sequence is somewhat self-explanatory. A question or issue has been raised within a sequence, regardless of the act in which it appears. That issue, question or obstacle must now resolve the sequence in a manner which addresses that issue, i.e., a response from our hero, which then leads us organically into the next sequence.

For one of my classes, I broke down the motion picture "Saving Private Ryan" into its sequences. To each sequence, I've assigned individual titles for identification purposes. I've also identified some of the principle story-structure moments within the sequences, i.e., the STORY TRIGGER, ACT BREAKS, CRISIS, CLIMAX, MOTIVATING FACTOR and RESOLVE.

You'll note that the opening scene of this film is a one-scene sequence. In this instance, the film used a story technique known as "bookending." An opening scene sets up the story at the beginning and a closing scene resolves the story at the end. What this generally tells us is that the story in between is told in flashback, and that's the case here.

Here is my sequence breakdown of "Saving Private Ryan," with some notes I've added along the way:

"SAVING PRIVATE RYAN"

Written by Robert Rodat

Sequences

OPENING SEQUENCE - (Opening Bookend - One Scene Sequence) Arlington Cemetery. An elderly man with his family arrive and walk to a grave in a section beneath the flags of The United States and France. MOTIVATING FACTOR: A curiosity hook, raising a question which must be answered.

RESOLVE: Sets up flashback. (HOOK) (Approx. 4 minutes)

SEQUENCE 2 - D-DAY ASSAULT

Establish Capt John Miller and Sgt Horvath. During battle, we meet Pvt Reiben, Pvt Jackson, Pvt Mellish, Pvt Capazo and Medic Wade.

Capt. Miller in shock, then recovers and takes charge. MOTIVATING FACTOR: Survival for Capt Miller and his men.

Object: Open "Dog One"; a designated area to break through the enemy lines.

Carnage and confusion, then a semblance of order; the tide turning.

Miller uses a mirror attached to a bayonet to see around a corner without exposing himself to enemy fire - an action which shows his capacity and training.

Miller calls for bangalors - explosives to blast through barbed wire.

DOG ONE IS OPEN - (ANCHOR SCENE)

Establish Capt Miller's weakness, (FATAL FLAW), an intermittent trembling in his hand, hinting at a neurological disorder.

Character defining moments for Miller's men at the end of the battle.

RESOLVE: The beach has been taken. A wide shot of bodies on the beach, zooming to one dead soldier with "Ryan S." stenciled on the back of his pack. (STORY TRIGGER) (Approx. 25 min.)

SEQUENCE 3 - THE LETTERS

A large office with dozens of secretaries typing letters to families of soldiers killed in battle. A typist discovers that three Ryan brothers have been killed, and reports it to her C.O. (ANCHOR SCENE)

The C.O, a Colonel, discovers that only one Ryan brother is left alive, somewhere in France. MOTIVATING FACTOR: Save the life of the last remaining Ryan brother.

The Ryan Home - An Army Chaplain arrives to tell the Ryan's of the loss of three of their sons.

Chief of Staff's Office - Discussion over the logic of risking a squad of men to save one man. Chief of Staff reads a letter written by Abraham Lincoln to a Civil War era mother who has lost five sons in battle.

RESOLVE: *"We are going to find Private James Ryan and get him the hell out of there."* (Approx. 7 min.)

END OF ACT ONE

SEQUENCE 4 - ASSEMBLING THE TEAM

Capt Miller is given the assignment of finding Private Ryan. (ANCHOR SCENE)

We gather the squad for the assignment. MOTIVATING FACTOR: Capt Miller has his orders, and must carry them out.

Add to the squad Cpl Upham, a journalist who has never been in battle, but is needed to be an interpreter. (Set him up as a coward - a subplot).

RESOLVE: The team is assembled, sets out to find Ryan. (Approx. 4 min.)

SEQUENCE 5 - THE WRONG RYAN

Character revelations on the move. The logic of the mission is questioned by one of Ryan's men and discussed. Capt Miller states the external goal; find Pvt Ryan because that is what they've been ordered to do.

French Town - Capt Miller's squad locates a town where Ryan is supposed to be. They become involved in the battle for the town.

The French family - A distraught family begs Capt Miller to take their young daughter away from the fighting. One of Miller's men, Caparzo, is killed by a sniper.

Miller's sniper takes out the enemy sniper.

Capt Miller meets the Captain in charge of the unit fighting for the French town, who sends for Private Ryan.

The man who arrives turns out to be James Frederick Ryan, from Pennsylvania. They're looking for James Francis Ryan, from Ohio. They've located the wrong Ryan. (ANCHOR SCENE) (PAGE 60 - MIDPOINT) - MOTIVATING FACTOR: They have not found their Pvt James Ryan, and therefore, have not completed their mission.

RESOLVE: The hunt for Private Ryan continues. (Approx. 23 min.)

SEQUENCE 6 - HOLDING UP

Miller's team holds up in an abandoned building. MOTIVATING FACTOR: Character revelation between Capt Miller and Sgt Horvath - their experiences together in the war. Character revelation reveals Capt Miller's dedication to his mission. Conversation about the mission. Miller knows exactly how many men he has lost (shows his compassion.) More on Capt Miller's shaking hand; neurological condition. Miller knows the writings of Emerson (shows his intelligence & education). (One-Scene Sequence) (ANCHOR SCENE) RESOLVE: After a much needed rest, the mission will proceed.(Approx. 23 Min.)

SEQUENCE 7 - THE CROSSROADS

German Prisoners being herded through the area. Wounded American soldiers also pass through. A glider, carrying a General has crashed, nearby. Few survivors.

Miller and his men search through dog tags of deceased G.I's, to see if Ryan is among the casualties. MOTIVATING FACTOR: New information must be acquired in order for the mission to continue.

Miller locates a wounded G.I. who knows Ryan, and directs them to a French town, where Ryan's unit is protecting a bridge. (ANCHOR SCENE)

Miller's men see the uncontrollable shaking in Capt Miller's hand,

and show concern.

RESOLVE: Follow the new lead to another French town.

SEQUENCE 8 - THE BUNKER

Miller's team comes across a German held bunker. There is disagreement over whether to attack it. *"This isn't our mission!"* from one of the men.

Attacking the bunker. Wade, the Medic, is killed. Cpl Upham, the journalist, reveals himself to be a coward.

They take the bunker and capture a German soldier. Conflict over whether to kill him or let him go. Division within the ranks. (ANCHOR SCENE)

Miller decides to release the prisoner. MOTIVATING FACTOR: Despite internal conflict within the unit, Capt. Miller must maintain control.

Miller buries dead bodies. The rest of his team joins in to help.

RESOLVE: The team is nearly divided, but unifies to press on. (Approx. 20 Min.)

SEQUENCE 9 - FINDING PRIVATE RYAN

Miller's team gets in a firefight with a German half-track. Another team of G.I.'s is also attacking it. MOTIVATING FACTOR: Survival.

It's a unit from the French town, and Private James Ryan is among them. (ANCHOR SCENE)

Miller explains to Ryan that they have come to find him and take him back. Ryan refuses to go. His unit has orders to protect the bridge in the French town.

Miller and Sgt Horvath discuss their options.

RESOLVE: Miller's unit will stay and help protect the town. (Approx. 11 Min.)

END OF ACT TWO

SEQUENCE 10 - DEFENSE STRATEGY

Miller takes charge, and designs a defense strategy for the town. (ANCHOR SCENE)

Ryan tells stories about his brothers, and their lives back in Ohio.

Character interaction and revelation, as they wait for the assault. MOTIVATING FACTOR: To prepare for and survive the German assault.

RESOLVE: The battle plan is set. (Approx. 7 Min.)

SEQUENCE 11 - BATTLE FOR THE BRIDGE

The Germans attack. (ANCHOR SCENE) (CRISIS)MOTIVATING FACTOR: Victory in battle and survival.

Upham, the coward, gets one of Miller's men killed.

The German who Capt Miller released at the bunker is here, and shoots Capt Miller. Upham finally gathers courage and kills the German soldier.

U.S. air support arrives, and the German's are defeated. (CLIMAX)

Capt Miller, gravely wounded, summons Ryan and tells him, *"Earn this."* Then, Miller dies.

RESOLVE: The bridge has been held, and Ryan is alive to return home, but Miller has been killed. (Approx. 36 Min.)

SEQUENCE 12 - THE RESOLVE (Bookend - One Scene Sequence)

Flash forward to the Arlington Cemetery scene. The man kneeling at the grave is an elder Private Ryan. In the grave is the body of Capt Miller. MOTIVATING FACTOR: To honor the man who gave his life for Ryan's survival.

Ryan asks his family if he is a "good man" who has led a "good life," recalling Miller's words to "earn this".

Ryan salutes Miller's grave.

Last shot: The flag.

RESOLVE: Ryan has earned his life. (Approx. 5 Min.)

In Summary: Sequences are made up of a combination of scenes, creating a through-line to deliver an important segment of the overall story. Breaking a story down into sequences, and attacking each sequence individually makes the writing task much more palatable than looking 120 pages or so down the road. It also aids in the outlining process.

CHAPTER 14

Dialogue

When silent films gave way to "talkies," filmmakers took full advantage of it. There were logistical problems, at first, because of the rudimentary beginnings of recorded sound. The cameras were large and cumbersome. Microphones couldn't move with the actors, so the actors had to come to the microphone. That meant hiding the microphone in, say, a vase of flowers, while the actors huddled around it and delivered their lines.

Even when filmmakers devised ways to overcome these obstacles, allowing for more movement, dialogue was still a dominant part of the filmed story. Romantic comedies of the 30's and 40's were rampant with crisp, rapid-fire dialogue, and dramas of the period contained long, ponderous dialogue exchanges.

This is no longer the trend, for better or worse, and a script that leans heavily on dialogue today faces an uphill battle in the commercial marketplace. There are notable exceptions, of course, but the general attitude toward dialogue-heavy scripts is a negative one.

Character-oriented stories demand a lot of dialogue, and it's tolerated more in a story of that genre, such as "The King's Speech." Yet, character stories are tough to sell, which, maybe, proves the point.

On a personal level, I love dialogue. I love writing it and I love hearing it, especially when it comes from writers at the level of Neil Simon or David Mamet. Then again, I still love Westerns, and a lot of good that does me. Just, be forewarned and cautious, before you fill your character's mouth with too many words.

Still, characters talk, and what they say and how they say it are easily as important in selling a character and story to the audience as anything they can do visually.

If dialogue doesn't work in a script, it's been my experience that there are three primary reasons:

1. There is too much text, and not enough subtext.
2. There is too much extraneous dialogue.
3. There is too much dialogue, period.

Dialogue Issue Number One

Too much text and not enough subtext results in what I term "blatant exposition." This is where a character tells us exactly what she's thinking. All motivations and conflicts are clearly stated. The character wears her emotions on her sleeve.

There is an appropriate time for blatant exposition. If we're watching a crime story, and the police Sergeant walks up to the Detective and states:

"The victim, a white male around 35 years of age, was found by the cleaning lady, just after midnight. He died of a bullet wound to the head. There was no I.D. on him."

That's blatant exposition. Just the facts, and quite appropriate. And, there are times when a character can use blatant exposition to emphasize an emotion, as when Jeff Bridges, as Rooster Cogburn in the revisiting of "True Grit" announces to the outlaw:

"I aim to kill you!"

He says exactly what he means, and it puts an emphasis on his intent. So, yes, there are times when it can work effectively.

Most of the time, however, characters, just like real people, have hidden agendas. It's considerably more interesting to have a character drop tidbits of veiled information in his dialogue, which forces us to analyze his true feelings or intentions for ourselves. Reading between the lines makes us think. Keeping us guessing keeps us interested.

That's where subtext comes in. If text is what the character says, subtext is what the character means. Consider Dirty Harry's famous line:

"Go ahead, make my day!"

That's subtext, of course, for:

"Please pick up your gun, because I really want to kill you!"

When Burgess Meredith as Mickey, wearily leans his forehead against Rocky's bathroom door and mumbles:

"I'm 76 years old."

He's really telling us:

"This is my last chance."

How a character says what she says is as important as what he says. Each line of a character's dialogue should be on-story and in character.

When a character expresses a thought, he will do so in a manner which is specific to his personality. When our characters are well-developed, that character's unique attitude and personality will determine how a thought is verbalized.

In "Butch Cassidy and the Sundance Kid," there is a moment on the cliff, just before our heroes jump, when Butch insists:

"The next time I say let's go someplace like Bolivia, let's go someplace like Bolivia!"

With a clenched jaw and in a caustic tone, Sundance retorts:

"Next time."

His delivery tells us what he's really saying:

"Yeah, like there's going to be a next time. We're going to die here, you idiot!"

It's an attitude of irony and cynicism; one which Sundance employs throughout this story, and which provides some of the conflict in the relationship between these two characters.

One handy exercise we employ is to swap lines between different characters. If a speech or significant line of dialogue can be expressed by any character, without distinction, then it may need tweaking.

Dialogue Issue Number Two

Extraneous dialogue is another troubling issue I frequently see in screenplays.

Dialogue become extraneous when:

- It is repetitive; driving home the same point over and over.
- It delivers information which can be better expressed through action.
- It talks about something we've already seen, or…
- It is simply unnecessary, not revealing anything important about the character or is "off story" and does not advance the plot.

Extraneous dialogue takes up critical space in your screenplay, and quickly wears thin on an audience.

Often times, I'll see what is referred to as "mirroring," which occurs when a character repeats what another character has just said, like so:

Character 1: *"What are you doing here?"*

Character 2: *"What am I doing here? I had to do something!"*

Character 1: *"You're a fool, to come back."*

Character 2: *"I'm a fool? What else could I do?"*

Character 1: *"You should have stayed home."*

Character 2: *"Stayed home? What good would that do?"*

It's surprising how much this tendency shows up in screenplays, and most of the time, it only results in wasted space.

We must examine our dialogue carefully, to be certain that what our characters say is meaningful; that it reveals aspects of our character, reflects our character's inner thoughts and feelings and progresses the story.

If our story works just as well without a specific line or speech, the dialogue is extraneous, and probably doesn't need to be there.

Dialogue Issue Number Three

Too much dialogue is one of the biggest problems I see in spec scripts. I was guilty of it, myself, in my early writing, and still struggle to avoid it. It's the primary culprit in screenplays that tend to run too long.

Even well-written dialogue can sink a good script, when there's too much of it. Movies are visual, and so we want to see things happen, not talk about them.

Overwriting dialogue results in what is termed "talking heads;" people delivering numerous exchanges and long speeches. No action, no movement, just talk.

While carefully crafted dialogue can advance story and character, and may thrive in heavily character-oriented stories, the danger is in slowing down the progression of your story.

When the pace starts to drag, because characters are doing a lot of talking, that's when we tend to disengage.

In Summary: When we consider the crucial role dialogue plays, it's easy to see why it demands at least as much of our attention as the action in our screenplay.

It must cover so many bases; revealing and reflecting a characters personality, expressing motives, delivering exposition, enhancing the theme and advancing the story. It must work in harmony with action, in just the right proportions, to maintain the proper rhythm and tone to make the story flow easily and logically from the page.

CHAPTER 15

Story Types

Story Types are often confused with Genres, but they really aren't.

Here's why:

When someone says, *"It's a sci-fi film,"* what do we visualize?

Space, advanced technology, aliens, spacecraft, high-tech weapons and futuristic settings, right?

If we hear *"It's a Western,"* then we're seeing cowboys, horses, six-guns, saloons and dusty streets.

A mystery will require a crime, usually a murder, a detective of some sort, several suspects, some red herrings and, if done well, a surprise ending.

But, when we hear, *"It's a fish-out-of-water story,"* while it does give us a general idea of the story arena, it doesn't give us much to visualize. No "where," no "when," no real frame of reference.

It's a story type, but it needs a genre to create a mental image, because any story type can be employed in any genre.

A Coming-Of-Age story, for instance, can occur in an Action Film as easily as in a Romantic Comedy, or Character Study.

Story types are also considered to be themes, by some. I don't consider them as such, but you sure can, if you want to. That said, here is a short list of story types, which I'm sure you can add to, with some thought.

The Fish-Out-of-Water

An easy way to evoke sympathy for a character and make him relatable is to take him out of his environment and put him in a place that is totally foreign to him.

This story type has been successfully exploited since the beginning of storytelling, from Greek Mythology's "The Odyssey," to the amazing adventures of Sinbad the Sailor to "Alice in Wonderland," and right up to "Sister Act" and "Legally Blond." It's always been a popular and effective story type.

"Crocodile Dundee" was quite a successful fish-out-of-water comedy, as were "Trading Places" and "My Cousin Vinnie." On the dramatic side, "Midnight Cowboy" was a Fish-Out-of-Water tale, and also a Buddy Story.

One of the nicest aspects of the Fish-Out-of-Water story is the ability to allow the audience to learn right along with our lead character. It's all new to him, this strange land he's found himself in, so we get to take that journey of discovery with him. It puts us immediately in harmony with our hero, and it sets up some nice complications generated by the environment.

When Eddie Murphy, as a detective from the mean streets of Detroit, shows up in Beverly Hills, in the film "Beverly Hills Cop," it's not much different in tone than Dorothy's unceremonious landing in Oz. It immediately puts us on the character's side.

How our character reacts to this unfamiliar environment aids us in learning who he is. It also provides some pre-established complications. Not only does our hero have to overcome odds to achieve his goal, he has to do it in a place where people think, talk and act differently. It forces our protagonist to adapt.

The Ensemble

The clear distinction Ensembles have is that there is no one central protagonist. That role is represented by several characters, who deliver the message of the theme as a unit. "The Big Chill" and "The Breakfast Club" were very successful ensemble dramas, and ensembles are quite popular in comedies, from "Animal House" to "Hot Tub Time Machine" and "The Hangover."

The idea is to tell the story through the relationships within a group of characters.

Although ensembles tend to spread the story responsibilities around, there will always be one protagonist who is prominent within the group; a leader. The leader of an ensemble usually turns out to be either a voice-of-reason character; the one who keeps the others in check, or the instigator, who leads the group into action, with either negative or positive results. Still, the group dynamic is the defining element of the story.

The ensemble story type fits neatly into most any genre. Aside from comedy and drama, we've had Action ensembles, like "The Dirty Dozen" and "The Expendables," Adventure ensembles like "Swiss Family Robinson" and "Star Wars," Western ensembles like "The Magnificent Seven" and "The Wild Bunch," comedy ensembles such as "Animal House" and War ensembles like "The Longest Day."

I doubt there is a common genre where the ensemble can't be and hasn't been employed, at some time or another. From a writer's perspective, it presents a very specific challenge, in that it requires us to juggle several "main" characters of basically equal stature to deliver our message. There are a lot of personal storylines and interpersonal storylines to develop.

One of the major commercial draws of this story type is the ensemble cast, itself. With a big enough budget, a film can be a star-studded feature, filled with "A" list talent. At a smaller budget, the theory is that several recognizable actors of mid-level stature can equal one big star.

The Buddy Story

The Buddy Story shares a distinction with the Ensemble, since our two principals basically represent one Central Protagonist.

While it would seem obvious that the overall theme of any buddy story would automatically be "friendship," it really isn't the case.

In "48 Hours" we had a buddy relationship between Eddie Murphy and Nick Nolte, but the story was about crime, and fell into the Action Genre. The same can be said of "Lethal Weapon," with the pairing of Mel Gibson and Danny Glover.

The Buddy Story is always present as a theme in the story, of course, and the charm and appeal of the story relies on the relationship, but it is not always the Master Theme.

The buddies involved in a Buddy Story equal two aspects of one hero. Though they may be as different as night-and-day, and though they may conflict constantly, they are still two characters with the same goal, facing the same complications and participating in the same climactic ending in our story. It takes both of them to deliver the message.

The beauty of this is that it allows us to create one multi-dimensional hero from two characters. Nice.

The Buddy Story has been around forever, of course, and there have been some wonderful pairings in films. The results turned out fine for Paul Newman and Robert Redford in "Butch Cassidy and the Sundance Kid," while Eddie Murphy and Nick Nolte in "48 Hours" were good enough to earn a sequel. Richard Pryor and Gene Wilder created solid comedic buddies in "See No Evil, Hear No Evil" and "Stir Crazy," and "Midnight Cowboy" showed us how it could be implemented to great effect in a gritty character drama.

Creating buddies is a wonderful way to open up opportunities we might not otherwise have for narrative, since helpful personal information can come out through verbal exchanges between our leads.

The Poor Fool

Chaplin gave us the perfect template for this, with his Little Tramp character. The Poor Fool was also a staple for Buster Keaton, W.C. Fields and most of the early films of Jerry Lewis.

In more contemporary times, stars like Rodney Dangerfield, John Candy, Steve Martin, Peter Sellers, Owen Wilson and Jim Carrey have created Poor Fool characters with great success. And, Poor Fool Buddy Stories are common, as we've seen in "Dumb and Dumber" and Cheech and Chong's "Up In Smoke."

Because of the obvious intellectual shortcomings of Poor Fools, they are highly vulnerable characters, and that allows us to easily evoke sympathy for them. The audience will not only root for them, but will fear for them. That's the positive side.

However, to have a Poor Fool overcome great odds from a powerful villain in order to succeed requires a certain suspension of disbelief from our audience. Often, a dumb character survives by dumb luck, and generally requires support from a character with a higher intellect.

We, the writers, must find credible ways to justify our hero's success, and that can be tricky. We can only hope the audience will want him to win so badly, they'll accept some small holes in logic. But, they still have to believe.

The Character Study

Character films are about a character. A character. There are character comedies, like "Arthur," character dramas like "A Beautiful Mind" and even character action films, like "Gandhi," "Patton" and "Braveheart."

Not every film that leans heavily on character, however, is a character film. Romantic Comedies certainly focus on character, as does most any relationship film, like "Driving Miss Daisy" or "Rain Man." But, those aren't true character films. Rather than examinations of a character, they are movies wherein a theme is explored through the relationship between two or more characters.

"Driving Miss Daisy" was a story about racism, and how two people of different races, cultures and social status overcame those stigmas through a growing friendship.

In the case of "Rain Man," a story of brotherly love, the relationship's struggle was an issue of responsibility for Raymond Babbit, as portrayed by Tom Cruise, and one of salvation for Dustin Hoffman's Charlie.

Academy Award winner "The Hurt Locker" is also a story which puts a heavy emphasis on character, even though played out in a War theme. The Active Theme, "war is a drug," is personified by one particular character, but the story is not specifically about that character.

The main convention, here, is that the character is the point, in a Character Study. The theme of our story is embedded in the character. If ever there were a story type where a writer could say, *"It's about this guy..."* and be pretty much right, this is it.

The struggle within a character-oriented story is always internal, with a man-against-himself source of conflict. It concerns matters of the heart, soul and conscience.

These internal conflicts can be driven by outside forces, in the form of physical or emotional obstacles, in the way Forrest Gump rose above his physical and mental handicaps to live a rich, full life, and Russel Crowe's John Nash in "A Beautiful Mind" fought to overcome a mental handicap.

The character of Joe Clay, played by Jack Lemmon in "The Days of Wine and Roses," battled alcoholism. In the case of historical biographical character studies like "Gandhi" and "Patton," there are external conflicts, galore, it's true, but the internal goals and struggles of one person are the point.

The basis of conflict in each of these stories lies in the character's strength of will to overcome his handicap.

Because the demands on our characters are at their peak, our characters must be fleshed out and better developed than in any other type of story. They are the story, and so the intricacies of their personalities and relationships become critically important.

These characters must be complex. They must have paradoxes; opposing characteristics to create internal conflict. And, they must be flawed, in fact fatally flawed, yet still possess redemptive qualities which attract us.

More than the characters of any other story type or genre, these characters can teach us. Their stories are generally about people trying to find themselves, or save themselves, or redeem themselves by overcoming some internal struggle which threatens their happiness, or sometimes their very survival.

They teach us about overcoming physical disability, as Forrest Gump did; about responsibility, as Tom Cruise did in "Rain Man;" about perception, as Peter Sellers' Chance, the Gardener did in "Being There," or about redemption, as with the Jeff Bridges character of Bad Blake in "Crazy Heart."

Character Studies force us, the writers, to dig deeply into our own psyche and instill our deepest, darkest secrets, fears and desires into our characters, then lay them bare before an audience.

One positive aspect Character Studies provide is their ability to attract talent. Stars are always looking for a powerful, meaty role that will allow them to stretch and display their acting prowess. Often a film or television star will take a considerable cut to perform a juicy role in a story that is all about them, or at least the character they will play.

Character Studies also can provide an opportunity for an actor with a television profile to make the leap into films, or a supporting character actor a chance to play the lead. It can also offer a budding nobody the showcase piece he or she is looking for.

A nicely written character story, even when produced on a low budget, can make the leap beyond the indie market into the studio fold. "Nobody's Fool" attracted the likes of Paul Newman, Bruce Willis, Melanie Griffith and Phillip Seymour Hoffman. Paul

Newman was nominated for an Academy Award for this little character film, and so was Bruce Benton for his screenplay.

And, look what "The Wrestler" did for Mickey Roarke, also nominated for a Best Actor Academy Award.

These were all small character films which could easily have been produced on low budgets with relatively unknown actors. The quality of the writing put them over the top and gave them a wider exposure.

Character Studies are also odds-on favorites when it comes to award nominations. A glance at the examples I've provided above will bear that out. Critics tend to favor character stories, since they're more profound and sophisticated in general, and the Award gods frequently smile on them.

There is a very real commercial down side to the Character Study, and that is in foreign marketing. The requirement for dubbing or subtitles is a hindrance, and often times, the subject matter is esoteric to a specific culture or region. If it's a biographical film, it may present a character who doesn't have an international profile, or appeal.

But, they do cross over. "The King's Speech" and "Forrest Gump," aided by a slew of Academy Awards, both did exceedingly well in the international marketplace. It's always within the realm of possibility to buck the odds.

The leads in Character Studies all have one thing in common: a flaw that is potentially fatal, which they must rise above. If they do, as Forrest Gump did, we get a happy ending. If they don't, as with Mickey Roarke's Randy "The Ram" in "The Wrestler," we wind up with a tragedy.

In every case, the character's story is the movie's story, and the outcome for the central protagonist provides the message, or Active Theme of the story.

Yes, in this case, it's all "about this guy."

The Coming-of-Age Story (Rites of Passage)

Watching a hero's emotional growth through a series of challenging events is the draw of this story type.

Coming-of-Age stories work dramatically or comedically with equal effect. Patrick Fugit's character of William in "Almost Famous" and Jaden Smith's Dre in "The Karate Kid" offer just a sample of the range of genres open to this story type.

Coming-of-Age stories work nicely with ensembles, as well. Witness the likes of "American Graffiti," "Stand By Me" and "The Breakfast Club."

It's all about the angst that comes with the process of maturing, and works because we've all been through it.

The stories have a soap-opera effect, the idea being to sweep us into the inner workings of our protagonist's heart and soul, and create a yearning for our hero to overcome the painful process of growing up; a pain we can all identify with.

When we think of the definitive Coming-of-Age story, it's only natural to envision our Central Protagonist as a youth, but that doesn't necessarily hold true in this story type. That's why I added Rites of Passage to the definition. A character of pretty much any age can experience a life-changing epiphany and grow, emotionally.

Tom Cruise has made this transition in several films, including "A Few Good Men," "Top Gun," "Rain Man" and "The Color of Money." Dudley Moore's comic turn as George Webber in "10" also demonstrated that we're never too old to grow up.

Even if the story you're writing is not a Coming-of-Age story overall, this Rites of Passage angle works very well in a character's personal storyline.

We want to see growth in a character, and watching that character go from immature to mature or irresponsible to responsible before our eyes fills the bill.

In Summary: These are all story types, and there are probably more I haven't noted, but again, the main difference between them and genres, in my personal definition, is the genre's ability to conjure an immediate visual image; an expectation of what is to come.

With that preface, let's take a look at the generally accepted major genres, and some of their sub-genres.

CHAPTER 16

Genres

My dictionary defines the word this way:

GENRE: "A class of artistic endeavor having a characteristic form or technique."

Virtually every story falls into a genre. In truth, it can't do otherwise. If it doesn't fit into a pre-existing genre, it would, by its very inception, create a new genre. "The Blair Witch Project" did this, and created the Found Footage genre.

When we talk about genre films, we're usually referring to a handful of major genres. These are the most common; the "evergreens," which account for the majority of the films made.

In the film world, genre refers to those story elements which an audience expects the movie to employ. If it's a Western, it has to have horses, and we expect a few gun fights.

In a Romantic Comedy, we're looking for a "meet cute," with the traditional boy-meets-girl, boy-loses-girl, boy-gets-girl-back story arc.

In Sci-Fi, we expect cool technology, futuristic settings, special effects and some aliens to deal with.

The conventions of each genre are its built-ins. Because of those built-ins, writing to a major genre does a lot of the work for us. It presents us with specific, familiar moments and incidents which we will employ in structuring our story. We have a wide array of story tools already determined, since there are so many familiar story devices in each genre.

On the negative side of that, because every common genre convention; car chase, meet-cute, gun fight, love scene, etc. imaginable has been written thousands of times and in as many ways, it's quite challenging to write something that doesn't come off as cliched.

For that reason, the stunts in big-budget action films have reached breathtaking levels, technologically. Sadly, often the stunts strain the limits of credibility to the point of becoming unbelievable. They're big, they're splashy and they're impressive to look at. They're just hard to believe, at times, and that can damage the credibility of any story. But, the need for it is understandable. It is simply a result of someone out there trying to squeeze something fresh from a well-used genre.

Admittedly, it's no easy task, but that should be our goal, and it is achievable. Look what Quentin Tarantino did with the Crime genre film "Pulp Fiction." He actually made two cold-blooded hit men empathetic and relatable. That little "What do they call a Quarter Pounder with cheese in France?" speech was all about achieving that, and it worked, providing a nice angle on an old genre.

The most common practice, and one that makes plenty of sense, is to mix genres, and that's what most mainstream films do, these days. Within the action story is a love story, for instance. We hear labels such as Action/Comedy or Romantic/Adventure.

"Scary Movie," in lampooning horror films, successfully combined the genres of horror and comedy, just as "Airplane" combined comedy and disaster to spoof the "Airport" series of films of the 70's, and "Naked Gun" married comedy to the crime genre. The logic is clear. The more genres we have, the more tools we have with which to create.

One positive aspect to genre films is the fact that we know who our audience is, and so do the distributors. That provides them a certain comfort level. They know how to market a film which fits neatly into a familiar mold.

Selling a mediocre genre film may not always guarantee a profit, but it generally reduces the risk of a loss. Even if it's a bad Sci-Fi film, there is a strong enough audience of hard core Sci-Fi buffs out there to support it. Distributors market hundreds of major genre-targeted films in the straight-to-DVD arena, and therefore have a good barometer with which to calculate a return.

Genre films are genre films because they have conventions. The audience is drawn to them because of those conventions. That means we must honor those conventions.

We can play with them, tweak them, turn them on their heads, but they must be there. They must be addressed, or our audience will feel cheated. They came to the theater expressly because they expected something, and we didn't give it to them. Are we really going to write an Action film with no car chase? A Western with no gunfights? A Romantic Comedy where boy never meets girl?

Now, like any good rule, this one has been successfully violated by some pretty notable films. William Goldman, the screenwriter of "Butch Cassidy and the Sundance Kid," commented on the fact that in constructing his story, he was forced to violate an age-old Western Genre convention.

He had his heroes run away from a fight!

This was when the Super Posse chased Butch and Sundance, ultimately driving them to Bolivia. The Super Posse presented a formidable foe, since it personified the unstoppable movement of progress.

Still, heroes don't run. John Wayne wouldn't have. But, it quite obviously worked in "Butch Cassidy and the Sundance Kid," considering that the screenplay won an Academy Award, and the film was nominated for Best Picture. The box office wasn't bad, either. Besides, the movie was still loaded with comforting Western conventions; gunfights, chase scenes, horses, holdups, saloon girls and a schoolmarm, to name just a few.

Woody Allen's "Annie Hall" violated a Romantic Comedy convention, because boy didn't get girl at the end of the film. Yet, it held to all traditional Rom Com standards, otherwise.

In almost every instance, however, if we stray too far from the comfort zone and ignore the genre conventions our story is expected to present, we do so at our own risk. I'm not saying, we can't do it. I am saying, we'd better know what we're doing, before we try.

The Common Genres

The Action Genre

Truly one of the staples of the industry, Action films have tremendous advantages in the marketplace, for several reasons.

For one thing, action films can be made at almost any budget.

What we're used to are large budget films with splashy effects and head-spinning stunts; things crashing and exploding everywhere. But creating action doesn't necessarily mean spending a lot of money. A foot chase can be as compelling as a car chase, and a lot cheaper to shoot, and a creative fight scene can be engrossing at any price. Robert Rodriguez made the action film "El Mariachi" for seven-thousand dollars, and it, in turn, made his career.

A second advantage to the Action genre is its popularity in the home video/Pay-Per-View market. Low budget action movies are frequently made for direct-to-video distribution, and can do quite well. Younger audiences, in particular, love films in the Action Genre, even when produced on lower budgets and without major stars.

The third advantage films in the Action Genre hold is that they travel well in foreign markets. Action is universal, has no cultural boundaries, and there is less dialogue, which is a positive, because dialogue requires dubbing or subtitles.

Some of the conventions we find in the Action Genre are:

- The Car Chase

A classic story device. Cars and movies found one another early in the twentieth century, and have had a thriving relationship since.

Take a look at some old Keystone Kops, Marx Brothers or W.C. Fields films, and you will see some of the best orchestrated, most creative stunt-filled chase sequences imaginable. No fancy camera tricks or CGI, just stunt drivers truly putting their lives on the line for their craft, at a time when the craft was raw and untested.

The Car Chase is an element that's pretty difficult to "one-up," these days. If there's anything new that can outgun the classic sequences in Steve McQueen's "Bullitt" or Gene Hackman's "The French Connection," I have yet to see it. However, this convention is so well-received by the action crowd, they'll willingly go along for the ride, as long as there is a modicum of imagination put into it.

An aspect of the Car Chase is the Car Crash, of course. Somebody has to slam at least one car into something, or flip it over something, or run it off the side of a hill, so it can burst into flames and explode. That brings up another Action Genre convention.

- Explosions

There pretty much has to be at least one. We love watching things blow up, and there are so many things to blow up, and so many ways to do it. Pyrotechnics are a must, and not just a plus, in an action movie. The bigger the explosion, and the bigger the structure being toppled, the better. Enough said.

- Gun Fights

This device rivals the Car Chase/Crash in popularity, which leads to the creation of a couple of Action Genre conventions. First, there are a lot of really cool guns out there, for those who appreciate them. In the "Dirty Harry" films, Detective Harry Calahan's .44 Magnum, "the most powerful handgun in the world" became a character in itself.

21st Century weapons of war have become more sophisticated, and Hollywood gleefully climbed on board the bandwagon. The more bullets they can spew and the bigger the bullets, the better, so automatic weapons are always in vogue. It makes one wonder how any single human being can possibly carry all the ammunition they use up.

No matter, because this leads to the need for something to shoot at, which, in turn leads to the need for "cannon fodder," another convention. We need lots of low-level, non-speaking bad guys to kill. Body count is the thing, and the more blood-letting, the better.

- Fist Fights

We must also see some mano-a-mano fisticuffs of some sort. We pretty much always see our action heroes mix it up with someone, if not a lot of someones.

While they require stunt actors and often meticulous staging, fight scenes are still, overall, pretty cheap to shoot. A good one can rival the Car Chase/Crash and the Gunfight in its effect.

James Bond always has exceedingly well-designed fight scenes in every film. He is usually pitted against an overpowering opponent, such as an "Odd Job" or "Jaws," since we know he can take an ordinary man with his hands tied behind him.

Good fight scenes are intense and creative, and are orchestrated by highly skilled Fight and Stunt Coordinators. The writer's job is to put the elements of physical and emotional conflict into place to create the initial source of conflict.

Some writers prefer to write detailed descriptions of fight scenes. It's optional, but really isn't necessary to do so, unless some specific action involved is needed for the story. For the most part, regardless of what we write, the Fight Coordinators and Stunt Coordinators will disregard the bulk of the written direction and create their own fight sequence. When the fists start to fly, we just sit back and let the specialists do their thing.

The Action Hero

Our heroes in the Action Genre will possess specific qualities which make them suitable for the perilous, danger-filled task ahead. "Macho" is the key word. We often find them to be stoic, strong-willed, rebellious loners, pursuing their own agenda with a vengeance, as their superiors struggle to control them. Hard drinking, knuckle-busting "man's men."

Of course, Tarantino turned that one on its head with the "Kill Bill" series, by putting an attractive woman in this role, a twist on the Action film hero type. It's been done in other films, as well, in the way that revenge-themed "The Brave One" twisted Bronson's "Death Wish" every-man hero into an every-woman. In general, however, Action Genre heroes stay pretty consistent in their makeup.

The Action Villain

Villains in action films are most often gifted with three common traits: they are powerful, they are smart and they are evil. You can substitute certain qualities for evil, such as "psychotic" or "ruthless," wherever appropriate, since the end result is basically the same, but powerful and smart are pretty consistent.

Tommy Lee Jones' character of Marshall Sam Gerard in "The Fugitive" was powerful, smart, and ruthless. In this case, we had a rare story of a good guy going after another good guy. A nice angle on an Action Genre convention, which almost always demands an actual bad guy. The one-armed-man doesn't really count, since he was more of a Maguffin in this film than a central villain.

We want our villains to have those traits of power and intelligence in order to create the most challenging opposition for our hero. In every instance, when we write a story, we want the odds against our hero to appear insurmountable. We want to put them where they don't want to be, and force them to do what they don't want to do.

In the Action Genre, this means creating obstacles which are physically demanding and life-threatening in nature. Thus, we end up with gunfights, fist fights, explosions and chase sequences.

In some instances, the Action Genre "villain" will actually be an organization, as in the Jason Bourne series, starting with "The Bourne Identity."

In this type of film, we will generally have a character who personifies the organization, but the organization, itself, is our Central Antagonist.

The James Bond films give us the best of both worlds in this category. Virtually every Bond film featured a smart, powerful, evil villain who also controlled an organization.

In some instances, while James brought down the organization and saved the world, the villain escaped to fight another day, in another Bond film.

You'll find that audiences are quite willing to suspend their disbelief in these films. We often see stunts performed in action films which defy not only logic, but the laws of physics.

As mentioned previously, the bar continues to rise in this area, making it more and more difficult to "wow" the viewer. If the stunt is imaginative and exciting, however, the audience will usually forgive the fact that it's also probably impossible.

Martial Arts Action

Here's a sub-genre that's as pure genre as a movie can get. When someone tells us it's a "karate flick," we know exactly what we're in for.

This is a very healthy direct-to-video product, and can be produced on a modest budget, since the level of martial arts proficiency and the creativity of the fight scenes and stunts are the draw. Rarely will we find a seasoned, serious actor who is proficient enough in martial arts to headline one of these films.

That means, generally, we wind up with great martial artists who are so-so actors. However, these films can also make stars of unknowns, as Bruce Lee, Jean Claude Van Damme, Steven Segal, Jackie Chan and Chuck Norris demonstrate.

Being a cut-to-the-chase film style, plot and character development require little attention. The bare-bones storylines cover familiar ground, delivering just enough information and backstory to provide a minimal setup, then it's on to the kicking and punching.

Initially, most of these films came with a built-in revenge theme, although break-out martial arts stars like Chuck Norris and Steven Segal have helped the sub-genre cross over into pure Action, where plot lines can vary. Rather than being "karate flicks," they are Action films with martial arts. It's pure escapist fare, and even without any star power, or potential star power, these films are easier to market than most, and play very well in foreign territories.

In Summary: Overall, the Action Genre is the fast-food of the film industry, always in demand to provide some good, old-fashioned heart-pounding, popcorn-munching fun. A writer who handles this genre well can often look forward to a long and lucrative screenwriting career.

The Adventure Genre

Adventure goes hand-in-hand with Action, in many respects. In fact, you'll frequently hear a film being touted as an Action/Adventure. The reason is simple, most Action films have Adventure, and vice-verse. However, there is a distinct difference which separates the two genres.

The Adventure Genre takes in an entire realm of stories which don't fit into the Action Genre.

Adventure films promise to take us on a journey, and while they may have some of the same elements as Action films, like chases or gunfights, their story structure is decidedly different.

Adventure films frequently feature exotic locales or introduce us to new worlds. Most epic, tentpole extravaganzas fall into the Adventure Genre. "Avatar," "Lawrence of Arabia," "Pirates of the Caribbean," and "Waterworld" are some examples.

Movies about a quest fit into the Adventure Genre, as well. Witness "Raiders of the Lost Ark." Plenty of action going on, and yet, we are clearly on a journey of discovery; a quest for a magical treasure, unlike, say "Lethal Weapon." Both films featured chase sequences and gunfights, but the difference between them, thematically, is dramatic.

Stories which pit man against nature fall into this category, as well, as in "Into the Wild," "The Impossible" or "The Perfect Storm." Nature can be a great villain. Climbing a mountain, traversing a jungle or crossing an ocean can provide numerous opportunities to test our hero's mettle.

The Adventure Genre is one which really plays well with others. When it comes to mixing genres, as we nearly always do, Adventure is a solid choice.

"Star Wars" is a great example of an Adventure/Sci Fi Genre, along with "Alien," "Blade Runner" and a host of others. "Romancing the Stone," "Titanic" and "Fool's Gold" show us that Adventure clicks with the Romance Genre, as well.

Also, let us not forget the coupling of Adventure and Comedy, a time-honored tradition. "Night at the Museum," "It's a Mad, Mad, Mad, Mad World," "The Princess Bride" and "Tropic Thunder" all mixed the genres with great success.

Adventure also provides fodder for parody, as witnessed in films such as "Monty Python in Search of the Holy Grail," "Land of the Lost" and "Hot Shots."

The Adventure Hero

Unlike the Action Genre, the Adventure Genre is much more conducive to flawed heroes.

The staunch, stern, tough-guy (or gal) of the Action Genre is not necessarily the best choice in an Adventure film.

What we tend to like, here, are heroes who are more like us, thrust into precarious situations. Spielberg's Indiana Jones is a college professor, not a particularly macho guy in his "real" life. He enters into the exotic Adventure world of each film on a quest, but he's not really looking for a fight.

While we certainly admire our Action heroes, we tend to identify more easily with Adventure genre protagonists. The "Average Joe" is not only acceptable, but often preferable.

Along with our pal Indy, think about the characters played by Cary Grant in "North by Northwest," Ben Stiller in "Night at the Museum," or Noah Wiley in "The Librarian" series. And, let us not forget our naive, young farm girl Dorothy, who landed smack-dab in the middle of Oz.

Even families get into the act, as in "Swiss Family Robinson" and "Honey, I Shrunk the Kids."

One simple rule of thumb differentiating Action Genre heroes from Adventure Genre heroes is this: We don't have to worry about our Action heroes, because they are always equipped for the job. Arnold, Stallone, Eastwood, Willis and the current flavor of James Bond are always up to the task, and we know it.

Not so, the Adventure Hero. Because they are most often average people taken out of their element and thrust into dangerous situations, we are encouraged to be concerned for their safety and survival. They are us, whereas Action heroes are what we aspire to be.

The Adventure Villain

Adventure Villains share the most of the same qualities as Action Villains. There is little distinction, except in a sub-genre of our Adventure Genre, the Fantasy Adventure. Villains in the Adventure Genre range from other-worldly to forces of nature to reality-based human villains and systems.

Indiana Jones faced the Nazis, a "system," for instance. "Blood Diamond," "The Man Who Would Be King" and "Sahara" all provided real-life villains to oppose our heroes.

Fantasy/Adventure

Magic, monsters and supernatural forces often come into play in this genre, and we never tire of them. From medieval worlds of sorcery and dragons to fantastic realms hidden deep within the universe, as in "Avatar," Fantasy/Adventure takes us far from the norm, into the deepest corners of our imagination.

This is an "anything goes" venue, where all things are believable, and possible.

The Fantasy/Adventure Hero

From "The Wizard of Oz" to "The Last Starfighter" to "Harry Potter," our Fantasy/Adventure heroes tend to be average people caught up in fantastic worlds and supernatural events.

The exception here is when our heroes are, themselves, endowed with superhuman qualities of their own.

The superhero trend which is currently hot demonstrates this clearly. While our heroes in such films as "Spiderman," "Batman," "Superman" and "Iron Man" (notice a trend?) appear to defy their common-man relate ability, they actually don't.

These characters all live normal lives, when not out fighting crime. They are motivated to action by their opposition, which is always of the super-villain ilk, possessing powers of evil which can only be defeated by some countering super-force.

The superhero protagonists always fight to protect and preserve mankind, demonstrating their humanity, while the super-villains threaten total destruction of, or an all-controlling power over mankind, a common convention of the Fantasy/Adventure Genre.

The Fantasy/Adventure Villain

Fantasy/Adventure villains take on more unique qualities than the norm. Since this genre takes us into strange, new worlds, we'll often encounter opposing forces which are, themselves, strange and new. From "The Wizard of Oz" to "The Last Starfighter" to "Harry Potter," to "Jumanji," our Adventure villains most often possess some supernatural advantage over our "Average Joe" heroes. This generally requires the support of a supernaturally endowed ally for our hero to survive and overcome these villains.

Nature/Adventure

Nature Adventures qualify as a sub-genre of the Adventure Genre, but their conventions differ, in many respects. Here, we find our heroes in more reality based surroundings, such as a wilderness, but certainly in that same out-of-their-element situation as in the standard Adventure Genre.

Man-against-the elements stories, such as "127 Hours," "The Perfect Storm," "Armageddon," "Never Cry Wolf" or "Twister," where nature is the central antagonist, fall into this category.

Man-against-animal stories wherein our "villain" is a wild animal also fall under this heading, as in "Jaws," "The Ghost and the Darkness," "Night of the Grizzly" and "Moby Dick."

Animal Adventures which feature animals as protagonists, from "Lassie, Come Home" to "Homeward Bound" to "Babe" fall within this sub-genre, also.

These days, this flavor of the Nature Adventure genre is generally seen in animated films, such as "The Lion King," "Finding Nemo" or "Ice Age."

In Summary: Adventure can compliment pretty much any other genre, and is a good commercial choice, to boot. In order to pull it off at a competitive level, however, it demands a high price tag, which usually limits it to studio production.

The Caper (or Heist) Genre

Everybody loves a good caper story. Caper, or Heist films come armed with a number of audience-friendly qualities. For one thing, just like Cracker Jacks, when you get to the end, there's a prize waiting.

A major genre convention, of course, is that there has to be something worth heisting. The goal for our protagonist can be a diamond, a painting, an historical artifact, just plain money or anything of great value. However, there doesn't always have to be a financial reward to justify a heist.

In escape films, freedom is the final reward, as in "Escape From Alcatraz," "The Great Escape" and "Argo." Revenge is sometimes the goal, as well, demonstrated in films like "The Sting" and "Trading Places."

Most of the time, Caper films will feature an ensemble cast, and each character will have a specific talent necessary to pull off the heist. Witness "Now You See Me," "Ocean's Eleven," "Tower Heist" and "The Usual Suspects." We also know, going in, that a Caper film will involve some subterfuge; an intricate plan to overcome the fool-proof security surrounding our treasure.

Caper films combine nicely with most any other genre, the most common being Crime, since the capers, swindles and schemes involved are frequently of the illegal variety. Caper fits quite comfortably within the Crime Genre, since a great number of crimes inherently involve some form of a caper. Bank jobs, museum thefts, blackmail and even kidnaps make the grade.

The Clint Eastwood vehicle "Kelly's Heroes" was a caper within the Action/War Genre, as was "The Dirty Dozen."

Combining Caper with Comedy has always paid big dividends for Hollywood. The classic "It's a Mad, Mad, Mad, Mad World" was an ensemble Caper Comedy, and the genres combined successfully in films like "How to Steal a Million," "Going in Style" and "To Catch a Thief."

The Caper Hero

This is a genre where we get to root for a "good" bad guy, since our heroes are often thieves or con artists. Audiences have always been attracted to the charming cat burglar or loveable con man, which have been portrayed by the likes of Carey Grant, Steve McQueen and George Clooney.

Although the bulk of caper films feature an ensemble cast, there is always one major player, around which all else revolves. It was Frank Sinatra in the first "Ocean's Eleven," George Clooney in the remake. In the original "The Thomas Crowne Affair," it was Steve McQueen, and in the updated version, Pierce Brosnan.

This character will not only be the leader; the brains of the outfit, but is most likely to be the one with the motivation to go after the prize in the first place.

Bear in mind, the real prize may not be a tangible object of value, at all. The true goal for our central protagonist can be purely personal, addressing an internal desire.

The aforementioned "Thomas Crowne Affair" is a good example. Citing the original film, Steve McQueen's character was already fabulously wealthy. Money wasn't the point. It was the challenge that attracted him; a purely personal motivation. And, as has been pointed out, revenge or justice can be the driving force.

Our heroes in this sub-genre are generally smart, charming, witty and seasoned with just enough larceny in their hearts to keep them interesting. Since, in most cases, our heroes are technically on the wrong side of the law, they should also possess enough positive characteristics to make them redeemable, or keep us on their side. That is, unless we're sending our protagonist to his doom, in a tragic ending, as suffered by the Dean Keaton Character in "The Usual Suspects."

The Caper Villain

In most instances, the villain of a Caper film is represented by an organization, such as a bank, a government, the police force or an art gallery, presenting a man-against-the-system form of conflict for our hero. The organization is then personified, giving us a human villain to contend with, one which represents the forces of the organization.

When we're dealing with a motivation of revenge or justice for our hero, where the goal is of a personal nature, we get human villains. In "The Sting," it was Robert Shaw's character, Doyle Lonnigan, who was responsible for the death of a friend of Robert Redford's Johnny Hooker. This was a blatant revenge theme.

In "Tower Heist," Arthur Shaw, played by Alan Alda, was the crooked businessman and perpetrator of a ponzi scheme, which obliterated the pension fund for some hard-working stiffs. In this case, our heroes were committing a criminal act in the name of justice.

In order to maintain the moral high ground for our Central Protagonist, his target, if that target is human, must be immoral, unethical or criminal, and thus deserving of being fleeced.

Caper films are a good bet in the marketplace. The big "sell" for them, along with a diverse cast of colorful characters, is the appeal of seeing an imaginative plan put into action to achieve the heist or fulfill the caper. Similar to the Mystery Genre, most of the fun is in getting there, and the obstacles within the story are all about preventing that.

In Summary: Caper films, like mysteries, challenge the audience to think, with plots that twist and turn throughout. For a writer, that means a lot of plotting, with the challenge to create an intricate story puzzle which must be solved in an entertaining and believable fashion. The obstacles to the goal will be both internal and external, and overcoming them will require skill and cunning by our protagonists. Likewise, the writer. A well-written caper film is a popular item in the marketplace, with a long shelf-life.

The Comedy Genre

Here's a genre that's pretty vague, on the surface, until you break it down into its sub-genres. Just saying "Comedy" doesn't conjure up any familiar images. All we know is, it's supposed to make us laugh. Instinctive in some and elusive to others, comedy is much more complex, when you dig into it, than it appears on the surface.

The rise and fall of comedy is that it allows every viewer to be a sophisticated critic. Either we laugh, or we don't. No deep analysis required. And, since we don't all laugh at the same things or for the same reasons, you can consider this genre a "mixer."

There always has to be another genre involved.

Comedy is about making fun of things; finding humor in familiar surroundings. Therefore, we need something to relate to, before we can mine the humor from it.

Every genre which exists has been mated, at one time or another, with Comedy. With that in mind, lets explore some of the broad strokes of Comedy, before we get into the sub-genres.

Early in my venture into Hollywood to take my shot at writing Situation Comedy, I spent considerable time around stand-up comics. The first rule I learned from them is that nothing is sacred in comedy. Anything can be played for laughs. It's all about context and, as the old saying goes, timing. And the raw, bare bones structure of Comedy, in general, can be found in a simple joke.

It begins with a premise. This is the thing I'm going to make you laugh at.

"Life stinks" is a premise.

So is "Life is Beautiful," but you know what? It isn't as funny.

Things going right never are. Things going right can be cute, sweet and heartwarming, but rarely funny. Not really. Only when something bad is happening to someone do we laugh.

That's why, when Rodney Dangerfield bemoaned the many reasons he got "no respect," we found it hilarious. Says something about we humans, don't you think? But, there it is.

It's the situation in Situation Comedy. It's where the potential for the humor lies. Two guys walk into a bar...a Priest, a Rabbi and a Buddhist Monk are on an airplane...I went to the doctor...this traveling salesman runs out of gas...there was a young man from Nantucket...got it?

Once we establish our premise, the next element of our basic joke is the setup. This is where we qualify that thing we're going to make fun of.

So, "Life stinks?" Why? How? What happened that caused life to stink? As I've pointed out, the revered joke-master Rodney Dangerfield made his career on one simple premise: *"I get no respect."* That premise was qualified by several thousand setups, over the years, all designed to demonstrate just how Rodney got no respect.

Our last basic element is, of course, the Punch Line. I'm pretty sure, we all know what that is. That's the part where we laugh, assuming, of course that we find the joke funny.

That means, do we relate to it? If we don't relate, we don't laugh. The comics I knew used the term "too hip for the room" to describe a joke that was so esoteric or obscure as to disconnect with the audience. That is a risk which is inherent in comedy writing, since pushing the boundaries is the goal.

Now, let's look at an example. Here's the joke:

Premise: *"I was feeling depressed, so I went to a psychiatrist."*

Setup: *"He told me, cheer up, things could be worse."*

Punch line: *"So I cheered up. Sure enough, things got worse."*

Now, apply that simple structure to our screenplay. In story terms, the premise is our first act, the setup is our second act and the punch line is Act Three. And, it's all about bad things happening to people. Things that turn out okay...but funny. We'll get into more detail as we examine the sub-genres in the Comedy fold, starting with...

Romantic Comedy

Widely considered a major genre all its own because of its unique conventions, Romantic Comedy has well-defined pros and cons.

On the plus side, it never goes out of vogue. The industry is never not looking for a good Romantic Comedy. It brings with it a loyal audience and is most often conducive to lower production costs.

Because it is cheaper to produce, Romantic Comedy doesn't need the wide audience base of Action or Adventure to achieve financial success. Action/Adventure budgets for tentpole movies run in the hundreds-of-millions of dollars. I have yet to see a Romantic Comedy that comes anywhere near that, even with major stars involved.

Speaking of stars, another reason for the popularity of this genre is that it offers an opportunity to showcase young, new actors. There are always plenty of pretty, handsome and sometimes even talented actors coming up through the ranks. Their popularity makes them likely candidates to showcase in a Rom Com.

For some teen actors, it becomes a rite-of-passage into more adult roles. If their faces are being splashed all over fan magazines and they're being talked about on entertainment shows, you're bound to see them in a Rom Com, eventually. That means, these young, hot actors will be looking for a good script.

One negative attached to the genre is its lack of critical appeal. Very, very rarely does a Romantic Comedy win, or even get nominated for an Academy Award. Frank Capra's "It Happened One Night" did it, back in 1934, but since then, Woody Allen's "Annie Hall" has been the only Romantic Comedy to make the grade. "Gigi" in 1958, "My Fair Lady" in 1964 and "The Apartment" in 1960 come close, because of strong romantic elements in their storylines, but the first two were primarily musicals and "The Apartment" more of a melodrama.

As mentioned previously, in the case of "Annie Hall," Woody Allen violated a standing Romantic Comedy convention, since boy didn't really wind up with girl at the end, but in every other respect, it fit the mold. The bottom line is, if you're looking for awards and critical acclaim, this probably isn't your genre of choice.

The main conventions of Romantic Comedy are as solidly entrenched as any could be. First and foremost, it will always, always have love as its Master Theme.

Since its the romantic style of love, that pretty much sets your Active Theme in stone, as well. In Romantic Comedy, the Active Theme is "Love Conquers All." I mean, really, that's what makes it a Romantic Comedy, right?

The pace of Romantic Comedy is another consistent trait. The stories are fast-paced and full of energy and forward motion, with quick, witty dialogue. Moments of reflection are few, and should be significant, when they occur. This results in a shorter story, and therefore a shorter screenplay. Rarely will we see a Romantic Comedy reach the two-hour mark. Ninety to 100 minutes is more in the range.

The Romantic Comedy Hero

Here, as in the Buddy Story, we have two Central Protagonists: our two lovers. Bringing them together at the end will complete our central storyline.

The Central Protagonists of Romantic Comedy come in all shapes and sizes; with varying characteristics and traits, but each must be flawed in a manner which can only be fixed by the other. They must not only be in love with each other, they must be good for each other. Their union is necessary for each to live a happy life.

The Romantic Comedy Villain

This role can be filled by a wide choice of sources. Basically, anything that threatens to keep the lovers apart qualifies.

Family often serves as an established source of conflict for our lovers. Family members can disapprove of John or Jill's choice of mates for a variety of reasons, and provide both an internal and external source of conflict.

The memorable "Guess Who's Coming to Dinner" explored the family machinations through a racism theme. Katherine Hepburn wants to marry Sidney Poitier, and families on both sides are dead set against it. The internal struggle for the families became the conflict between "I'm not a racist" and "But, not with my daughter/son." Family dynamics also provided a significant complication for Cher and Nicolas Cage in "Moonstruck."

Ethnicity and religion provide conflict fodder, as we've seen in "My Big Fat Greek Wedding," and many other Rom Coms. A forbidden romance in the workplace, political rivals in love; any societal obstacle will do.

Very often, a Man vs Himself conflict is the culprit. Internal, rather than external forces become primary. Holly Golightly in "Breakfast at Tiffany's" was determined to marry for money, not love. Dustin Hoffman's Ben in "The Graduate" had to overcome Elaine's shame and outrage over his affair with her mother. Tom Hanks' Joe Fox and Meg Ryan's Kathleen Kelly in "You've Got Mail" were kept apart by a matter of personal principle.

The internal conflicts within our leads play a big part in a Romantic Comedy story in any circumstance, but they do nicely in providing us with a central force of antagonism; a villain.

Romantic Comedy Structure

From a structural perspective, we're bound by the most rigid of conventions you'll find in any genre: Boy meets girl, boy gets girl, boy loses girl, boy gets girl back. It is the basic spine of every Rom Com story.

Boy Meets Girl

The boy-meets-girl requirement is usually fulfilled by another Rom Com convention: the "meet cute."

We're looking for a fun, creative way to put the guy and girl together for the first time. Most often, the meet cute will occur in the first act, early in the story, sometimes serving as an Story Trigger. There is room for variations, here, but very little.

In "Sleepless in Seattle," Nora Ephron gave us a twist by keeping our principals apart until the very end. In this case, the meet cute moment became their connection through a radio talk show. Ephron directed another film which twisted the convention with "You've Got Mail," wherein the lovers met online anonymously, then again in real life, where their e-mail identities were unknown to one another.

In any case, boy must meet girl at some point, early on, and since it's romance plus comedy, the meeting should be humorous and yes, cute, if possible. It's also a nice opportunity to establish our source of conflict between our characters, and there will nearly always be an inherent conflict between them, or within them, at the outset.

If the goal is to get them together, then we need obstacles to keep them apart. He's just coming off a bad break up, she's engaged to someone else. He's blue collar, she's high society. In George Axelrod's script "Breakfast at Tiffany's," based on the book by Truman Capote, Audrey Hepburn's Holly Golightly was determined to marry for money and status, paired with George Peppard's starving writer "Fred," who, though jaded, still believed in love.

The classic Academy Award winner "It Happened One Night" is a film which, at least to my mind, established the contemporary Romantic Comedy form. In it, the conflict hinges on the fact that Clark Gable, a newspaper reporter, hooks up with runaway rich girl, Claudette Colbert, on the premise of helping her escape, when what he really wants is a story.

This is an example of establishing a nice external source of conflict which then creates internal conflict for our characters, once they fall in love.

Internal conflict is not just necessary, but critical in Romantic Comedy, because, while it isn't a Character Study, it is a character story. It's about love, and internal conflicts are the only kind which can threaten love. Physical obstacles can keep lovers apart, but only internal obstacles can drive them apart. If Johnny goes off to war and dies, his love for Jill lives on. It's just unrequited. Not to mention, a lousy ending for a Romantic Comedy.

The same kind of internal conflict is demonstrated in "You've Got Mail." Our leads, Tom Hanks and Meg Ryan are anonymously infatuated with one another, online. We yearn for them to meet, because it's obvious they're perfect for each other. They must get together. But, there is a problem.

We know that Tom is an executive for a large bookstore chain, which drives small, neighborhood bookstores out of business. Guess what Meg owns? A small, neighborhood bookstore, of course. I feel an "uh-oh" coming.

It follows that when they meet in real life, as executive and small business owner, they conflict on an important matter of principle. Another established external conflict giving rise to internal conflict.

But, it doesn't stop there. Each of them is currently in a relationship! Wow, yet another established conflict, both internal and external.

But, screenwriters Nora and Delia Ephron weren't finished turning the screws, yet. It isn't enough that Tom owns a bookstore chain. He's opening a superstore! It's certain to gobble up every little bookstore within miles! And, it isn't enough that Meg owns a small, neighborhood bookstore. It's a children's bookstore! And, she reads stories to the little tykes!

Tom, how could you?

As you can see, a certain level of conflict will nearly always exist between our two romantic interests before they meet. That conflict is often at the root of our "meet cute" moment.

Boy Gets Girl

Once boy gets girl, the relationship must spark, although not without problems or conflict. At this point, we must have an underlying issue which threatens the relationship. The audience will know that trouble looms ahead, even when the characters do not.

We all know the conventions of this form, by now. This means that we, the writers, must plant that time-bomb early in the story. We establish that point of conflict, then let it bubble on low for awhile, only to spring it to life at the critical Boy-loses-girl moment, later.

In the boy-gets-girl sequence, the audience must arrive at that these-two-must-fall-in-love moment. This is the sequence where we discover why they are perfect for each other, even if appearances indicate otherwise. There can't be a happy ending unless they end up together, so we yearn for our lovers to overcome the obstacles they will face.

"Annie Hall" defied this part of the rule by not allowing our leads, Woody Allen's Alvy Singer and Diane Keaton's Annie Hall, to remain together. However, they did maintain a fulfilling relationship and the resolve was satisfying. We came away feeling as if they both wound up better off, even though the love relationship between them didn't hold up.

By resolving the film in this way, "Annie Hall" actually answered the question posed by Billy Crystal and Meg Ryan in "When Harry Met Sally":

Can a man and a woman be just friends, without a romantic entanglement?

Ironically, the answer in "Annie Hall" was "yes," while in "When Harry Met Sally," the film that explored the question, the answer turned out to be "no."

Boy Loses Girl

Boy-loses-girl is step three in this Rom Com structure. This step can appear in several places where a primary story beat occurs. It can provide our act break at the end of Act One, though it doesn't often, or it can serve as our mid-point turn, or it can come at the end of Act Two and work as an act break there.

We can structure our story to accommodate any of these choices. What is consistent is that boy must lose girl somewhere in the second act. Since this moment is always the crisis point of the story, it will generally show up as a second act ending. It serves quite neatly as an Act Two break, leading us into the high-energy climax in Act Three.

Let's go back to my template, "It Happened One Night." Clark and Claudette began their relationship with an established conflict. She's the heiress trying to run away from an arranged marriage, he's the reporter who wants to exploit her story, a fact which we, the audience, know, but she doesn't. That's a wonderful story device, since it puts the audience in a superior position to our character.

If Claudette knew this little tidbit of info; that Clark was playing her for a story, the chances for a relationship would go right down the drain. That's the threat to our goal of getting these two together. If she falls in love with him and finds out the truth later, well, that's exactly what happened, and we knew it was coming, didn't we?

It's been hanging over our heads since Act One, building up tension and anxiety in us. But, she had to find out, to create the crisis moment the story demanded, and to meet our structural requirement.

When Claudette did find out, it led us to the inevitable hijinks in the third act.

There are a couple of conventions in the genre which can accommodate the boy-loses-girl story beat. The first is misunderstanding. Often, Boy will lose Girl because one or the other is suffering from a misconception. She thought she saw him kissing another girl, or he finds a note that she wrote for someone else, and thinks it's for him. Whatever the device, the evidence is incriminating, but the character is innocent.

The love triangle is another popular convention, and a clear, relatable element in the boy-loses-girl plot point. Jill is going to marry Jack, when we all know that John is the guy for her.

Now, Jack is usually a nice enough guy, at least on the surface. He has to be, otherwise, we'd question Jill's judgment for picking him. And, Jack generally has some advantages over our chosen suitor, John. Jack is a professor. John is a high school dropout. Jack is fabulously wealthy. John makes minimum wage. Jack is witty and charming. John is witty, but awkward.

Outwardly, we can at least understand why Jill has chosen Jack for a mate, and he may even be deserving of Jill's affection, but still be wrong for her.

Jill may be manipulated into her relationship with Jack due to outside influences. Maybe, her family is pushing her into marrying Jack ("It Happened One Night".) Or, she might be making the wrong choice due to internal influences. She listens to her head, rather than her heart ("Breakfast at Tiffany's".)

Another option is for Jack to reveal himself to be a jerk, or all glitter, but no substance. This, too, relies on superior position by the audience. It only works if we see it and Jill doesn't, until that critical moment in the climax.

Maybe, Jack is "Mr. Perfect" with Jill, but shows his dark side when he's away from her, so we can see it and cement our belief that Jack is actually "Mr. Wrong." In fact, not only is he wrong for her, but now, by hiding Jack's dark side from Jill, we've increased the threat to her.

Boy Gets Girl Back

The last spoke in our wheel is the boy-gets-girl-backstory beat, leading to another reliable Romantic Comedy convention, the Stop-The-Wedding sequence. This sequence appears in Act Three to provide our story's climax.

It's clearly demonstrated, I mean, literally demonstrated in "The Graduate," with Dustin Hoffman physically racing, first in his car and finally on foot, to the church. He gets there just at the critical *"Do you take this man?"* moment, pounds on the glass window and screams out her name. And, it stops the wedding.

The Stop-The-Wedding sequence works well for several reasons.

Structurally, it gives us all the right beats for a third-act, boy-gets-girl-back climax. It creates tension with the race to stop the union in the nick of time, and it addresses the greatest possible threat to the relationship we're pulling for.

It can also be done well comedically, since it provides a "set piece"; all the trappings and supporting cast of a wedding ceremony, which opens opportunities for fast-paced physical hi jinx to ensue.

Of course, we can't end every single Romantic Comedy with a stop-the-wedding sequence. But, if we use this sequence as a metaphor in our story development, then we know what our third act climax needs to accomplish.

We want a moment when the relationship is at its greatest risk of going down in flames. That can mean a "stop-the-girl-from-getting-on-the-plane" sequence or "stop-the-guy-from-taking-another-girl-to-the-prom" sequence, or anything else, as long as it creates the same ticking-clock sense of urgency.

If we can mimic the tone and intent of the stop-the-wedding sequence with a different action or location, we'll hit the right mark.

The resolve of our Romantic Comedy is pretty much of a lock. Our lovers must wind up together and it must lead to a happy ending.

How we arrive at that conclusion without stepping into a thousand cliches is the challenge, because, ultimately, we must end our story the way every Romantic Comedy ends. Boy gets girl, happily ever after.

In Summary: There is enough charm in the premise and commercial appeal in the genre to make Romantic Comedy worth the challenges inherent to it. A good Rom Com script also serves as a fine calling card for a writer, since it offers an example of the writer's ability to develop strong characters. And, if we make them laugh, at the very least, we'll gain a fan.

Slapstick Comedy

I would venture a guess that Slapstick was the first form of comedy ever embraced by mankind. I picture some caveman tripping over a rock and falling on his face, sending his caveman buddies into a fit of laughter.

The comedy here is physical, of course, and generally speaking, is a series of pratfalls and blunders, all strung together in what is usually a pretty thin plot. From Charlie Chaplin and the Keystone Kops through "The Pink Panther" and "The Three Stooges," slapstick has been and will always be a film staple.

The Slapstick Comedy Hero

Our heroes in this genre are not usually all that bright. We identify with them, because their general dim-wittedness automatically makes them underdogs to just about every living, thinking creature on earth. They are flawed, but always comically, not tragically flawed.

We want them to succeed because, at heart, they are good people. We relate to them, because we've all experienced those moments in our lives; those times when we were monumental klutzes, even if briefly. Those times when we were the ones being laughed at. These heroes give us comfort in our fallibility, and actually put us in a superior position that makes us feel better about ourselves.

The Slapstick Comedy Villain

The villains in these stories are quite often not Rhodes Scholars, either. Our blundering heroes are rarely pitted against seriously intelligent foes. The audience just wouldn't buy it.

Creating villains who are also comically flawed gives the success of our heroes credibility. I mean, if they were opposed by people who were really, truly smart, they wouldn't stand a chance. And, we want them to not only stand a chance, but succeed. Sometimes, fate plays a role in that success. Our hero just gets lucky. It's pretty much how Inspector Clouseau solves every case.

Slapstick comedy, as with all comedy, is basically a commentary on a social condition. But, in the case of slapstick, it isn't enough to just poke fun at our "civilized" society. We must trash it, slap its face, step on it a few times and deliver the message that the world is absurd, we are all comically flawed to some extent, and we might as well accept it. Even as we laugh at our hapless hero, the "little guy" inside of us roots for him to triumph, as he ultimately will.

In the way today's Action films must push the limit of stunts to thrill us, so must a Slapstick Comedy push the limits of gags, in order to put a fresh face on an old premise.

In Summary: Elaborate and creative physical jokes are no easier to come up with than the next new car crash. In Slapstick, though, it's hard to go too far with a joke. The reality established in these films is equal to the reality found in cartoons. We can just as easily accept the tragedies befalling poor Inspector Clouseau as we do those of Wiley Coyote, in his pursuit of the Roadrunner. When it comes to broad, physical comedy, the sky's the limit.

Black Comedy

Simple. This is comedy deeply rooted in tragedy. It's a fart at a funeral. When we hear "black comedy," we get a good sense of what's coming. It's going to be some very serious stuff made fun of, like "Dr. Strangelove" making light of nuclear war, or a couple of average guys plotting to kill each others spouse and mother in "Throw Momma from the Train."

No comedy ensemble was ever better at Black Comedy than the Monty Python group, and that makes them worth studying, for any writer delving into this sub-genre. "The Meaning of Life," "In Search of the Holy Grail" and "The Life of Brian" are all replete with dark, ironic humor taken to the extreme.

The Black Comedy Hero

This is another one of those genres where, like The Caper, we often have a "good" bad guy as our protagonist. Sometimes, our good-bad guy is simply misguided, or misled into his nefarious deeds.

Sometimes, the protagonists are just bad guys with positive human qualities, and not beyond redemption, which is generally achieved in the end. If we didn't know that John Travolta's Vince Vega in "Pulp Fiction" was a hit man, we might think he's a regular guy, actually kind of charming.

Jack Nicholson and Kathleen Turner were hit-man and hit-woman in love, who have been hired to kill each other in "Prizzi's Honor." We encountered hit-man bad-good guys again in "In Bruges."

The Black Comedy Villain

Beyond redemption is key, for some Black Comedy villains. Since our hero is often not without sin, the villain must be morally bankrupt. He must possess enough evil to justify our flawed hero's often unsavory actions needed to defeat him, as were the villains in "Beetlejuice" and "Fargo," or the zombies in "Shawn of the Dead."

In Summary: Black Comedy explores the dark side of human nature, and done well, makes us squirm and laugh at the same time, by tapping into social taboos. It is intelligent comedy, relying on complex characters and subtext at every level.

The Youth Oriented "Raunch" Comedy

I kind of gave this my own label, throwing in the "raunch" factor, because it nearly always exists. In fact, it's more prevalent today than at any time I can recall, though every generation of filmmakers has spawned several of these.

"Animal House," "Fast Times at Ridgemont High," "Porky's" and "American Pie" were highly successful efforts in this genre. Even low-budget Raunch Comedies can be produced and find a market without breaking the bank.

One convention of this genre is the use of an ensemble cast. Nearly all comedies in this genre sport an array of characters, and generally, our Central Protagonist is, once again, the voice of reason. There is a slightly older-skewing angle on this genre, as seen in films like "The Hangover" and "Old School," where our ensemble is of a more advanced, although no more mature age. Yet, the conventions remain the same.

At the low-budget level, smaller distributors chew through these things like candy, and at the studio level, they can lead to breakout hits, as in the examples above. They do limit our market, in that they generally require an "R" rating to work. This prohibits the highly desirable market demo of under 17's from viewing the films in theaters, at least theoretically.

But for various reasons, including cable and home video, it doesn't seem to hinder their financial success. Don't look for any major awards, of course, but a film in this genre can keep the residual checks rolling in for a good, long time.

A number of themes can be explored Y.O.R.C. Genre. A coming-of-age theme is common, as in "Fast Times at Ridgemont High" or "American Pie," while "Porky's" and "Animal House" each had a revenge theme.

Lowbrow humor is a major trait, providing the "raunch" part of the puzzle. Body parts, body functions, physical flaws and sexual references are all fair game.

On a personal level, I have one primary objection to this brand of humor. It's just too easy. It's the kind of stuff that challenges neither the writer nor the audience. But, my personal feelings aside, it works.

When Cameron Diaz, as Mary in "There's Something About Mary," rubs the "hair gel" into her hair, the audiences roared in approval. Lest we forget, there is nothing sacred in comedy.

The Y.O.R.C Hero

Our heroes, if they can be termed as such, are, of course, young. high school or college age is the norm, and this genre is nearly always of the ensemble story type. They'll lean toward immature, sometimes heavily so, and tend to be borderline unlikable. Yet, they are always united in a just cause, and fearless in their pursuit of it.

The Y.O.R.C. Villain

The majority of the time, villains will be represented in the form of an organization, giving us a Man vs The System form of conflict. That system will be personified by an antagonist who is an authority figure of some sort, be that high school principal, military officer or college dean.

In Summary: Raunch Comedies have a lot going for them, when it comes to marketing. Because they contain elements of "forbidden fruit," that is, socially unacceptable subject matter, they bring with them a sense of rebellion. They make us laugh, while at the same time, we cringe in embarrassment. These films can have a tremendous longevity in the marketplace, and translate well in foreign markets.

The Spoof (or Parody) Genre

This genre is all about making fun of things that we normally take seriously, be they historical events, iconic personalities, current fads or popular culture. The more serious the subject matter, the easier it is to lampoon it.

The Spoof is also a genre which can overcome the studio stigma against period pieces, as demonstrated by "Monty Python in Search of the Holy Grail," "Blazing Saddles" and "Young Frankenstein."

The reference is the concept, so if the pitch is simply "I'm making fun of King Tut," the imagery is clear. That's enough to hook them. The biggest gripe from the studios against period pieces is the expense of the locations, and though the stories take place in historical locations, they are usually confined enough to keep the budgets within a reasonable range.

The strength of The Spoof is dependent on the familiarity of its reference point, that being the subject matter being spoofed. We have to know something about the Cold War to fully appreciate "Dr. Strangelove" or "The Russians Are Coming, The Russians Are Coming," and "Young Frankenstein" would lose a lot in translation, had we never seen a "Frankenstein" movie.

The conventions of every genre; those familiar elements which become stereotypes and cliches, become the butt of the jokes when they are spoofed. Because we've seen them so many times, there is great joy in seeing them turned on their heads.

Spoof Heroes and Villains

There are really no specific requirements for either the Heroes or Villains in this genre. If we're spoofing an historic character, then that character is portrayed in the most absurd manner, as were the Knights of the Round Table in "Monty Python in Search of the Holy Grail" or the classic characters in "Robin Hood: Men in Tights."

In Summary: The marketing prospects in this genre are quite favorable. Even with their esoteric subject matter, Spoofs seem to play well in foreign markets. They are never outdated and there is a tendency for them to be viewed more than once, creating a solid shelf life to generate long-term income.

The Drama Genre

Stories in the Drama Genre are socially relevant, in nature. This is where we most often find stories with a Man vs Himself or Man vs The System sources of conflict. Dramas make statements on such themes as addiction, racism, corruption and morality.

While dramatic stories are generally reality-based, nearly any story type can be employed. It also mixes well with other genres, such as Sci-Fi, Action, Horror and War, which primarily serve as backdrops in which the dramatic conflicts occur.

Character studies are nearly always dramatic in nature, and in this case, the drama is mined purely from an internal struggle, as our protagonist seeks love, redemption, validation, freedom from the bonds of addiction, or matters of conscience.

Family dynamics are frequently explored in dramatic fashion, in this genre, as we've seen in "Kramer vs Kramer," "Field of Dreams" and "Rain Man."

Stories of a character in conflict with himself are also common, in the vein of "A Beautiful Mind," "The Rose" and "The Man With The Golden Arm."

Nature can also provide an arena for dramatic conflict, illustrated by such survival-story films as in "127 Hours" and "Cast Away."

Issues of social struggle can be found in dramas such as "The Help" and "Philadelphia."

The Drama Hero

Because the subject matter of stories in the Drama Genre can be wide and varied, so, too are their heroes. What they share in common, however, is a great measure of depth and dimension. Since drama demands empathy, and sometimes sympathy for our hero, these characters must be rich and well-developed. Their struggles are based in reality, driven by internal goals and conflicts. Their flaws are potentially fatal, and therefore, the consequences of failure for them will be devastating.

The Drama Villain

As previously noted, the major source of conflict in a drama is frequently our Central Protagonist, himself. Society and survival also come into play. When personified in a Man vs Man source of conflict, the drama villain can be as wide-ranging as are our heroes. However, since our Central Protagonist in the Drama Genre is nearly always dealing with internally based conflicts, our villains will be a primary obstacle to those internal conflicts. Therefore, the struggle will tend to be an emotional, rather than physical one.

The Melodrama Genre

Melodrama can be described as an exaggeration of Drama. The Websters dictionary defines it this way:

A work (as a movie or play) characterized by extravagant theatricality and by the predominance of plot and physical action over characterization.

By that definition, the depth and dimension of the characters involved will not be as intricately developed as in Drama.

Melodramas go straight for the heart, with little subtext or subtlety. They take the emotion to an extreme level. Most any Lifetime or Hallmark Channel presentation fits into this category, but from a theatrical standpoint, films such as "Little Women," "Forrest Gump" and "Jerry Maguire" are examples in the genre.

In Summary: If you're shooting for a major award, or just drawn to more personal stories, Drama is the genre to explore. Well-written dramatic stories are always marketable, domestically. While stories in this genre face difficulties in foreign territories, films such as "The King's Speech" demonstrate their ability to sometimes overcome those barriers. In their favor, dramatic, personal stories generally won't require exorbitant budgets, since they rely so heavily on character, rather than action. While the returns on these films won't often reach blockbuster proportions, they can garner great critical success.

The Science Fiction Genre

A mother lode of motion picture stories have come from the Science Fiction Genre, starting with "A Trip To The Moon," by French Director Georges Melies in 1902. It's a genre which allows a writer room for his imagination to roam. After all, no matter what today's reality dictates, there will always be a future, and how that will look is subject to anyone's conjecture.

George Orwell's famous novel "1984," eventually to twice become a film, portrayed a world which looked nothing like the reality of 1984 when that year arrived, but who cares? It's still a classic, and certainly must have seemed pretty profound, when it was published in 1949.

Same goes for the old "Star Trek" series, and those little communicator gadgets they all carried. You know, the ones that flipped open and beeped? Remind you of anything you've seen recently, maybe, hanging off of your belt or in your purse? But, back in the 60's, it was pretty cool, futuristic stuff. That's part of the fun of Sci Fi: delivering the promise of as-yet undiscovered technological advances.

The Sci-Fi conventions are familiar to us all. The aliens, space craft, lasers and other sophisticated weapons lend themselves to a tone of excitement and discovery. And, themes in this genre are virtually unlimited.

Nearly any kind of story theme can be played out in a high-tech, futuristic setting. "Star Wars" has often been described as a Western in outer space, while "Planet of the Apes" was a blatant statement on the decline of humanity, as was "A Clockwork Orange" and Orwell's "1984."

Science Fiction is often a chosen venue for statements on modern society's ills, sometimes using alien beings and worlds as metaphors for our own.

"The Day the Earth Stood Still" "The Hunger Games" and "Avatar" all delivered critiques on the human condition, exploring themes like nuclear proliferation and greed.

The Sci-Fi Hero

Since so many themes and story types can be delivered in a SciFi story, the protagonists in these films are many and varied.

The tough-guy action hero is not uncommon, or the fearless adventurer exploring new worlds, but our protagonists need not be exceptional. Plain old, average people have been shot into space. Even families make the grade.

The Sci-Fi Villain

The villains, our forces of antagonism, tend to be limited to two types:

Man vs. Man or Man vs. The Elements.

In the case of the aforementioned blockbuster "Star Wars," the Man vs. Man conflict was employed, even though some of those "men" were alien beings.

Man vs. The Elements is the preferred choice. Space, itself, can present the challenge, containing forces beyond our control. Aliens fit into this category, as in "Men in Black," "Alien," "War of the Worlds," "Mars Attacks" and "Earth vs the Flying Saucers."

From a marketing standpoint, Science Fiction is a strong seller, but from a budgetary standpoint, it is mostly limited to studio production. Nothing fails quite like a bad Science Fiction film, and to do it right requires a lot of money and a high level of talent on the technical side.

In Summary: The future is in the hands of the writer, in this genre. An active, colorful imagination, combined with good story skills can create a highly marketable screenplay. While Sci-Fi brings with it considerable budget requirements which limit it to production at the studio level, this is a solid choice for a spec script.

The Horror Genre

We love stories that get our adrenaline pumping, and this is one that can do it as effectively as any.

Horror brings with it many of the same advantages found in the Action Genre, in terms of marketability. There is and always will be a large audience for horror films.

As with the more extravagant stunts now seen in Action films, the graphic nature of horror films has also intensified. Today, one can see considerably more gore on an episode of "C.S.I." than was ever allowed in any early horror film made for the big screen.

More gore, achieved in more brutally creative ways, has become necessary to appease an audience grown desensitized over the years. What they'll do to surpass the "Saw" series, one can only speculate...and shudder.

In earlier incarnations, the tendency in horror films was to have the audience identify with the victim. Thus, the central story thread was to put an innocent victim in the path of a horrific monster or psychopath, and root for the victim to survive.

This basic structure still survives, of course, however, in the late 60's and early 70's, a horror sub-genre dubbed "Splatter Films" emerged, with the arrival of movies like "Nightmare on Elm Street" and "Texas Chainsaw Massacre."

Splatter Films are currently referred to as "Grindhouse" films, and include the likes of the "Saw" and "Evil Dead" series. In these films, and countless others like them, we suddenly began to see these sadistic acts from the villain's point-of-view, as he stalked what were usually morally flawed characters, then graphically disposed of them.

There is no real "hero" to speak of, in these types of films. Even though on the long list of victims who are butchered, there will often be one or two left alive, probably for the sake of the sequel, they are rarely portrayed as heroic.

In movies like those mentioned above and others, like "I Know What You Did Last Summer" and "Scream," our protagonist-victims demonstrate imperfections which are designed to make them more-or-less deserving of their fate. That, in turn, makes our Villain the focus of the story, often attaining celebrity status.

In the same way we used to embrace Dracula or Frankenstein, we now embrace Freddy Kruger, Chucky, Leatherface and Jigsaw. We seem to find them creepy, frightening, repulsive and yet, fascinating.

The Splatter Film sub-genre then generated...or, perhaps degenerated into what is now known as Torture Porn, also referred to as "Gorn;" the combination of gore and porn. It's the uncomfortable marriage of sex and graphic violence.

Sex has always been a staple convention in horror films, of course, but as the depictions of violence have become more graphic, so, too has the sexuality increased in prominence. It is another example of filmmakers continually pushing the limits, in order to get beyond the cliches and stereotypes, and deliver something new.

The suspense instilled in many horror films uses the reverse point-of-view device quite frequently, wherein the audience, through the deranged killer or monster's eyes, stalks the victim right along with him.

Recently added as a sub-genre is the Found Footage Genre, demonstrated by "The Blair Witch Project" and "Paranormal Activity." These films basically provide the same horror conventions as any horror film, yet on a much smaller scale. The significant difference comes in the filming technique, which gives us an entirely new point-of-view through the lens of either an amateur or security-type camera.

The Horror Hero

Unless you consider the Freddy Kruger and Leatherface types as "heroes," which I do not, most Horror Genre heroes are actually victims, fighting for their lives. They are reactive characters, battling forces of pure evil. In most cases, they will be young and flawed, possessing traits which, at least in some part, justify their gruesome demise. Some will be innocent victims, such as the Jamie Lee Curtis character of Laurie Strode in "Halloween," but this brand of horror character has fallen from grace in recent years.

The exception to this arises in zombie-laced features which have exploded in popularity, and still give us protagonists whose survival we can root for. Rarely are the innocent-victim style heroes well-equipped for the monstrous villains they will face, but endowing them with intelligence and creativity; an ability to think on their feet and react spontaneously to danger can validate their ultimate survival.

The Horror Villain

This one is pretty easy. Horror villains are monsters, plain and simple. They can be cunning, but rarely are they smart, relying mostly on sheer strength and brutality to wreak havoc on their victims.

They also need very little in the way of motivation, to justify their actions, although revenge is sometimes employed as a motivating factor, as in "I Know What You Did Last Summer."

These characters are easy to create and write, since they are void of the majority of characteristics we want to employ in any character. Internal goals and conflicts are virtually non-existent, and external goals are basic and clear. They are monsters, therefore, all they want to do is kill. Designing creative ways for them to do this seems to be the greatest challenge for the writer.

In Summary: Films in the Horror Genre have a niche market, although an expansive and favorable one. A writer must possess a certain morbid imagination in order to push the boundaries beyond what the Horror audience is familiar with, but the payoff can be substantial. Of all Genres, horror probably has the best chance of financial success when produced on a low budget. While there are some technical requirements in filming the gore involved, those requirements are generally not so substantial as to increase the budget to any significant degree.

The Suspense Genre

Also known as Thrillers, Suspense films require the same type of plotting and story work as The Caper or The Mystery. They are intricate stories, and must be meticulously designed to work properly.

The pace of Suspense films is generally slow, until the climax in the final act. It works that way for a couple of reasons. First, these stories lean heavily on character, which means a lot of setup and exposition. We really need to get involved with our characters, particularly our Central Protagonist, so we can feel the fear, foreboding and anticipation; the mainstay emotions of Suspense films, through them.

Primarily, though, the slow pace is designed to build tension. Long moments of silence with little action create a waiting-for-the-other-shoe-to-drop sensation.

A woman walking slowly through a dark house for two straight minutes would be unacceptable in an Action film, or most any other genre. That's a lot of screen time, with no forward movement in the story.

In a Suspense film, it's a required convention. When a woman walks slowly through a dark house in a Suspense film, our hearts pound faster with each room she enters. The more slowly she makes that walk, the more agonizingly sweet it is for the audience.

Additionally, if she takes that walk through the dark house in Act One, that's when the cat jumps out at her. The cheap scare. There are usually several. That's often a moment when the audience is aware of an impending threat, but our potential victim is not.

If the walk comes in Act Two, then often, the threat is indeed real, but somehow thwarted. Supporting characters may be disposed of in this act, but rarely our heroine.

However, if she takes that walk in Act Three, it's likely that the threat is real and must be dealt with by our protagonist. This is the climactic confrontation. The killer is in the house.

This form of manipulation is one of several psychological tools Suspense films utilize to control our emotions. Tension is built through the constant anticipation of a looming threat, then relief when that threat is removed, only to build into the next, more ominous or imminent threat.

Key to good suspense is the surprise factor. You'll frequently encounter the "look out behind you" tool in the storylines. In fact,

Hitchock's very definition of suspense was: *The audience knows what is going to happen, but the hero doesn't.* The fun is knowing that danger is imminent, but never knowing when or where it will strike.

Suspense also gives us those "aha" moments, as when a critical piece of information is revealed. The plots keep us thinking through the use of red herrings, hidden information and misdirection. Mysteries employ these devices by design, of course, and thus Mystery blends seamlessly with the Suspense Genre.

Suspense films evoke constant fear for the welfare of our Central Protagonist. We hold our breath each time a character opens a suspicious door, or walks past a dark alley. We get those "look out behind you" moments, when we know the threat is there, but our hero doesn't.

Even humor is not left out of the mix in many Suspense films. Alfred Hitchcock once pronounced:

"For me, suspense doesn't have any value unless it's balanced by humor."

The Stanley Donen directed "Charade" employed character humor and witty dialogue with success, and the cheeky, but fun "Snakes on a Plane" gave us ironic humor in an absurd situation.

While Suspense has often been merged with the Comedy genre, as in the "Pink Panther" series, even a pure Suspense film benefits from lighter moments. The relief of tension is a marvelous tool in developing our much needed roller-coaster pace and tone.

Another tool used effectively in Suspense films is that of altering the point-of-view of the action, by putting the audience into our hero's shoes.

This device, seeing the action through the character's eyes, keeps the viewer intimately attached to that character. We see what he sees, we fear what he fears and we share his anxiety.

The Suspense Hero

Our protagonists in this genre are either victims or potential victims. Suspense hero characteristics are similar to those of Adventure heroes, in that the "every man" hero is the most common choice. Since the idea is to heighten the fear and concern from the audience for our hero. The more relatable that hero is, the more effective will be the suspense built around him.

Often times, we will find a Suspense hero who has the circumstances of the story thrust upon him, rather than pursuing a goal at the outset. Carey Grant, in Hitchcock's "North by Northwest," was such a hero, as was Tippi Hedron in "The Birds."

In "Wait Until Dark," Audrey Hepburn played a blind woman menaced by criminals searching for a child's doll, stuffed with heroin, they believed to be in her apartment. This film utilized the "look-out-behind-you" device, since the audience knew about the doll, but our Protagonist did not. The fact that our heroine was blind compounded that threat, and heightened our concern for her safety.

In "Psycho," our heroine, Janet Leigh, had no clue that she was dealing with a deranged killer, when she checked into the Bates Motel. The real suspense came after her character, Marion Crane, was killed by Norman Bates. That's when a detective, played by Martin Balsam, and Marion's sister, Vera Miles, came searching for answers. By then, we knew what Norman was capable of, and the threat intensified. Therefore, as exists in the Horror genre, we frequently wind up with a reactive protagonist; someone we can fear for.

The Suspense Villain

The human villains in the Suspense Genre are particularly nefarious characters. Sometimes, they are evil for evil's sake, but always they are some brand of evil. Whether real or alien, they always represent the threat of death for our hero, and sometimes a gruesome one, at that.

While villains in most genres are encouraged to display some redeemable characteristics, not so in Suspense films. These villains are as wicked, deranged and ruthless as they come, and that's just how we like them.

The Central Force of Antagonism in a Suspense film doesn't always have to be of the human variety, of course. Animal villains like the shark in "Jaws," forces of nature, as in "127 Hours" and alien villains of the kind we met in "Alien" also fill the bill.

In Summary: The Suspense/Thriller Genre is a good commercial choice for a screenwriter. It is another "evergreen" genre; always in vogue.

The challenge for a writer in this genre is the ability to manipulate the tone of the story, by creating moments of high tension balanced with moments of relief, ahead of a heart-stopping climax.

The War Genre

War is the ultimate conflict with the highest possible stakes, so it only makes sense that it's ideal story material.

War Genre conventions are as obvious as those of Westerns. We're getting big battles with big weapons, wielded by big armies. Uniforms, chains-of-command, heroes and cowards, lots of blood and mostly exterior shots all create the mold. These stories are generally packed with extras to provide literal "cannon fodder."

The plots of War films can be reality based, as in "Saving Private Ryan," "All Quiet on the Western Front," "The Longest Day" or "Reds," or they can be completely fictional, as portrayed in the film "Red Dawn," which depicted the invasion of the United States by the Soviet Union, at least, in its first incarnation. The remake, for political reasons, changed those villains to North Koreans.

We also frequently find fictional wars in Sci-Fi films, such as "War of the Worlds," "Iron Man," "Battlestar Galactica" and the "Star Wars" series. While these films are primarily Science Fiction in their settings, the conventions of the War Genre were prominent.

Keeping things simple, the good vs evil conflict is pretty black-and-white in these films, and the stakes are clear. Most of the time, however, films in the War Genre are not about the war, itself, but employ war as a backdrop for more personal stories.

The inherent drama encompassed in the life-or-death urgency of the heat of battle makes a fine setting in which to exploit the most extreme aspects of human behavior. Consider films like "Platoon," "Apocalypse Now" and "The Hurt Locker," all of which examined not war, itself, but war's effect on the human psyche.

The War Genre gives us the best of two worlds: spectacular visuals in the form of gun battles, explosions and high-tech weaponry, and at the same time an opportunity to portray characters in the most stressful and demanding of situations.

The War Hero

Since virtually any Master Theme can be played out in the War Genre, the heroes are just as varied. Typically, the War Hero meets the very definition of a hero: brave, self-sacrificing and physically adept. John Wayne, Arnold Schwarzenneger and Sylvester Stallone, among others, demonstrate one Hero type; the capable, battle hardened warrior.

But, our hero can also be an "Average Joe," forced to rise above his limitations, as Tom Hanks' character of Captain John Miller, a high school math teacher, showed us.

In a Redemption Themed story, our hero can even be a coward at the outset, who grows into a heroic figure, thus gaining his redemption. In the end, though, the traits of heroism must prevail for the War Hero to satisfy his obligations.

The War Villain

The war itself is the Villain in a story with a Master Theme of

Conflict, as seen in "The Longest Day," "In Harm's Way" and "The Thin Red Line." In these cases, an opposing military provides the main opposition.

War can threaten love, as in "Dr. Zhivago," "A Farewell to Arms" and "The Americanization of Emily."

But, while War can be a villain at some level, it isn't always the Central Force of Antagonism in a War film. In a story with a Cowardice theme, for instance, Man-vs-Himself provides the primary conflict, one that is internal. As pointed out, most any Theme can be played out in the War Genre.

In Summary: War films give us another good commercial choice, but the physical requirements, and therefore the budgets, are substantial, relegating this genre to films at major studio level production.

The Mystery Genre

There is a dearth of pure mystery films, these days, in the Agatha Christie, or original Sherlock Holmes style. Maybe, it's because studios feel they move too slowly, and require too much concentration by the audience, but that's just speculation.

Maybe, it's because they just don't get any good Mystery scripts to consider. The genre is still embraced by television, as we've seen in numerous examples like "Elementary," "Monk," and "The Mentalist," the new incarnation of "Sherlock," and supernatural versions like "Ghost Whisperer" and "Medium."

The trend we currently see in motion pictures, however, takes a slightly different tack, by combing Mystery with Action or Adventure. "Raiders of the Lost Ark" did it, along with "The Da Vinci Code" and "National Treasure."

The mystery at hand doesn't have to involve a murder, but most pure mystery films seem to do that. If, however, revealing the perpetrator of a crime is not the issue, then there is most often a "Maguffin" involved; an object of desire sought by all parties. That object will often possess a value far beyond monetary, such as an historical artifact, or one endowed with some supernatural power.

For a writer, Mystery has some pretty unique requirements. The plotting in these films is intricate, planting suspects and red herrings, while successfully hiding the truth until the critical reveal at the end.

Twist endings are a must, and with audiences growing more and more sophisticated, they are harder than ever to deliver.

Mysteries are incorporated as a convention in most Crime Genre stories, since it's all about uncovering clues and tracking down criminals. However, Crime stories are about crime. The mystery involved in solving that crime is secondary.

The Mystery Hero

A Mystery Hero must demonstrate the characteristics of intelligence, perception and perseverance, but aside from that, most any character type will suffice.

While Mystery Heroes of the Sherlock Holmes, Phillip Marlowe, Hercule Poirot ilk dive headlong into the mystery, many Mystery Heroes are more of the common man/woman variety.

In any case, our Mystery Heroes must be gifted with exemplary deductive powers and an unquenchable curiosity, strong enough to keep them moving forward, even when the danger in doing so is clear.

The Mystery Villain

The same qualities apply to villains as to heroes in this genre. Our Villains should be smart, cunning and just as determined to stop our hero as our hero is to solve the mystery. They are, most often, mirror images of our heroes, except on the "dark" side.

Matching wits is a necessary staple of this genre, and therefore, our villains must possess at least as much intelligence as the heroes pursuing them. Consider Sherlock's foe, Moriarty as an example.

Organizations can provide the obstacles we need, or forces of nature. Whatever deters our Central Protagonist from unraveling the clues to solve the puzzle can provide the Central Force of Antagonism.

In Summary: A Mystery film can be made at any budget level, of course, but marketing can be quite a challenge. As I've pointed out, they are difficult to sell, unless combined with a more commercial genre, and they don't travel well into foreign markets. As television has consistently shown us, however, there is a hunger for them, by a loyal audience.

The Crime Drama Genre

A close relative to the Mystery Genre, since a mystery is frequently employed as a plot point. However, it isn't always the case. Crime Genre films often expose our villain and the goal to capture him, rather that utilizing the "whodunnit" factor. Clues in a mystery become "leads" in a crime drama. Therefore, the pursuit becomes the focus.

Many films in this genre follow the criminal, as often as the law enforcement officials trying to track him down. "Silence of the Lambs" serves as one example. The gangster films of the 30's and 40's, with titles such as "Little Caesar," "Scarface" and "The Public Enemy" were quite popular. More recently, we've seen the trend continue with "The Godfather" trilogy, and films like "Pulp Fiction," "Goodfellas" and "The Departed."

Earlier Crime Dramas employed film noir techniques to define the genre, and were mostly filmed in black-and-white and highly stylized, yet most other conventions of the genre have been retained in contemporary films. These films feature tragic endings almost exclusively, generally deliver a "crime doesn't pay" message.

The Crime Drama Hero

Whether our hero is a detective, beat-cop or Private Eye, most Crime Drama heroes are cynical, hard-bitten heroes. While Humphrey Bogart personified the type in films of the 40's, Jack Nicholson in "Chinatown" and Clint Eastwood's Dirty Harry picked up the mantel in later films. These protagonists are rule-breakers, relentless and tough. They may have time for sexual encounters along the way, but rarely for romance.

The Crime Drama Villain

Crime Drama villains reflect many of the same qualities as do our heroes, just on the opposite side of the law. While just as tough and ruthless as our heroes, they also possess more negative qualities, such as greed and a lust for power.

They may have their own warped sense of fairness and loyalty, but ultimately, they are out for themselves, with little or no regard for the innocents who may fall in their wake. These characters are basically beyond redemption. Since Crime Dramas most frequently employ a "justice will prevail" Active Theme, the ending for these villains is inevitably tragic.

In Summary: The public's endless fascination with notorious criminals makes the Crime Drama a safe genre choice for a writer. While these are films with strong negative emotional qualities and depictions of graphic violence, they nevertheless satisfy, since the basic "good vs evil" theme is easily embraced by an audience.

The Western Genre

Talk about falling from grace! Westerns once dominated the film and television worlds, but no longer. However, that doesn't mean this genre is dead. Occasionally, an ambitious producer or studio will take a chance on a Western, though results in recent years have been mixed. Remakes of classic Westerns, such as "3:10 to Yuma" and "True Grit" fared quite well, but "Wild, Wild West" and "The Lone Ranger," not so much.

Whatever one may think of the Western in general, there can be no denying that some of the greatest films of all time were made in this genre, including such classics as "Shane," "High Noon," "Stagecoach," "The Magnificent 7," "The Wild Bunch" and the previously mentioned Academy Award winner "Butch Cassidy and the Sundance Kid."

While the genre will likely never disappear completely from the landscape, Westerns are a hard-sell under the best of circumstances. The conventions within them largely reflect the period. Before car chases became the rage, chases on horseback were already old news. Same goes for gunfights, which were romanticized to a great degree in early Western films and television programs. So horses, saloons, stagecoaches, cowboys and Indians (of the Native American ilk) are as familiar to us as any genre convention can be.

Though much of what is portrayed in the majority of Western films has become stereotypical, virtually any type of story can be told within this genre. Westerns have been utilized as a backdrop for character studies, historical films, dramas, comedies, even Science Fiction.

A writer should bear in mind the difficulty of selling a screenplay in the Western genre. However, that doesn't mean it should never be considered. A good story is still a good story, whether the hero wears a white hat or not.

The Western Hero

The typical Western hero is the very epitome of masculinity, yet not all Western heroes fit this definition. The story type employed within the genre will dictate the role. Gary Cooper's portrayal of Marshall Will Kane in "High Noon" is in direct opposition to the standard, macho hero in the genre, and Paul Newman's Butch Cassidy certainly goes against the grain. Comedies often sport awkward and inept cowboy protagonists, as Gene Wilder's portrayals in "The Frisco Kid" and "Blazing Saddles" demonstrate.

The "anti-hero" character has been portrayed numerous times in this genre, as well, as best illustrated in the Spaghetti Western series of the 60's, which featured Clint Eastwood in his "Man-with-no-name" persona.

Yet, the macho, self-assured, John Wayne style Western good-guy still stands as the template for a Western protagonist, and likely always will.

The Western Villain

These are usually pretty nasty characters; sometimes driven by greed or power, as we find in the typical cattle baron, corrupt Sheriff or big banker. Other times, these villains seem to thrive on pure blood-lust as gunfighters or outlaws of the most nefarious kind. The actor Lee Marvin must have played a dozen of these, in his stellar career.

There is rarely anything sympathetic to be found in these characters, since most Western genre themes tend to be pretty black-and-white, with little subtlety or complexity involved.

In Summary: Marketing a screenplay or film in the Western Genre is challenging in the current atmosphere. Still, the genre survives, and likely always will. A writer with designs on creating a story in the Western Genre has an uphill climb, but a solid story with compelling characters can overcome the current perceptions.

The Musical Genre

A bit elusive, this one. In order to truly be a musical, the music must be a part of the narrative; i.e., the music, just like the action and dialogue, must be there to tell the story. In its purest form, it's opera, and that is the last thing I will say about opera.

In this definition, films such as "The Music Man," "My Fair Lady," "Les Miserables," "The Sound of Music" and "Chicago" all apply, and it's no coincidence that all of these films were based on stage plays.

If a film has music built into the storyline; actually there to help tell the story, it's a Musical. However, just having music in a film doesn't make it a Musical.

Many times, films in this genre are actually Character films, built around a real-life musical talent, as were "Walk the Line," "The Doors," "Coal Miner's Daughter" and "Lady Sings the Blues," or fictional talent, as in "A Mighty Wind," "This is Spinal Tap" and "The Rose."

There was a lot of music in "Almost Famous," but this was a coming-of-age story in a musical setting. A similar case could be made for "That Thing You Do."

Musicals share a common bond with Westerns. They're a hard-sell, yet there always seems to be someone making one. The challenge for a screenwriter is painfully obvious. You don't have a script unless you have the music.

If you want to use existing music, there are rights involved, and that translates to money. The other options are to either create the music yourself, which requires an entire, unique set of job skills, or to involve a composer with a body of work worthy of supporting a film.

There are really no defining characteristics for either Heroes or Villains in this Genre. Any type will do, the only caveat being that the performers who portray these characters must not only be able to act, but also to sing, and frequently, to dance, as well.

In Summary: The obvious obstacles, plus the limited arena for Musicals, make writing a Musical a pretty "iffy" proposition for a screenwriter, particularly a writer in the early stages of her career.

Not only must the story appeal to a wide audience, but the music must, as well. Pursue this genre at your own risk.

The Sex Exploitation Genre

Sex sells. It just does. It's as compelling as a car chase and a lot cheaper to shoot. Do I have to tell you there's a market?

Movies of the "R" rated, soft core variety thrive in this genre, and do well on cable and in DVD sales and rentals. The hard core offerings; plain old pornography, have been relegated to DVD sales and rentals, pay-per-view cable, a smattering of adult theaters and, of course, the internet.

In the mainstream, many movies have been produced which feature some pretty graphic sexual situations. "Basic Instinct," "The Girl With the Dragon Tattoo," "Blue Velvet" and "Last Tango in Paris" all featured sexuality prominently in their storylines, yet not in an exploitative manner, and therein lies the difference.

The returns on these hastily slapped-together Sex Exploitation productions must be pretty good, since the porn industry remains healthy. Estimates of how much is spent on adult entertainment each year reach as high as ten billion dollars, and there are hundreds of production companies dedicated to adult product.

That doesn't represent a boon to screenwriters, as one might think, since the scripts are merely rough blueprints, and don't require much literary talent. Storylines in Sex Exploitation films are generally thin, and not actually taken seriously. They only exist as a framework for the required "slap-and-tickle" scenes.

I won't even delve into the hero/villain aspects of these films, since the requirements are mostly superficial: be attractive and willing to have sex on camera. Real actors need not apply.

In Summary: While Sex Exploitation is a booming market, here's the rub (sorry, I couldn't resist). It brands you. If producers in the mainstream industry, particularly at the studio level, know you write this kind of content, they probably won't touch you. So, use a pseudonym, or just don't do it.

Genres In Summary: The genres and story types I've covered are not all-inclusive. I'm certain someone can come up with a hybrid, or a common genre I've overlooked, but the ones I've presented represent a substantial portion of the genres and story types most frequently employed.

Understanding genres and the conventions within them are critical to a screenwriter. These are patterns which have been established and time-tested, with elements audiences not only want, but demand. Finding unique and interesting ways to deliver on these genre conventions is our job. If we do it well, we can reap big rewards, both creatively and financially.

CHAPTER 17

The Process

"Writing is easy. All you do is sit, staring at a blank sheet of paper, until the drops of blood form on your forehead." - Gene Fowler

Let me preface this, in case I haven't emphasized the point enough, by saying that what follows is my personal approach to the screenwriting process. It is the way I've grown to understand it.

I'll offer some alternatives which are employed and touted by others, all of which work for someone. Mostly, though, this will be what works for me. Again, take from it what you will and leave the rest behind.

The first part of this process begins with one simple act: sitting down at the keyboard.

I'm often asked if I have a favorite place or time to write. Not really. All I look for is quiet time, to limit interruptions as much as possible. Writing late at night, sometimes into the wee hours of morning used to be my routine, but that was mostly out of necessity.

I must admit, it worked. The phone didn't ring, the TV was off, there were no errands to run or chores to do, and no one knocked at my office door. But, I didn't write any better or become more inspired than at any other time.

We've all heard the old adage "Write every day." That would be fine, in a perfect world. Idealistic, but not realistic. Anyone who said they wrote every day, I always figured was lying. I've refined my thinking on this point, over the years, because I grew to understand that writing is a process that doesn't have to end when we're away from the computer. In fact, it shouldn't. Our imaginations don't stop working, just because we've stopped writing.

Along with the "Write every day" adage, another one you've probably heard is "Write what you know." Well, we simply can't always do that. Experience is a great tool, but trying to write only from personal experience is profoundly limiting. Margaret Mitchell didn't experience the Civil War, but "Gone With The Wind" turned out just fine, thank you.

You don't have to be a cowboy or a soldier or a jock or a Wall Street Wizard to write those characters. If you don't have that intimate knowledge of the character type you're writing, then it's time to do some research.

Besides, there is a more important internal aspect to the write-what-you-know philosophy. We all share universal experiences of fear, elation, anxiety and the like. We've all bee lied to or manipulated, angry with, in love with or suspicious of someone, at some point.

These shared emotions are the wells we go to, when we create a character. They are characteristics common to us all. If you truly have that mysterious gene that makes you a writer, you have a unique and inherent ability to relate to the human condition, and that's really where the magic lies.

Aside from an active imagination, I think observation is the most important tool a writer possesses. There are scads of wonderful stories to be found, simply by being keenly sensitive to the world around us. Most of us really aren't. We tend to forge through our day with a rather myopic view of life; caught up in our own little world and focused on the immediacy of the moment.

Unless you consciously make a choice to pay attention to the people and events surrounding you, it all remains in the peripheral. Just paying attention, then, becomes a wonderfully useful tool in your creative process. We live in a world filled with unique and interesting characters, and each of them has a story.

You can garner story material by listening, really listening, to conversations, both overheard or engaged in, and taking bits of information that can help you build a story or a character.

Current events gleaned from the news offer a wealth of inspiration. Grabbing a spiffy headline and applying the "what if?" tool to it can get your imagination going.

Writer's block is another nagging problem we all deal with, and there are no simple solutions, since the "block" is usually unique to each individual. Unless you know what's causing it, you can't know how to fix it. The only solution I've found is to just keep at it.

Rather than quitting a project outright, try using a free moment here-and-there, while you're away from the keyboard, to mull a problem in a script. It's the same process we all go through when we can't remember someone's name. It nags at us, in the back of our heads, off-and-on throughout the day until, bingo, it comes to us, that great story idea or solution to a story problem that has been blocking our progress.

Applying that thought process to the development of a script can save time when you do get back to the keyboard. Time that might otherwise be spent staring at a blank screen and agonizing over the problem then. It helps to keep those story problems ever-present in your mind; a mental lookout for the answers to your question, or a solution to the problem at the root of the block.

Here's another suggestion, and yes, another adage:

Write what you watch.

What movies attract you? Obviously, there's some common

thread within them that you relate to. Find it.

You must discover, within yourself, where your passion lies. This might take a little digging around, but steering your creative engine in the direction of your own viewing habits can serve as a guide.

On the flip side, beware of the inherent "traps" within the industry; those which can easily lead you away from your creative path.

Agents, managers, producers, directors, teachers, family, friends and associates will all be there at various times to tell you, for your own good, of course, what you should be writing.

Opportunities that make you salivate will come with the caveat that you change what you do, which is tantamount to changing who you are.

If only you would turn your romantic comedy into a romantic comedy slasher film, then they could sell it.

If only you could alter this part to suit that actor. If only it wasn't a period piece, because, you know, period pieces are dead. Ditto Westerns.

If only you wrote sci-fi.

If only the hero didn't die.

What if you made it a musical?!

It will never end.

Writing "to the market" is a farce, too. The film market has one thing in common with the stock market. Nobody ever knows what the hell it will do. Today's fad is tomorrow's distant memory.

Now for my next adage:

Writing is re-writing.

This is one I heard frequently, in my early days in the industry. There is a lot to that, which I'll go into in the rewriting section, but I would take this little truism to another level.

Writing is writing.

No way around it.

All too often, I've encountered (and you will, too) people who like to get together and brainstorm ideas. They talk about the story and make suggestions and give notes and call themselves writers, convinced that "we're writing it together." However, someone else has to be there who will actually put the words on the page, structure the action and create the dialogue.

Make no mistake, the person who does that is the writer. I've actually had people tell me (and you will, too) *"I have this great idea for a story. You can write it and we'll share the credit!"*

No, thank you. If we're going to share the credit, you're going to write, not just talk. Put the writers and the "idea people" in separate rooms, alone with a pen and paper, typewriter or computer and you'll find out who the writer is.

You also need to think about the industry, and your life within it. I've known highly successful television writers who amassed great fortunes and burned themselves out pumping out jokes on sitcoms for years. All of those creative juices down the drain, and they never really got to say what they wanted to say. But, they're driving a Mercedes.

Some writers actually have disdain for what they write. They're extremely talented and quite successful, but their talent feels wasted, because they're writing the kind of content they feel is beneath them, or trivial. They're writing mindless commercial films when they'd rather be writing the great American novel. But, the big, fat Hollywood carrot is too hard to resist.

Now, if I'm sounding too idealistic, here, let me back off, a bit. There is no shame in writing for money. You have a right to make a living, and while sacrificing for the art sounds noble, it doesn't pay the rent.

However, just because you take writing jobs for the money doesn't preclude you from telling our own stories. Even a writer with the good fortune of finding steady work, and there are a limited number of those, can always find time to write that personal story, make that all-important statement on life, put his "mark" on the industry.

In Summary: Each writer must determine his own best process in deciding when and what to write. However, outside influences can lead a writer astray. When we write out of love and passion, regardless of what "the market," friends or associates might counsel, we write our best, and that will create the greatest opportunity for success.

Choices

If I were asked for one word to describe the process of putting a story down on the page, that word would be "Choices."

Storytelling is all about choices, those you make for your story and those our characters make within the story. That's true, no matter whose method you employ. The trick is to not limit those choices; to explore every possible option and angle, before settling on one. That's what ultimately separates "fresh and unique" from "predictable and cliched."

Too often, when I read screenplays from nascent writers, I find options which have been overlooked; opportunities to add more depth to the story, which are never discovered or considered. It's as if the writer is in a hurry, and so, makes the first, most familiar story choice, in a rush to get the story down on the page.

I can relate to that urge. There is an adrenaline-fueled creative moment which occurs when a story gushes into your brain, and the need to write it before it dissipates can be overwhelming. But, it's risky, because when you hurry, you often don't make the best choices, and what you wind up with is a story with too much "familiar" and not enough "unique."

A stand-up comic friend of mine used to do a bit in his act; a Charles Bronson impersonation. He set it up by saying:

"Now, here's a scene from all of Charles Bronson's movies!"

That kind of familiarity is what you want to avoid; to not settle for the first choice that hits you, just because it works, structurally.

That's usually a choice that's been made many times in many films. We've all seen it before. That's why it's the first one that pops into our brains. It's an easy choice, because it's comfortable.

But, in order for it to work and be comfortable, but not cliched and predictable, you have to find a way to add the "unique" to it, otherwise, you're not bringing anything fresh to the table.

One option is to pull a simple misdirection tact, just like you'd see in a magic show. You set up the old, familiar scene. The audience says, *"Oh, yeah. I know what's coming,"* then, you surprise them with something that they aren't expecting; a new angle on the old, familiar scenario.

Another option is to simply go in a completely different direction from the get-go, using that familiar scene as a reference, only in regard to the information or emotion that needs to come out of it. Consider that the story cliches and genre conventions are there to guide you. They provide you with information which is required to progress the story.

Each old, familiar scenario represents a natural building block in the structure of the film. Now, you must find a new way to do it; to bust those cliches and bend those conventions.

As pointed out previously, Nora Ephron tweaked the "meet cute" moment in "Sleepless in Seattle" by having the characters not actually meet until the end of the film. Their interaction was all by telephone, through the filter of a radio station. That's taking a convention in a different direction, but at the same time, honoring it.

You must send your mind out on a quest in uncharted directions. You never know where it will take you, and if you go too far, you can always come back. Personally, I love seeing moments in films that work and leave me shaking my head, saying to myself, *"I never would have thought to go there."*

Beyond story choices, the choices you create for your characters are critical in defining your characters, as well as in moving the story forward. Once again, those choices should never be easy.

The second act is specifically designed to force difficult choices onto your protagonist. That's what complications and obstacles are all about, forcing your character to adjust to ever increasing threats to his goal. A hero can only become a hero by accomplishing a heroic feat. As the old saying goes, if it was easy, anybody could do it.

Because the characters supply the heart and soul to the story, you want their challenges to be not only physical, but moral. The way in which an audience identifies with a character is based on its perception of a character's moral choices.

One early screenwriting proverb went like this:

A dog lays out in front of an old West saloon. A cowboy comes out of the saloon, stops and pets the dog. Afterward, another cowboy comes out of the saloon and kicks the dog. Any question about which is the good guy and which is the bad guy?

My advice to beginning screenwriters is to slow down and savor the creative process. Take some time to dig deeply into your story and explore every option, before settling on a choice. Don't stay married to a particular direction for a scene, just because you're in a hurry to reach THE END, and this one works okay. "Okay" is not what they're looking for.

In Summary: Every scene; each moment of your story will come as a result of a choice you have made. Poor choices equal sub-par stories, and therefore your choices must be made with the optimum of careful consideration. Rushing through the process; making convenient, rather than considered choices will likely result in a "pass" from the readers who will determine the fate your screenplay.

Writing to a Budget

Something else you must keep in mind, when choosing the scenes and locations in your screenplay, is the reality of physical production. If you write something "big," like large crowd scenes, exotic locations, stunts and the like, you are creating certain budget requirements for your story.

In that respect, you are placing your screenplay within a certain marketing niche. If you incorporate a lot of expensive locations, stunts or crowd scenes, you'll be taking yourself out of the low-budget, independent film arena. And, if you do create big scenes, you must be certain they are justified. If your cool, splashy scene doesn't really add much to your story, it's probably going to be cut.

Writing to a specific budget level is not something I thought about when I started writing, but I've learned that there are times when it needs to be considered, particularly when working in the indie market, where those budgets are notoriously low. In Hollywood, of course, budget is much less of a concern to the screenwriter, but still can be an issue.

Ideally, I would like to advise every writer to just not think about it. You have no budget. Just write the story. What it costs to bring it to the screen is someone else's problem. The truth is, sometimes, it can be your problem, too.

Hollywood is currently in love with tentpoles; extravagant, high-budget action pieces, laden with special effects, CGI and 3-D. Comic book heroes are in vogue, so much so that they're creating new comic book heroes to make movies about. And, sequels to those movies.

Not every movie they make is a tentpole, of course, but if you can sell one of those babies, you're in for a nice, fat paycheck. The drawback in this is the fact that your options for a sale are very limited. Either a major studio is going to purchase it, or no one will.

These types of movies are most frequently developed "in-house," meaning the studio buys a property, be that a novel, a comic book, or the rights to a comic book hero, then assigns a high-end, "A" list writer to write it.

Very rarely are they purchased as spec scripts from freelance writers, but that shouldn't necessarily stop you from writing one. If you have a great idea for a tentpole type script, and a passion for the story, you should write it. If it's well done, it will, at the very least, arm you with a solid writing sample, and from that, anything can happen.

On the other end of the spectrum are the independent producers. As mentioned previously, indie budgets are generally low, so that's the market for less demanding scripts.

The indies are generally looking for three elements:

- Genre films, as in Horror, Action, Martial Arts and similar standard fare.
- Character pieces, such as "The King's Speech" or "Silver Linings Playbook."
- Art Films, as in "The Guard" and "We Need to Talk About Kevin," and quirky, off-center projects like "Little Miss Sunshine" and "Napoleon Dynamite."

The budgets for these can vary somewhat, but are always within the low-budget range. While a writer isn't going to retire from a script sale in this market, it provides us with opportunities to get our scripts produced; opportunities which probably don't exist in Hollywood.

A low-budget indie film can be the entry-way to a screenwriter's career, by endowing her with that elusive and all-important first credit.

In Summary: Although securing a film's budget is not within a writer's job description, the physical requirements of the screenplay will, in large part, determine the financial requirements. Therefore, a screenwriter should always consider the cost of production when determining his target audience.

CHAPTER 18

Development

The Idea

Ideas. They're just like...let's say bellybuttons. Everybody has one.

Every story in every form starts with an idea, of course. Where that idea actually comes from is a subject that is well above my pay grade, but I'm convinced that the answer is very mystical and profound. At any rate, the idea is the starting gun. Now, I doubt you'll find a single soul who won't tell you about the "great idea" they have for a movie, and sometimes, they really are great ideas. But, let's put ideas in their proper perspective.

If you wake up one morning and say to yourself, *"Gee, I need a new shirt,"* and then someone drops a bale of cotton on your front porch and says *"Here you go,"* that's the equivalent of an idea in relation to a screenplay.

If you need a shirt, and the only way to get one is to make it, you're going to go out and learn how to make a shirt, right? But, even if you know all of the intricacies of crafting a shirt, and have all of the tools to do so, it's still going to be a chore. And, your level of talent and craftsmanship will determine how good that shirt looks and fits.

That's where the first line in the sand is drawn. Every time you are hit with "a great idea for a movie," what you actually have is a bale of cotton, when what you need is a shirt.

The Outline

So, how do you turn your idea into a screenplay? You flesh it out with an outline; a first step in the process, and one which is approached in a variety of ways.

Some writers are proponents of using cards on story boards. They stick a cork board on the wall, write their scenes on cards and pin them to the board as they develop the story. This allows them to move scenes around, eliminate them, replace them, add new scenes and still have the overall structure of the story in front of them. They can color code the cards into day and night scenes, action scenes, act breaks, etc.

This method of outlining has been around for a long time, and I greatly suspect, stemmed from the fact that writers, at the time of its inception, were relegated to writing on typewriters. I've been around just long enough to know what a nightmare it is to do rewrites on a typewriter, so having scenes on cards, stuck on a board, provided a nice flexibility.

It's nothing you can't now do on a computer, of course, but some writers still go "old school" and use the cards, for a variety of reasons, but mostly because it works for them. That's the only criteria that matters.

Some writers and teachers of screenwriting advocate extensive outlines, before getting into the writing process. I mean, extensive outlines, sometimes nearly as lengthy as the finished script. Each story beat is meticulously plotted, from beginning to end.

This type of full-blown, detailed outline never worked for me. I have two major problems with the approach: I'm lazy and I'm impatient. Okay, those aren't really the two major problems, but they do factor in. My first real problem is that a highly detailed outline makes me feel locked in. When I tried it, it began to feel like a fill-in-the-blanks process, like working a crossword puzzle.

Just fit the words into the squares. Logical enough.

Yet, somewhere along the line, I always found my story drifting away from the original outline. Maybe, something in the outline seemed like a good idea, but the actual writing of it; seeing it on the page, tells me otherwise.

Sometimes, the characters just don't want to go to my pre-determined location, or make the choice I thought they would. I've given them minds of their own, and dammit, they're changing them!

That, in my view, is the inherent danger in a detailed outline. An outline is dry. It is emotionless. It's math. The passion comes through in the screenplay.

I believe that we subconsciously know how we want to tell our story. While our evil-but-necessary left brain dominates our thoughts by focusing on structure, our right brain struggles to compete, because it knows exactly what we want to say.

I like leaving myself open to that right-brain influence, rather than stifling it, as a rigidly structured outline can do. Plus, I'm lazy and impatient.

At the opposite end of the scale are those writers who boast that they never outline. They just sit down and start writing. Well, okay, if they say so, but I don't think so. Every writer outlines, in some form, whether they'll admit to it or not.

What I really suspect is that those writers have the ability to formulate an outline in their minds, and somehow retain it in an orderly fashion. Maybe, they've spent hours and hours mulling the story before they ever sit down at the keyboard. Kudos to them. I envy the ability.

However, the structure of the story must exist somewhere, before you start writing. Developing a story "on the fly" is an extremely risky way to approach the process, and you're much more likely to abandon the project after the first flash of inspiration fades than you are to complete it.

My favored process at this stage falls somewhere in between the above examples. I do need something tangible on the page, but I also like to retain some flexibility. What I've found that works for me is the Beat Sheet.

The Beat Sheet

I first encountered the Beat Sheet process when I started writing sitcom, where it is ideally suited, and later found that it also works well for developing a long-form screenplay.

One of the reasons I like it is its ability to evolve. In fact, that's the very basis of how it works. It is flexible. It lets me build my story, piece-by-piece, without locking me into a rigid structure from FADE IN to FADE OUT. It allows me to outline as I write, but not blindly.

The idea is to lay out the major beats dictated by screenplay structure; the major story points that create the spine of the story, then develop the story around and between those points.

Using a road map as a metaphor, it's akin to driving a car from one city to another. I know where I'm going, but there are a number of alternate routes that will get me there. The Beat Sheet process is like waiting until I'm on the road to decide which route I will choose. Maybe, I'll take a detour for the scenery.

I'm left with the basic spine of the story, which is a firm, but not rigid structure which still allows me to explore and remain open to new directions as I write.

I've determined that I need six critical pieces of information in my initial Beat Sheet. If I have those points in place, I have a story, although in its most rudimentary form.

The Six Starting Points of a Beat Sheet

1. The Opening Hook
2. The Story Trigger
3. Page 60 (Midpoint turn)

4. Crisis

5. Climax

6. Resolve

My first job is to supply those six story beats. In the very raw stages of creating a screen story, the Beat Sheet will consist of answers to the following questions:

1. Opening Hook - What event grabs the reader/viewer and pulls her into the story?

2. Story Trigger - What event occurs which sets the story into motion?

3. Page 60 (Midpoint Crisis) - What event nearly stops my hero in his tracks?

4. Crisis - What event creates the most critical challenge for my hero; an "all is lost" moment?

5. Climax - The hero's all-or-nothing battle to achieve his goal.

6. Resolve - The hero wins or loses.

These are the bare-bones story moments I need to have some concept of, at the outset. These six beats are the ones which are critical to determining the viability of a story.

As you can see, it leaves plenty of flexibility. Odds are, when I choose a story to write, I have even more of this information predetermined. Fine. The more beats, the merrier. If I have scenes in my head, I'll include them in the Beat Sheet where they occur.

Now, I build on this basic, six-point Beat Sheet before I start writing, focusing on the first act. Once I'm comfortable with the beginning, I can start writing. When I finish writing through the beats I've fleshed out, I begin developing the beats of the next sequence. I'm outlining as I go, with the basic six-point beat sheet to keep me from going astray.

I find that having brought the story to life by writing the early sequences, fleshing out the sequence that follows is easier. I have more information about the story and the characters to help guide me.

Personally, I make it a habit to end my writing day by outlining the beats of the next sequence I need. That way, when I come back to the story, I'll be able to dive right in to writing the scenes and get my rhythm back.

I should point out another advantage of the flexibility of the Beat Sheet. I can write a single beat to represent an entire sequence of scenes, i.e., "Joe and Jim chased by bad guys at the amusement park." That can cover quite a few pages, but it only needs one beat to describe it.

Once I get to that story moment, I can now flesh out the sequence and write it. I'll have the entire backstory of the script I've written, up to that point, to help decide my next move. I find it much easier to maintain continuity this way.

In Summary: Creating an outline, in some fashion, is an absolute must. Utilizing the Beat Sheet gives you the benefit of having a basic structure from which to work, one which is pliable enough to allow for further development during the writing process.

Man Bites Dog

So, let's say I've hit on a great idea for a story: Man Bites Dog

I now must set up the primary beats for the story. At this point, the choices are virtually unlimited, because the premise is so scant. Is it going to be about the man or the dog?

That makes a pretty big difference, doesn't it? I can't know if my protagonist will win or lose until I know who my protagonist is.

I could use this premise to tell a Disneyesque dog story, for instance. Dog gets bitten by man and is somehow affected by it.

 Maybe, the man in question was infected by a radiation-type-thingy from an alien space craft. Now, when he bites the dog, it becomes SUPER DOG!

A bit "out there," right? Okay, let's say I want my "man bites dog" story to be about the man. Ah, but what kind of man? Do I want him to be a nice, likeable guy? It's always a safe choice for a protagonist, but it isn't the only choice.

Maybe, my guy is a jerk. Maybe, he bites this dog because he's a jerk. Really, what kind of a guy bites a dog? It's okay if he's a jerk when we meet him. He just can't be a jerk when we get to the end of the story. Or, if he is, he must have received his proper comeuppance.

So, am I going to start out with a jerk, and redeem him by the end? The act of man-biting-dog ignites a chain of events that will leave him forever changed; evolved. That's a possibility.

The answer that helps me make these determinations is found in my old friend, the Theme. What, exactly, is this story going to be about? What is it going to say?

In this case, let's say I've decided that the theme will be "Fame." Man biting dog will make the man famous, or, perhaps, infamous.

Now, let's surmise that I've put anywhere from five minutes to five years of thought into the story, and I've come up with this:

Jack is a mail carrier for the Post Office. He's three weeks from retirement. At one particular house on Jack's route lives a dog; a big, mean-tempered mastiff, that loves to make Jack the object of his ire, each time Jack passes.

After several years of dealing with this, Jack has discovered ways to evade and avoid the dog, but it's always a challenge. But, not today. Jack is retiring soon, and has decided that today, the dog will not win. Jack will stand his ground. Right on cue, the cur comes after Jack. When the dog sinks its teeth into Jack's pant leg, Jack descends on it..and bites it, sending it yelping back to its house!

Jack feels a glorious sense of victory and resolve from the incident, but unknown to him, a kid from across the street caught the whole thing on his cell phone camera. When the kid posts the video on the internet, all hell breaks loose.

A lot of people who don't like vicious dogs running loose in their neighborhoods cheer Jack's actions, and view him as a hero. But, the owner of the dog doesn't feel that way, and he files suit against the Post Office. As a result, the Post Office fires Jack, thereby depriving him of the pension he's counting on to retire. And the A.S.P.C.A hears about the incident, and files animal cruelty charges against Jack.

Jack has no choice but to defend himself, aided by a Public Relations man of dubious integrity. Jack goes on talk shows. Jack writes a book: "The Man Who Bites Dogs."

Jack's entire life is turned upside down. Ultimately, he is acquitted of the animal cruelty charges. He doesn't recover his pension, but his book goes through the roof, and he winds up with more money than he ever dreamed of. The End.

Okay, there's my story. Still pretty sketchy, at this point, but enough to create my Six-Point Beat Sheet. Here are how the beats will lay out.

"Man Bites Dog" Beat Sheet

1. Hook - A mail carrier retaliates against a vicious dog by biting it.
2. Story Trigger - A kid videos the man-bites-dog incident and posts it on the internet, to a huge response.
3. Page 60 - The Post Office fires Jack just weeks before retirement, depriving him of his pension, and the dog owner and A.S.P.C.A both file charges against him.
4. Crisis - Jack's fame and notoriety grow. He goes on talks shows to defend and explain his actions, to no avail. It looks like he's going to fail, losing everything.
5. Climax - In a brilliantly planned defense in court, Jack has the offending dog brought in, where it promptly latches

onto the leg of the prosecutor and won't let go. Jack wins his case, but still doesn't recover his job or his pension.

6. Resolve - Jack writes a book, which goes through the roof, due to the media's fascination with his trial. He makes a fortune; more than his pension would ever provide. Meanwhile, the prosecutor who was bitten brings charges against the owner of the dog.

Now, I can confidently continue fleshing out my "Man Bites Dog" story, knowing where I'm going, what I want to achieve and how my story will end. I can actually start writing at this point, or continue developing until I have more info, in which case, I'll be adding more beats to my Beat Sheet. My choice.

What I learn from this part of the process is whether I actually have a story that is worth writing. Is my initial flash of inspiration actually worthy of a complete story?

If I come up with some great scenes and choices for the major story beats, with a fresh approach that excites me, then I'm off and running. If I struggle to find those story beats, and they ultimately feel flat and lifeless, then it's on to another project.

In Summary: The process you will use to lay out the beats of the story you will write is purely a personal choice. Just as I suggest that writers not get locked in to any one screenwriting guru's philosophy, I make the same recommendation for outlining. If one teacher's outlining style is uncomfortable for you, either adjust it or dump it and develop your own. There is no right or wrong, here. There is only what works and what doesn't.

CHAPTER 19

Rewrites

A lot of writers dread the rewrite process. I used to be among them. I've just racked my brain and sweated bullets to get this thing finished, and now, I'm supposed to go back and start all over? Yep. That's exactly what I need to do, and I may do it again, several times, before I actually shop it.

Whether we want to admit it, or not, the fact is, we cannot produce the best possible script in the first pass. Over the years, I've learned the value of rewriting, and have actually come to enjoy it.

There are two kinds of rewrites you will encounter: those you will do based on someone's notes and those you will do for yourself.

Notes

When you give anyone in the industry a copy of your screenplay and ask for their opinion, guess what? You're going to get notes! No one is going to come back to us with, *"I think it's perfect!"* If they do, then they probably didn't read it.

Taking notes is generally one of the more unpleasant tasks in our business, and how you approach the process is critical to your success, and to your emotional well-being. Like agents, unions and lawyers, notes are a fact of a screenwriter's life.

The major qualities you need to survive this process with the least amount of pain and anguish are objectivity and confidence in your work. If you don't have confidence in the story you've written, you'll succumb to the urge to immediately address every single note you get, because you don't trust your own choices. You'll find yourself questioning every scene you write; every choice you make. You'll be rewriting incessantly, only to wind up with an incoherent script that doesn't represent your original inspiration at all.

Without objectivity, however, you'll have a tendency to let your ego control your agenda, and reject every note without giving it the proper consideration. Yeah, you want people to read it, and you'd like their opinion, as long as it's positive. You must keep an open mind, understanding that an objective reaction to your story may supply you with ideas which will make your story stronger.

It's difficult, at first, when you haven't been validated, to trust in your own instincts, and not cater to the whims of someone in a superior position. Highly qualified industry pros won't always agree with your choices, but just because they are who they are doesn't automatically mean their note is sacrosanct. It does, however, signal an issue that might be worth your attention.

Some note-givers will give you only the negatives; what doesn't work. They don't think you can benefit from being told what is right in your script. In their view, that's not what notes do.

Others will not only tell you what doesn't work, they'll tell you how to fix it. That's another land mine. Even if they have a way to fix it, they may not have the best way.

Then, there are some who just seem to enjoy tearing you down and undermining your self-confidence. Why remains a mystery, to me, but they're out there. I've met them.

You can best reduce the number of notes you get by becoming your own harshest critic, so that all others pale by comparison. When your work is not up to snuff, if you're honest, you'll know it before anyone else does. I recall, more than once, having a particular script problem pointed out to me, and thinking to myself,

"Damn! I knew that was an issue! I should have fixed it!"

Sometimes a note will sound like something out of left field, on the surface. It might make no sense to you, but that doesn't mean you should dismiss it, outright. If the problem isn't immediately clear, you have to look deeper to find the root of it.

What generated the note? For this reader, it's obvious that something didn't work. Why not? Once you find the problem, if there really is one, you can fix it in your own way. Ultimately, only you can determine how tightly you're willing to cling to your choices.

A good note will hit you instantly, sending your mind racing with the possibilities it presents. It will just feel right. You'll see the benefit of it to the story immediately.

A bad note is generally just as obvious in the other direction. It falls flat, feels confusing and doesn't fit. Other times, it's one of those red car/blue car notes I mentioned previously.

"See, here, where you have the red car? I think it should be a blue car."

What they're suggesting doesn't make the story better or any worse, just different. In that case, what you have already is probably fine, but if you give them what they want and turn the car blue, that will be fine, too.

The note-taking process gets even more involved when your script has been purchased, and you're doing rewrites for "the company." That's when they get input that you have no choice but to address, and it can manifest in many ways.

I've been given notes from seven or eight different executives during a rewrite phase, none of whom had compared their notes with anyone else, so one set of notes would often conflict with another. On top of that, the executives involved didn't all work for the same entity. Some were the producers who sold the project, while others worked for the company that would distribute it, and still others from the company who actually made the movie.

This was an extreme case, but when you sell a script, no matter to whom, many fingers will get into the pie. The producers, director and actors, at a minimum, will have notes.

Personally, when I get mired down in such a convoluted situation, I go to my immediate contact; the person I can trust, and ask:

"Who do I need to please in this crowd?"

Because, there's always a pecking order. Those are the notes that get the most consideration. I can't possibly satisfy everyone, so my best defense is to try to please the top dog.

The best approach I've discovered for dealing with notes is to lobby for time to consider them, rather than giving a knee-jerk response in the moment. I take the notes, make sure I understand them, then ask for a day or two to study them, after which time I'll respond with my thoughts on how to approach them. This way, if I disagree with a note, I'll have a chance to build my case against it, and deliver it in a tactful, logical manner. Sometimes it works, sometimes it doesn't.

Wherever notes come from, it is important that you judge them objectively and fairly, and that means setting your ego aside. We all want approval, and getting a note means someone found something of which they don't approve. A flaw, at least in their eyes. Our initial reaction to that is to take offense, and therefore a defensive posture. That is rarely productive.

After a scathing review of one of my screenplays by a producer, he capped it off by saying:

"It's not personal."

Of course, it is! At least, from my point-of-view. Can he really think that this story I've poured my heart and soul, sweat and toil into isn't personal for me?

That's where your own internal conflicts come to the surface, and you must quell them for the better good of the end game. You must force yourself to maintain your objectivity. Yes, it's personal, but you can't take it personally.

When you dive back into your screenplay, you must scrutinize every scene and examine every line of dialogue to make certain they've achieved their maximum potential. Your goal, first and foremost, is to enhance and strengthen the emotional impact of your story. If it's a comedy, make it funnier. If it's action, find ways to pump it up.

In Summary: Because the making of films and television programs is a collaborative process, a screenwriter must accept input from a variety of sources, before his project makes it to the screen. Confidence in your story choices, coupled with objectivity and an open mind will make the note process much easier to survive.

Edits

The last piece of the puzzle in the rewrite process, and generally the last thing you'll tackle, are the edits.

When editing for length, there are two major factors you need to keep in mind.

1. It probably isn't as long as it looks, and...
2. It is probably longer than it needs to be.

The first category, that it probably isn't as long as it looks, is the first area to attack when editing a script for length. The reason for this is simple. You want to retain as much of what you've written as you can, so you first want to take the least damaging approach. There are little "cheats" you can use to accomplish this.

First, look at the action blocks. If you have a "dangler," one or two words on the last line of the action block, find a way to condense the information in the block to eliminate those two words.

A line like "Joe turns to the old bum with a sympathetic look." can just as easily read "Joe gives the bum a sympathetic look."

Now, an action block that was five lines long becomes four lines long. Do that 52 times and you've saved a page, but lost nothing in terms of story context.

Approach dialogue in the same way. Find speeches that can be condensed, combined, and much of the time, completely eliminated without sacrificing anything in the story or the tone. This approach, alone, with a few passes, can often give you back two or three script pages. That's significant.

But, it's still too long, so enter phase two. Is it longer than it needs to be?

When I say needs, in this instance, I'm not talking about what the marketplace needs, in terms of page length, I'm talking about what the story needs. Can you tell the same story, with the same emotional impact, in less time?

Almost always, the answer is "yes." It takes a critical eye and some serious re-thinking, but in nearly every case, it can be done. The changes at this stage are far more important than the minor trims you made in phase one. They will truly alter the story, to some extent. The trick is, to alter the story in a positive way.

Are there scenes you can eliminate? It's great, when you can find them, because it lifts a big chunk of space out of the overall length in one fell swoop.

But, it's an entire scene! Surely, there must be something important, there. Otherwise, you wouldn't have written it. Right, so the next step is to lose the scene, but retain the information that was delivered in that scene, by incorporating it into an existing scene.

Let's say, you're looking to shorten a nice boy-meets-girl scene for a Romantic Comedy screenplay. They meet at an amusement park. They're both there alone, for their own personal reasons. It's a nice, poignant, four-page scene. Your first determination is whether this scene actually deserves four pages. Maybe, you can do the scene differently, but with more impact, in two pages.

Your options, now, are three:

1. You can rewrite this scene in a condensed version.
2. You can replace it with an entirely new scene, which can be effectively delivered in two pages, rather than four.

3. You can leave it alone.

You can only find the best option by working the scene.

If your four page scene is based on the premise that the meet-cute between my boy and girl comes in an awkward, embarrassing moment, i.e., she spills her milkshake all over him, or he accidentally breaks the Kewpie doll she just won, then your new scene should retain that character moment.

Awkward and embarrassing meet-cute stays, just in fewer pages, and perhaps, a different scenario. The nice thing is that you have a barometer. We've already written a scene, so you have it to compare, and to harvest from it the needed story elements for your new scene.

You now have to make certain that your new scene, or a tighter old scene, is just as good or better. If you take a few stabs at it, and none of the new stuff measures up to the original scene, that is when you should leave the original scene alone. Find your cuts elsewhere.

And, then, there are times when, upon close scrutiny, you'll discover that you've written a scene that doesn't need to be there, at all. It's fine, there. It works nicely. Sometimes, it's a really cool scene; one you're absolutely in love with.

Yet, when you lift it from the script, something surprising happens. The story works without it, just fine. Nothing is lost!

Time to kill one of your darlings. Time to remove that scene. If it doesn't advance the story; if it contains information that can be delivered elsewhere, in a more efficient and economical manner, with the same emotional impact, then it needs to go.

You may as well remove it, because the odds are, if you don't, someone else will. It happens all the time. Even when they survive the development process and are filmed, entire scenes still wind up on the cutting room floor, during the editing process, without damaging the overall story. As much as possible, you want to be the one who makes the decision as to what will go and what will stay.

You'd rather not have the director or editor do it, and if you don't do it during the writing process, they will do it during the development or editing process. They're smart enough to recognize an unnecessary scene when they see one.

Another rewrite issue which you may face, at some point, is the task of rewriting another writer. Having been on both sides of that issue, I can tell you that it's rarely pleasant, for either party. No writer, if he's being honest, relishes messing with another writer's work, and heaven knows, he doesn't want someone messing with his.

Of course, it isn't the original writer who will engage you to do the rewrite, it's a producer, production company or someone else who controls the rights to the screenplay, and that is who you need to please. If they're looking for a rewrite, then obviously, they want something different than they got in the original screenplay, and they don't feel like the first writer can deliver it.

While you may be sympathetic to the original writer's pain, and your hope is to enhance, rather than denigrate his work, your responsibility is to the party who hired you.

On the other side of the table, where the "abused" party sits, it's difficult to not feel insulted, at the least. They liked your script enough to buy it, and now, they want to change it. And, they want someone else to do the changing!

It takes a pretty tough shell to sail through this process with an unscathed ego. Yet, top level writers go through it all the time. I've seen writers who command six-figure sums for rewrites be rewritten by other six-figure writers. No one, at any level, is immune to the process.

One option, if you are the offended party is to have your name removed from the script. I've only done this once, and it was a tough decision. Credits of any kind are hard to come by, and trashing one should not be taken lightly.

If, however, the finished product not only doesn't represent your original work, but actually stinks up the theater, it might be worth considering. No sense taking credit for something that tells people you're a lousy writer, particularly when the end result doesn't reflect your vision.

On the up side, both writers will get a paycheck out of this deal. A lot of aspiring writers would be thrilled with that. There are times when you just have to let go; do what you can, the best you can, pick up your toys and move on.

As my hypercritical, note-giving producer put it:

"It's not personal."

Well, for him, it's not. It's business. Regardless of how painful it may be for us, we can only accept that bottom-line mentality.

In Summary: Editing can be a tedious process, to be sure, but it is critical to the ultimate success of a screenplay. The objective for the screenwriter is to commit to the editing process wholeheartedly, before someone else, up the ladder, gets a shot at it. Understand that it is inevitable that your screenplay will undergo intense scrutiny and ongoing refinement. Do the lion's share of the work yourself, to minimize the changes.

CHAPTER 20

Marketing

When you market your script, you probably already know, by now, that you won't have much luck with the direct approach.

"Will you read my script?"

Usually, the answer to that is "no." Sometimes, the answer is "yes," in which case, they're generally lying. They'll tell you "yes" to make you happy and get you off their backs, but they won't actually read your script.

That's why you have to give them something that makes them want to read your script, and that something is what is termed the "treatment."

The Treatment

People define treatments differently. For some, it means, simply a LOGLINE (aka SLUGLINE) and a SYNOPSIS. It could be a long synopsis of three-to-five pages, or it could be a short synopsis of less than a page.

Others feel, and I was taught, that a full treatment means a logline, a one-to-three page synopsis, and a STEP OUTLINE (aka BEAT OUTLINE, aka SCENE OUTLINE) which takes the reader through the story, via a brief description of each scene.

In some cases, particularly in a treatment for television, it also may include a CONCEPT PAGE, which tells us why the story is commercial, why it has long-term potential, who the target audience is, cast recommendations and the like.

In addition, if you're pitching a TV series, it can also include character bios and storylines for future episodes.

You won't see too many full treatments floating around, these days. The marketing of screenplays has, like most everything else, been abbreviated to the equivalent of a sound bite. This philosophy is aided, I suspect, by the infiltration of internet marketing. But, it goes deeper, to an issue that existed long before the internet figured in to the equation.

They hate to read!

In their defense, they have a right to hate to read. Now, more than ever, they are inundated by screenplays to consider. Greater access from the outlying landscape, a boon for writers, has created a deluge of critical mass for those on the other end; those people you're trying to get to.

At one point, early on, when I met with an agent, I was awed by the sight that beset me when I entered his office. There were bookshelves on every wall, each stuffed to overflowing with screenplays. But that wasn't enough. There were screenplays stacked on top of the bookshelves. They were stacked waist-high on the floor. They were stacked on every desk and credenza.

I initially suspected that this decorating choice was designed to dishearten the writers who passed through these doors, heightening their desperation and making them feel lucky that this overwhelmed agent would grant them an audience. That suspicion was quickly dispelled when I began to see the same sight in the offices of producers and story executives, all over town.

There are screenplays everywhere, in Hollywood. Roughly fifty-thousand scripts and treatments are registered with the Writers Guild of America, west, each year. They all beg to be read by someone. Even if you're diligent and fortunate enough to get your screenplay into the office of a legitimate producer or story exec, your screenplay is likely to be read by a "reader" before it ever gets to the person who actually has the clout to buy it.

Being a studio reader is generally considered an entry-level position, or a part-time income for some. They may be film school grads or apprentices at studios or agencies. Their sole job is to read scripts and either reject them or recommend them for consideration.

In the case of the latter, it means someone else, probably still not the "green light guy," will then read it, and we repeat the process. If your script makes it all the way to the top, you've probably been approved by a number of people. This process is less involved in smaller companies, of course, but there will nearly always be someone between your screenplay and the executive who can finally say "yes."

That should help you understand the importance of a good logline and synopsis. For our purposes, let's say the short synopsis. Used to be, a page was considered short. Now, it's a paragraph.

Websites often ask for approximately 400-500 words, tops, because that posts nicely on an internet site and can be read in a flash. Instant gratification is the mantra for the times, and screenplays are no exception. They tell you that you have ten pages of a script to grab their interest. You have even less than that to grab their interest enough to get them to read those first ten script pages.

The Logline

So you need a treatment. What's your first step?

The logline, also referred to as a slugline. It is just what it implies; a line. One single sentence, and it must pique the readers interest.

A logline is, to a screenplay, what a trailer is to a movie. Let's consider a few examples, as I might write them, using familiar popular films.

A man is obsessed with finding the truth behind UFO sightings, but the government is determined to stop him.

Two guys crash weddings to meet women, and wind up learning some hard lessons about love and relationships.

A poor orphaned boy in India is accused of cheating when he wins a million dollars in a game show.

An aging pro wrestler learns he has a heart condition, but returns to the ring for one last shot at glory.

Likely, you won't have to think very hard to discover which movies I've listed, here. They are, in order of appearance:

1. "Close Encounters of the Third Kind"
2. "The Wedding Crashers"
3. "Slumdog Millionaire"
4. "The Wrestler"

Now, let's look at what they have in common. All four loglines tell us three critical things: The concept, the goal and the conflict.

In the "Close Encounters of the Third Kind" logline, the concept is "alien visitations." We know it's a sci-fi story. The goal is discovering the truth behind the UFO visitations. The complication is the government's cover-up.

In "The Wedding Crashers," the concept is in the title - guys crashing weddings to meet women. The goal is to score with women. The complication is love.

In "Slumdog Millionaire," the concept is a poor boy winning a fortune on a game show. The goal is to keep his winnings: a million dollars. The complication is the accusation of cheating he faces.

In "The Wrestler," the concept is, again, in the title (notice a trend?) We're examining the life of a pro wrestler. The goal for that wrestler is to return to the glory of the ring. The complication is a heart condition.

That's really pretty much it. There is no time or space for details. It will be the concept, the goal and the conflict which sells the initial pitch. Therefore, you should highlight the aspect of your story that makes it unique or interesting; chasing UFO's, picking up girls at weddings, winning a million in a game show, finding redemption in the wrestling ring.

The ultimate goal of your logline is to make the reader "see" the movie, in one line. What they really see is the potential for the movie, but they should get a strong sense that there is a movie there.

What do you think this goes back to? Uniquely familiar! The concept is unique, the story is familiar. That's what they're looking for from a logline. Once the logline has grabbed them in that way, they'll be interested in just how you're going to approach this concept. That leads them on to the synopsis.

The Synopsis

Writers truly agonize over this process, and it's easy to understand why. I learned the lesson when I delved into the situation comedy world. The fact is, it is harder to write less than more. The fewer pages you have to tell your story, the tougher the going gets.

Inevitably, you feel like you're being forced to leave out some really important points in your story to get it down in such a limited space.

Don't despair. It isn't the job of the synopsis to tell the story. It is the job of the synopsis to get the reader to read the story.

In order to do that, you must fulfill, in your synopsis, the potential of the story. You do this by alluding to those moments of action, suspense, conflict, high comedy or high drama. You must show them a character with a worthy goal, and the odds stacked against her.

Let's look at an example. First, the logline.

Marketing

The Sheriff of a small, New England coastal town teams with a marine biologist and a crusty shark hunter to find and kill a Great White shark.

This is, of course, a logline (mine) for the film "Jaws." Now, the synopsis:

Martin Brody is a transplanted New Yorker, recently moved to a small tourist town on the New England coast with his wife and three children. Elected Sheriff shortly after his arrival, he faces his first critical problem when a Great White shark attack in local waters kills a swimmer. Brody's first instinct is to close the beaches, but he meets strong resistance from the Mayor and City Council, since the July 4th holiday; the biggest weekend of the summer, is upcoming. Closing the beaches will threaten the livelihood of the town, resulting in financial ruin for some of the town's merchants. Brody relents, but on the July 4th weekend, another swimmer, a young boy, is killed by the Great White. Panic ensues, and town-folk set out to find the shark on their own. When a large shark is brought in, the town celebrates, certain that they've caught the killer shark. But, Matt Hooper, a Marine Biologist who has been brought in to advise Brody, disagrees. Again, the Mayor stops Brody's attempts to close the beaches. Brody and Hooper track the shark on Hooper's boat, and come upon the heavily damaged boat of a local fisherman, who they find dead inside, another victim of the Great White. A crusty, tough shark hunter, Quint, is enlisted to find and kill the shark, but Brody insists that he and Hooper accompany Quint in the hunt. Brody, Hooper and Quint set out on Quint's boat, The Orca, to find and kill the giant shark. After a couple of initial sightings and failed attempts to kill the Great White, the shark goes on the offensive, attacking the fishing boat in open waters, ultimately sinking it, and leaving the ill-prepared Brody to attempt to destroy the animal by himself.

This is a synopsis of the page-or-less variety. Now, let's trim it down to an acceptable "internet" level:

When a swimmer is killed by a Great White shark in the waters off a small New England town, Sheriff Brody wants to close the beaches, but meets resistance from the Mayor and City Council. But, when another swimmer is killed by the shark, Brody teams with a Marine Biologist and a local shark fisherman to hunt it down. But, the shark takes the offensive, attacking and sinking their small boat, leaving Brody to face the animal alone.

As you can see, it's just the "meat;" our concept, our hero, our goal, our opposition, flavored by the critical high points of conflict; moments that allude to the excitement, danger and suspense contained in the story. Enough, hopefully, to spur someone into reading the script. It should be easily read, easily understood, concise and economical.

Studio readers read thousands of these. It's your first chance, and probably your last, to grab them.

In Summary: Treatments are valuable tools, and absolutely necessary in the marketing of any screenplay. Learning to generate them; laying out the bare essence of a story in a limited space is critical for you to master. It can determine the fate of your screenplay.

The Query

Query letters, whether sent through the mail or electronically over the internet, are an important part of a screenwriter's marketing process.

A writer may send dozens, even hundreds of queries to garner a single response, but one never knows if that single response will be the one that leads to a produced screenplay.

Therefore, knowing how to properly compose a query letter to achieve the greatest chance of success is of paramount importance.

Often, a producer, agent or studio executive will judge a writer's professionalism based on his query letter.

Following is a list of "do's and don'ts" in the writing of a query letter, along with a sample letter which may serve as a basic guide.

Query Letter Rules

Always....

Call or email first, when possible. This allows you to establish contact and get a specific name to whom you can direct your query. It also means that your query will not fall into the category of "unsolicited," a fact you should mention in your letter.

Keep it brief. One page is enough.

Include a single paragraph description of your story.

Include appropriate background information pertaining to your writing experience, if you have any.

Check it carefully for typos and spelling errors.

If sent through snail mail, enclose a stamped, self addressed envelope.

Follow up! Give the recipient two-to-three weeks to respond, then send a brief, politely worded note to inquire as to whether your query was received.

Never....

Include personal information. Stick to business.

Over sell! Don't brag on your incredible talent, or the brilliance of your screenplay. They'll be the judge.

Come across as condescending or desperate.

Reveal too much information about your story, especially the ending. (This is my personal choice, but is optional.)

Cast specific actors who would be "perfect" for the piece. They may not have relationships with those actors.

Never, never, never pay a reading fee! If you are soliciting professional notes or feedback on your screenplay, you can expect to pay for that, but not when marketing your completed script. Companies or agencies that charge fees for simply reading your screenplay are rarely legitimate.

NOTE: Query letters to agencies vary slightly from those directed to production companies or studios. The opening paragraph should contain information stating that you are a screenwriter seeking representation for your screenplay and/or screenwriting services.

Sample Query Letter

January 1, 20xx

Dear Mr./Ms. Executive:

I am a screenwriter with a recently completed screenplay which I would like to submit to you for consideration. Judging by your past production history, I feel this story will meet the needs of your company.

(Unless you have a specific contact name, address to Vice President of Development, Head of Development or Creative Executive. If querying an agency, directing it to Agent is okay.)

The screenplay, entitled "My Screenplay," is a story of the redemption of a troubled young woman with a tainted past who is on the road to self-destruction, until she falls in love with her therapist. Geared for a female lead, the story combines elements of "Pretty Woman" and "Girl Interrupted."

(Follow the opening paragraph with a brief description of your screenplay. Not too much detail! Just enough to, hopefully pique the interest of the reader.)

"My Screenplay" is the third project I have written for the screen. The first, "My First Screenplay," won honorable mention in the Toledo Screenwriting Competition, and is currently under consideration by Big Time Productions of New Jersey. Prior to my screenwriting endeavors, I had three short stories published by Romantic Love magazine. In addition, I have a Bachelors degree in Creative Writing from East Podunk University.

(Any background info of note, i.e., personal references, college degrees, previous work published or recognition in a screen-

writing competition goes here. If you have no prior writing experience, don't say anything about it! Just skip this paragraph.)

Please find enclosed a self-addressed, stamped envelope for your reply. At your request, I'll be happy to send a synopsis or copy of the completed screenplay for your perusal. I look forward to your comments.

(If using snail-mail, Always include an SASE to make it easier for them to reply to you.)

Very best regards,

Sammy Scribe

(555) 555-5555

Finding a Buyer

The markets for screenplays have expanded, over the years, as technology has created more distribution outlets. Theatrical, while still the brass ring in terms of aspirations, is but one small piece of that distribution pie.

We have gone, in a startlingly short period of time, from theaters-only to theaters and television, then cable, then VHS and quickly to DVD, and now digital, via the internet and mobile devices.

At the same time, foreign distribution has grown in stature, until it has actually overwhelmed domestic distribution.

Additionally, there was a time, not so long ago, when there was no such thing as shooting a film strictly for home video release. Now, it's commonplace.

Even though access for screenplays, thanks to our techie friend, the internet, has grown exponentially, there are still considerably more available spec screenplays than places to put them. It has always been the case, and it always will be.

So, when it comes time to go shopping; to get your script out there, it's wise to be realistic about your particular market. If you write a small, low-budget action film, you can't expect to "wow" the major studios with it. While it's possible, it will only happen under rare and extremely favorable circumstances.

In the current climate, small action films are of little interest to studios which would rather pump a hundred-million-plus into a film with a major star and cream-of-the-crop stunts and effects, worthy of high-dollar CGI and/or 3-D.

So, where does that small action film go? Film festivals?

Probably not. The festivals can't compete with Hollywood, and they know it, and therefore, what shines at a festival may very well fall flat in the major markets.

Sometimes, a Hollywood-friendly film can slip through the cracks, but it's usually one that is produced by a major Hollywood entity, like Quentin Tarrantino or Robert Rodriguez or Clint Eastwood.

While these filmmakers are technically "independent," let's face it, they're insiders. The true independents aren't about to tackle projects designed to compete with the studios.

Your best bet, in this realm, is to look for a small, independent distributor whose forte is home video or foreign distribution.

You'll likely get more mileage out of a quirky, low-budget character piece in the festival circuit, where the focus is more on the art than production values.

The benefit of this is, if your low-budget character film does manage to cross over into mainstream distribution, as "Napoleon Dynamite" or "Little Miss Sunshine" did, it can make a killing, since the profit margin is so high.

Same goes for low-budget films of certain genres, like "Paranormal Activity" or "The Blair Witch Project." It is a rare event, when a film of this type breaks out of the "art" market and into the mainstream, yet, as we've seen, it does happen.

Even that relies on big-league distribution entities to ultimately get on board. Marketing a film in the mainstream is expensive, and if the filmmakers didn't have a big budget to make the thing, odds are, they won't have a big budget to sell it. Only the major distributors have the necessary financing.

In Summary: The time to determine your target market is after you've written your screenplay, not before. Trying to write to the market is, as mentioned, always risky, and your best bet is to write your story based on your passion for it, rather than on its niche in the marketplace.

CHAPTER 21

Pitching

The thought of pitching a story to a potential buyer strikes fear in the hearts of most screenwriters. After all, if we wanted to perform, we would have become actors, wouldn't we?

Pitching a completed screenplay, or a story idea we hope will become a screenplay, requires a set of tools which are foreign to most writers. For that reason, I have included in this book a reprint of an article I wrote for SCRIPT magazine, which encompasses my thoughts on the dreaded pitching process.

10 Simple Rules for Surviving the Pitch

I've pitched a lot. Movies, sitcoms, series concepts...a lot; and it strikes me that certain similarities keep popping up at each pitch; road signs, trends, tendencies, call them what you will. Learning to identify these similarities may help writers read the situation and avoid the many pitfalls. Because the fact is, there are rules to a pitch, and woe to the writer who breaks them.

These rules aren't written down anywhere, mind you, but there's a certain pitch etiquette that you must observe. If you violate that etiquette, the meeting is over, and no one will even bother to tell you why. I'm here to tell you why.

Here are some rules based upon pitch situations that I or my brothers (and sisters)-in-arms have encountered.

RULE NUMBER ONE: Their Time Is Valuable

We all know about putting on our game face, prepping the dog-and-pony show and treating the pitch like performance art; but don't overdo it. Most producers and story executives who read scripts won't go much past 20 pages unless you've given them a reason to. In other words, if you haven't hooked them by then, it's too late. A pitch session is no different. When you step through the door, the clock starts ticking.

With that fact in mind, understand that one to two minutes of small talk up front is about the most you can hope for, and that should be orchestrated by the executive. A comment or a small compliment from you about a project the company has produced or is now producing may get you off on the right foot by letting the executive know you're familiar with what his company does. If you have friends or business associates in common, dropping a familiar name may help establish a certain comfort level. Beyond that, *"Looks like rain"* or *"How about those Lakers?"* will only eat up valuable time.

My first pitch was at "Mork & Mindy." I was writing with a partner at the time, and we had done our homework. We had sneaked onto the Paramount lot, then onto the set and watched rehearsals and run-throughs from the shadows. We had managed to lift a script or 10 from the show and sweet-talked an agent into a "casual relationship," one where we made the calls and set the meetings, simply using his name to clear the way. Once we actually got ourselves a job, the agent would sign us.

The point is, we were ready. We set up a meeting with a story editor, went in and pitched ... 16 stories!

Yes, you read it right - 16. We were there for nearly two hours. It was only our good fortune that the gentleman to whom we were pitching, George Zateslo, was a supremely nice guy. (Bless you, George, wherever you are!) He listened patiently. He took notes. He gave us feedback. He didn't nod off once. (Falling asleep qualifies as a "warning sign," of course, but if you can't figure that one out, you're already doomed.) Only later did we discover our blatant violation of pitch etiquette. We had taken far too much of George's valuable time.

My best advice is to go in with three brief, well-prepared story ideas and pitch the hell out of them. Keep a couple more loosely sketched out ideas in your back pocket, just for insurance.

Consider that you've probably been allotted 20 to 30 minutes, tops, to do your job. Don't leave it to the executive to devise a creative lie of some kind just to get you out of there. Be finished within that time frame. If you've just bowled him over, he'll grant you more time and attention. If you haven't, the last thing he wants is to be trapped in a room with you listening to 16 pitch ideas for two solid hours.

RULE NUMBER TWO: Know Thy Producer

It doesn't matter whether we're talking TV series or film. The point is, you don't treat every producer the same way. If you're pitching to a film producer, study up on him to find out what he's produced. It'll give you an idea of what attracts him. Then, gear your pitch to those tastes.

If it's a series, then for heaven's sake get a bible beforehand. The last thing you want to do is pitch something he has already done, or worse, something the show has already rejected for reasons you're unaware of "because you didn't get a bible." If you come to the meeting uninformed, you'll never meet in this town, or at least with this producer or executive, again.

RULE NUMBER THREE: Be Brave

Not brazen. Not cocky. Just brave. After all, it is a stressful situation. But, it's only stressful for you, not the executive. Whatever he throws at you, you somehow have to smile without twitching, breathe without gasping and sweat without, well, sweating.

Some executives like to test our mettle. Some executives or producers like to see what we're made of, because pitching isn't only about stories. It's about people and relationships. It's collaborative; and once you've sold this script and been given many thousands of their precious dollars for you to go off and do your thing, that's when the stress really begins. If you can't handle it in a pitch session, well...

So, be appropriately condescending at the appropriate times and respectful all of the time, but never grovel. Just remember, they need you as much as you need them, even if they are currently being paid for their time and you are not.

RULE NUMBER FOUR: Keep It Simple - meaning "conceptual"

What I'm advocating here is to deliver a pitch that can easily be re-pitched by the person you're pitching to. Still with me? Because here's the cold, hard truth: the executive to whom you're pitching will not be the one who will make the final decision. Your executive has a boss who is much too busy to meet with a lowly writer because he's meeting with the really important people.

This person is generally referred to as "The Greenlight Guy," or "The Big Giant Head," or something considerably less eloquent that you wouldn't call them to their face. This is the one true person who can turn your pitch into an assignment. Therefore, when your pitch is finished, understand that your fate now rests in the ability of your current story executive to pass on your dynamic idea with the same passion and commitment with which you've pitched him. And, just like some people can't tell a joke...well, you get the picture.

So keep the high points high. Make the concept unforgettable and hang a "visual" on it that he can't get out of his head. Most importantly, outline the major pitch points in written form, just a paragraph or so. That way you can hand him something tangible and hope that if he can't pitch, at least he can read.

RULE NUMBER FIVE: Don't Explain

"Oh," you may be thinking, *"I thought that's what pitching was, explaining my idea."* No! This one is hard, fast and etched in stone. If he raises an objection, never disagree and never explain!

The reason is simple. It will do no good. If he's confused about the story or suffering from a misconception of some kind, that's your fault anyway. The upshot is, he's found a fatal flaw, and you'll never convince him that he hasn't.

The situation is akin to trying to explain to someone why a joke is funny. It doesn't matter. Either he laughs or he doesn't. If he voices a question pertaining to your story, that's one thing. If he voices an objection, immediately dump the story and move on to the next one. Trying to counter a specific objection with logic is pointless for one good reason: The objection is only the text. The subtext is "No." Learn to recognize the fact, accept defeat and move on.

RULE NUMBER SIX: Get Excited!

Just like the audience sitting in a darkened theater watching your story unfold on the screen, the executives to whom you pitch are waiting for you to tell them how to feel. If you're excited about the story, they'll get excited about the story. Hopefully. Energy begets energy. Let them know that you really LOVE this story, "truly, madly, deeply," and you're just busting at the seams to write it.

There is a tendency among studio story executives to not feel positive about something unless somebody else feels positive about it first. Obviously, it's more advantageous if that someone is their boss, in which case the decision becomes a slam-dunk. However, since you are the only other person in the room, it's going to be left to you to generate the excitement necessary to sell the story.

RULE NUMBER SEVEN: When They Stop Listening, Move On!

How will you know? It's easy. Just watch their faces. Of course, we're not talking about the obvious things here, like yawning, looking at their watch or answering a phone that hasn't rung. These are highly educated people, well-versed in the fine art of hiding their true feelings. Most of them will at least make some small effort at politeness and try to appear interested even when they're not. So you have to look beneath the surface.

When you drop that killer story twist on them, that big emotional moment you've been building up to, it should warrant more than a slight smile and a barely perceptible nod. You're looking for raised eyebrows, genuine surprise, active interest or most importantly, what you hope will occur in the next rule.

RULE NUMBER EIGHT: If The Executive Starts Talking, Shut Up!

"My story takes place at a remote mountain resort..." you begin, and the executive says, *"Like in Alaska?" "Yes!"* you shout gleefully as you secretly scratch the word "Colorado" off your note pad. *"And, the hero is a hunter..."* The executive jumps in, *"Of bears!"* My God! It's uncanny! Of course, it was originally mountain lions, but hey. Because, you see, you know you've got the executive hooked when he begins to add elements to your story, when he starts to run with it.

If it's something he likes, something that shows promise, the immediate urge to put his personal stamp on the story takes over. If he starts pitching back to you, let him! It means you've won. For God's sake, don't correct him! (*"Actually, Colorado is better, because..."*) No! You've sold your story. Don't fight it. Of course, the resulting changes may not resemble the story you originally started with, but that's not the point. The point is, you got the job and that's what you're here for.

So, don't stay married to your original concept. Instead, fall in love with the one he pitches back to you, regardless of how much it might suck. Fight those creative battles later, after you've signed the contract.

RULE NUMBER NINE: Use Your Last Pitch To Set Up Your Next Pitch

The technique is a lot like name dropping at an industry party. It lets people know you're in the loop. You've already pitched at one honest-to-goodness company, so you must not be a complete flake. When you call in hopes of setting up another meeting, feel free to let it slip that you just met with Producer Joe Dynamic over at Residual Films. Maybe it was even Joe who suggested you call them because you've got a couple of hot ideas that are just right for their company. At least, that's what Joe thought.

RULE NUMBER TEN: Follow Up

There are many reasons for following up. For one thing, it keeps the door open and it is an excuse for you to call someone who otherwise might never take your call. It keeps your name familiar.

It's also an opportunity to bond, however slightly, with some of the most important people you will ever encounter in the business: the receptionists and personal assistants. Don't make the mistake of looking down your nose at these "underlings." They are a direct pipeline to the people you need, and their feelings about you could mean the difference. Besides, some day soon they might be running the show. Acknowledge them. Learn their names and make them your friends.

The most important reason for following up, though, is to let those producers know how grateful you are that they allowed you to pitch to them. And you should be grateful. In a nation of more than 300 million people, on a planet of billions, there are a meager 11,000 or so privileged enough to claim membership in the Writers Guild of America. Of those, only a fraction will be granted an audience with a legitimate producer or story executive in the course of a year.

It's an elite club, and now you're in it. Whether your stories were accepted or rejected, you've already won. Enjoy it.

In Closing

If you've read this entire book, rather than just flipping to the back to see how it ends, then you've picked up on a recurring theme: there are many ways to approach this process. What is written here has been my approach, and some of the influences which helped to form it. I hope the information enriches your screenwriting career in some small way.

Every screenwriter has a unique story to tell, and that is part of the joy of this profession. While there are many things all screenwriters share in common, it is a distinctly personal journey.

Just like any good screenplay, it is one in which you, the hero, set your sites on a goal (to get your screenplay produced,) overcome myriad obstacles and complications (too numerous to mention) and emerge victorious, with your vision exploding on the silver screen for the world to witness. And, that brings us to....

FADE OUT:

The End

About the Author:

A professional screenwriter for thirty years, Robert Gosnell has produced credits in feature films, network television, syndicated television, basic and pay cable, and is a member of the Writers Guild of America, West and the Writers Guild of Canada.

Robert began his career writing situation comedy on the staff of the ABC series *Baby Makes Five* and freelanced episodes for *Too Close for Comfort* and the TBS comedies *Safe at Home* and *Rocky Road*. In cable, he scripted numerous projects for the Disney Channel, the Showtime original movie *Escape from Wildcat Canyon* and the Denver produced film *Tiger Street*.

Robert's feature credits include the Chuck Norris/Louis Gossett Jr. film *Firewalker* and the independent features *Dragon and the Hawk*, *Siren* and *Juncture*. Robert currently conducts screenwriting classes and workshops in the Denver area.

Connect with me at:

Website: http://robertgosnellscreenwriting.com/

Facebook: https://www.facebook.com/robert.gosnell.9

Stage 32: https://www.stage32.com/profile/807/robert-gosnell

Films Referenced in This Book

Following is a list of the films and television programs referenced in this book, along with their writing, directing and/or created-by credits.

The Films:

127 HOURS - Screenplay by Danny Boyle & Simon Beaufoy
Directed by Danny Boyle

3:10 TO YUMA (2007) - Screenplay by Halsted Welles, Michael Brandt & Derek Haas; based on a short story by Elmore Leonard
Directed by James Mangold

40 YEAR OLD VIRGIN (THE) - Written by Judd Apatow and Steve Carell
Directed by Judd Apatow

48 HOURS - Written by Robert Spottiswoode and Walter hill & Larry Gross and Steven E. de Souza
Directed by Walter Hill

A BEAUTIFUL MIND (2001) - Written by Akiva Goldsman, based on the novel by Sylvia Nasar.
Directed by Ron Howard

ABSENCE OF MALICE (1981) - Written by Kurt Luedtke
Directed by Sydney Pollack

A CLOCKWORK ORANGE (1971) - Written by Stanley Kubrick, based on the novel by Anthony Burgess
Directed by Stanley Kubrick

ADVENTURES OF PLUTO NASH (THE)(2002) - Written by Neil Cuthbert
Directed by Ron Underwood

A FAREWELL TO ARMS - Screenplay by Benjamin Glazer and Oliver H.P. Garrett, based on the novel by Ernest Hemmingway
Directed by Frank Vorzage

I

A FEW GOOD MEN (1992) - Written by Aaron Sorkin (from his play)
Directed by Rob Reiner

AIRPLANE - Screenplay by Jim Abrahams & David Zucker & Jerry Zucker
Directed by Jim Abrahams and David Zucker and Jerry Zucker

AIRPORT (1970) - Written by George Seaton, based on the novel by Arthur Hailey
Directed by George Seaton

ALICE IN WONDERLAND (2010)- Written by Linda Woolverton, based on the novel by Lewis Carrol
Directed by Tim Burton

ALIEN (1979) - Story by Dan O'Bannon and Ronald Shusett, Screenplay by Dan O'Bannon
Directed by Ridley Scott

ALL THE PRESIDENT'S MEN (1976) - Written by William Goldman, based on the book by Carl Bernstein & Bob Woodward.
Directed by Alan J. Pakula

ALL QUIET ON THE WESTERN FRONT (1930) - Screenplay by George Abbott, based on the novel "Im Westen nicht Neues" by Erich Maria Remarque.
Directed by Lewis Milestone

ALMOST FAMOUS - Written by Cameron Crowe
Directed by Cameron Crowe

AMERICAN BEAUTY - Written by Alan Ball
Directed by Sam Mendes

AMERICANIZATION OF EMILY (THE) - Screenplay by Paddy Chayefsky, based on the novel by William Bradford Huie
Directed by Arthur Hiller

AMERICAN GRAFFITI (1973) - Written by George Lucas and Gloria Katz & Willard Huyck

Directed by George Lucas

AMERICAN PIE (1999) - Written by Adam Herz
Directed by Paul Weitz

A MIGHTY WIND (2003) - Written by Christopher Guest and Eugene Levy
Directed by Christopher Guest

AND JUSTICE FOR ALL (1980) - Written by Valerie Curtin and Barry Levinson
Directed by Norman Jewison

ANIMAL HOUSE (1978) - Written by Harold Ramis & Douglas Kenney & Chris Miller
Directed by John Landis

ANNIE HALL (1977)- Written by Woody Allen and Marshall Brickman
Directed by Woody Allen

APARTMENT (THE) (1960)- Written by Billy Wilder and I.A.L. Diamond
Directed by Billy Wilder

APOCALYPSE NOW (1979)- Written by John Milius and Francis Ford Coppola, based on the novel "Heart of Darkness" by Joseph Conrad
Directed by Francis Ford Coppola

ARGO - Based on the Wired Magazine article "The Great Escape," also based on a selection from "The Master of Disguise," by Antonia J. Mendez.
Screenplay by Chris Terrio
Directed by Ben Affleck

ARMAGEDDON - Story by Robert Roy Pool and Jonathan Hensleigh, Screenplay by Jonathon Hensleigh and J.J. Abrams
Directed by Michael Bay

A STAR IS BORN (1954) - Story by William A. Wellman and Robert Carson, Screenplay by Moss Hart and Dorothy Parker & Alan Campbell & Robert Carson

Directed by George Cukor

ARTHUR - Written by Steve Gordon
Directed by Steve Gordon

AVATAR - Written by James Cameron
Directed by James Cameron

AVENGERS (THE) - Story by Zac Penn and Joss Whedon, Screenplay by Joss Whedon
Directed by Joss Whedon

BABE - Screenplay by George Miller & Chris Noonan, based on the novel "The Sheep Pig" by Dick King-Smith
Directed by Chris Noonan

BASIC INSTINCT - Written by Joe Eszterhas
Directed by Paul Verhoeven

BATMAN - Story by Sam Hamm, Screenplay by Sam Hamm and Warren Skaaren, based on characters Created by Bob Kane
Directed by Tim Burton

BATTLEFIELD EARTH: A Saga of the Year 300 - Screenplay by Corey Mandell and J.D. Shapiro, based on the novel by L. Ron Hubbard
Directed by Roger Christian

BEETLEJUICE - Story by Michael McDowell & Larry Wilson, Screenplay by Michael McDowell and Warren Skaaren
Directed by Tim Burton

BLAZING SADDLES - Story by Andrew Bergman, Screenplay by Mel Brooks & Norman Steinberg & Andrew Bergman & Richard Pryor & Alan Uger
Directed by Mel Brooks

BUTCH CASSIDY AND THE SUNDANCE KID - Screenplay by William Goldman
Directed by George Roy Hill

BEING JOHN MALKOVIC - Written by Charlie Kaufman
Directed by Spike Jonze

BEING THERE - Screenplay by Jerry Kosinski, based on his novel
Directed by Hal Ashby

BEVERLY HILLS COP - Story by Danilo Bach and Daniel Petrie, Jr. Screenplay by Daniel Petrie, Jr.
Directed by Martin Brest

BIG CHILL (THE) - Written by Lawrence Kasdan and Barbara Benedek
Directed by Lawrence Kasdan

BIRDS (THE) - Written by Evan Hunter, based on the novel by Daphne Du Maurier
Directed by Alfred Hitchcock

BLADE RUNNER - Written by Hampton Fancher and David Peoples, based on the novel by Philip K. Dick
Directed by Ridley Scott

BLAIR WITCH PROJECT (THE) - Written by Daniel Myrick and Eduardo Sanchez
Directed by Daniel Myrick and Eduardo Sanchez

BLAZING SADDLES - Screenplay by Mel Brooks & Norman Steinberg & Andrew Bergman & Richard Prior & Alan Uger
Directed by Mel Brooks

BLOOD DIAMOND - Story by Charles Leavitt and C. Gaby Mitchell, Screenplay by Charles Leavitt
Directed by Edward Zwick

BLUE VELVET - Screenplay by David Lynch
Directed by David Lynch

BOURNE IDENTITY (THE) - Screenplay by Tony Gilroy and William Blake Herron, based on the novel by Robert Ludlum
Directed by Doug Limon

BRAVEHEART - Written by Randall Wallace
Directed by Mel Gibson

BRAVE ONE (THE) - Story by Roderick Taylor & Bruce A. Taylor, Screenplay by Roderick Taylor & Bruce A. Tayler and Cynthia Mort

Directed by Neil Jordan

BREAKFAST AT TIFFANY'S - Screenplay by George Axelrod, based on the novel by Truman Capote
Directed by Blake Edwards

BREAKFAST CLUB (THE) - Written by John Hughes
Directed by John Hughes

BRIGHT LIGHTS, BIG CITY - Written by Jay McInerney, based on his novel
Directed by James Bridges

BULLITT - Written by Alan Trustman and Harry Kleiner, based on the novel "Mute Witness," by Robert L. Fish
Directed by Peter Yates

CANDIDATE (THE) - Written by Jeremy Larner
Directed by Michael Ritchie

CASABLANCA - Written by Julius J. Epstein and Philip G. Epstein and Howard Koch, based on the play "Everybody Comes To Rick's," by Murray Burnett and Joan Alison
Directed by Michael Curtiz

CAST AWAY - Written by William Broyles, Jr.
Directed by Robert Zemeckis

CATCH 22 - Written by Buck Henry, based on the novel by Joseph Heller
Directed by Mike Nichols

CHARADE - Story by Peter Stone and Marc Behm, Screenplay by Peter Stone
Directed by Stanley Donen

CHICAGO - Written by Bill Condon, from the musical play by Bob Fosse and Fred Ebb
Directed by Rob Marshall

CHINATOWN – Written by Robert Towne
Directed by Roman Polanski

CITIZEN KANE - Written by Herman J. Manciewicz and Orson Welles

Directed by Orson Welles

CLERKS - Written by Kevin Smith
Directed by Kevin Smith

CLOSE ENCOUNTERS OF THE THIRD KIND - Written by Steven Spielberg
Directed by Steven Spielberg

COAL MINER'S DAUGHTER - Written by Thomas Rickman, based on the autobiography by Loretta Lynn and George Vecsey
Directed by Michael Apted

COLOR OF MONEY (THE) - Screenplay by Richard Price, based on the novel by Walter Tevis
Directed by Martin Scorsese

CRANK - Screenplay by Mark Neveldine and Brian Taylor
Directed by Mark Neveldine and Brian Taylor

CRAZY HEART - Written by Scott Cooper, based on the novel by Thomas Cobb
Directed by Scott Cooper

CROCODILE DUNDEE - Story by Paul Hogan, Screenplay by John Cornell and Paul Hogan and Ken Shadie
Directed by Peter Faiman

CRYING GAME (THE) - Written by Neil Jordan
Directed by Neil Jordan

CUJO - Screenplay by Don Carlos Dunaway & Lauren Curriers, from the novel by Stephen King
Directed by Lewis Teague

DARK KNIGHT RISES (THE) - Story by Christopher Noland & David S. Goyer, Screenplay by Jonathon Nolan and Christopher Nolan
"Batman" character created by Bob Kane
Directed by Christopher Nolan

DATE NIGHT - Written by Josh Klausner
Directed by Shawn Levy

DAVE - Written by Gary Ross
Directed by Ivan Reitman

DA VINCI CODE (THE) - Written by Akiva Goldsman, based on the novel by Dan Brown
Directed by Ron Howard

DAY THE EARTH STOOD STILL (THE) (1951) - Story by Harry Bates, Screenplay by Edmund H. North
Directed by Robert Wise

DAYS OF WINE AND ROSES - Written by J.P. Miller
Directed by Blake Edwards

DEATH WISH - Screenplay by Wendell Mayes, based on the novel by Brian Garfield
Directed by Michael Winner

DEPARTED (THE) – Screenplay by William Monahan
Directed by Martin Scorsese

DIE HARD - Screenplay by Jeb Stuart and Steven E. de Souza, based on the novel "Nothing Lasts Forever," by Roderick Thorp
Directed by John McTiernan

DIRTY DOZEN (THE) - Screenplay by Nunnally Johnson and Lukas Heller, based on the novel by E.M. Nathanson
Directed by Robert Aldrich

DIRTY HARRY - Screenplay by Harry Julian Fink & R.M. Fink and Dean Riesner
Directed by Don Siegel

DJANGO UNCHAINED - Written by Quentin Tarantino
Directed by Quentin Tarantino

DOORS (THE) - Written by Randall Jahnson and Oliver Stone
Directed by Oliver Stone

DRIVING MISS DAISY - Written by Alfred Uhry, based on his play
Directed by Bruce Beresford

DR. STRANGELOVE or: How I Learned to Stop Worrying and Love the Bomb - Screenplay by Stanley Kubrick & Terry Southern & Peter George, based on the novel "Red Alert," by Peter George
Directed by Stanley Kubrick

DR. ZHIVAGO - Screenplay by Robert Bolt, from the novel by Boris Pasternak
Directed by David Lean

DUMB AND DUMBER - Written by Peter Farrelly & Peter Yellin & Bobby Farrelly
Directed by Peter Farrelly

EARTHQUAKE - Written by George Fox and Mario Puzo
Directed by Mark Robson

EARTH VS THE FLYING SAUCERS - Screen Story by Curt Siodmak, Screenplay by George Worthing Yates & Bernard Gordon, based on the novel "Flying Saucers from Outer Space," by Major Donald E. Keyhoe
Directed by Fred F. Sears

EL MARIACHI - Written by Robert Rodriguez
Directed by Robert Rodriguez

ERIN BROCKOVICH - Written by Susan Grant
Directed by Steven Soderbergh

ESCAPE FROM ALCATRAZ - Screenplay by Richard Tuggle, from the book by J. Campbell Bruce
Directed by Don Siegel

ESCAPE FROM WILDCAT CANYON - Written by Robert Gosnell
Directed by Mark Voizard

EVIL DEAD (1981) - Written by Sam Raimi
Directed by Sam Raimi

EXPENDABLES (THE) - Story by David Callaham, Screenplay by David Callaham and Sylvester Stallone
Directed by Sylvester Stallone

FARGO - Written by Ethan Coen and Joel Coen

Directed by Joel Coen

FAST TIMES AT RIDGEMONT HIGH - Written by Cameron Crowe, based on his book
Directed by Amy Heckerling

FIELD OF DREAMS - Screenplay by Phil Alden Robinson, from the book by W.P. Kinsella
Directed by Phil Alden Robinson

FINDING NEMO - Story by Andrew Stanton, Screenplay by Andrew Stanton & Bob Peterson & David Reynolds
Directed by Andrew Stanton, Co-directed by Lee Unkrich

FIRST BLOOD - Screenplay by Michael Kozoll & William Sackheim and Sylvester Stallone
Directed by Ted Kotcheff

FOOL'S GOLD - Story by John Claflin & Daniel Zelman, Screenplay by John Claflin & Daniel Zelman and Andy Tennant
Directed by Andy Tennant

FORREST GUMP - Screenplay by Eric Roth, based on the novel by Winston Groom
Directed by Robert Zemeckis

FRANKENSTEIN (1931) - Screenplay by Garret Fort and Francis Edward Faragoh, adapted from the play by Peggy Webling, based on the novel by Mary Shelly, based on the composition by John Balderman
Directed by James Whale

FRANCIS, THE TALKING MULE - Written by David Stern, based on his novel
Directed by Arthur Lubin

FRENCH CONNECTION (THE) - Screenplay by Ernest Tidyman, based on the novel by Robin Moore
Directed by William Friedken

FRISCO KID (THE) - Written by Michael Elias and Frank Shaw
Directed by Robert Aldrich

FUGITIVE (THE) - Story by David Twohy, Screenplay by Jeb Stuart and David Twohy
Directed by Andrew Davis

FULL METAL JACKET - Screenplay by Stanley Kubrick & Michael Herr & Gustav Hasford, based on the novel "The Short Timers," by Gustav Hasford
Directed by Stanley Kubrick

GANDHI - Written by John Briley
Directed by Richard Attenborough

GHOST AND THE DARKNESS (THE) - Written by William Goldman
Directed by Stephen Hopkins

GIGI - Screenplay by Alan Jay Lerner, from the novel by Colette
Directed by Vincente Minnelli

GIGLI - Written by Martin Brest
Directed by Martin Brest

GIRL WITH THE DRAGON TATTOO (THE) - Screenplay by Steven Zaillian, from the novel by Stieg Larsson
Directed by David Fincher

GLADIATOR - Story by David Franzoni, Screenplay by David Franzoni and John Logan and William Nicholson
Directed by Ridley Scott

GODFATHER (THE) – Screenplay by Mario Puzo and Francis Ford Coppola, from the novel by Mario Puzo
Directed by Francis Ford Coppola

GOING IN STYLE - Story by Edward Cannon, Screenplay by Martin Brest
Directed by Martin Brest

GONE WITH THE WIND - Screenplay by Sidney Howard, based on the novel by Margaret Mitchell
Directed by Victor Fleming

GOODFELLAS – Screenplay by Nicholas Pileggi & Martin Scorsese, from the novel "Wiseguy" by Nicholas Pileggi

Directed by Martin Scorsese

GOOD WILL HUNTING - Written by Matt Damon & Ben Affleck
Directed by Gus Van Sant

GRADUATE (THE) - Screenplay by Calder Willingham and Buck Henry, based on the novel by Charles Webb
Directed by Mike Nichols

GREAT ESCAPE (THE) - Screenplay by James Clavell and W. R. Burnett, based on the novel by Paul Brickhill
Directed by John Sturges

THE GUARD - Written by John Michael McDonagh
Directed by John Michael McDonagh

GUESS WHO'S COMING TO DINNER - Written by William Rose
Directed by Stanley Kramer

HALLOWEEN - Screenplay by John Carpenter and Debra Hill
Directed by John Carpenter

HANGOVER (THE)- Written by John Lucas and Scott Moore
Directed by Todd Phillips

HARRY POTTER AND THE SOURCERER'S STONE - Screenplay by Steve Kloves, based on the novel by J.K. Rowling
Directed by Chris Columbus

HELP (THE) - Screenplay by Tate Taylor, based on the novel by Kathryn Stockett
Directed by Tate Taylor

HIGH NOON - Screenplay by Carl Foreman, based on the magazine story "The Tin Star," by John W. Cunningham
Directed by Fred Zinnemann

HOMEWARD BOUND, THE INCREDIBLE JOURNEY - Screenplay by Caroline Thompson and Linda Woolverton, based on the novel "The Incredible Journey," by Sheila Bum-

ford
Directed by Duwayne Dunham

HONEY, I SHRUNK THE KIDS - Story by Stuart Gordon & Brian Yuzna & Ed Naha, Screenplay by Ed Naha and Tom Schulman
Directed by Joe Johnston

HOT SHOTS - Screenplay by Jim Abrahams and Pat Proft
Directed by Jim Abrahams

HOT TUB TIME MACHINE - Story by Josh Heald, Screenplay by Josh Heald and Sean Anders & John Morris
Directed by Steve Pink

HOWARD THE DUCK - Written by Willard Huyck & Gloria Katz, based on the character "Howard the Duck," created by Steve Gerber
Directed by Willard Huyck

HOW TO STEAL A MILLION - Story by George Bradshaw, Screenplay by Harry Kurnitz
Directed by William Wyler

HUD - Screenplay by Irving Ravetch and Harriet Frank Jr., based on the novel "Horseman, Pass By," by Larry McMurtry
Directed by Martin Ritt

HUDSON HAWK - Story by Bruce Willis & Robert Kraft, Screenplay by Steven E. de Souza and Robert Kraft
Directed by Michael Lehmann

HUNGER GAMES (THE) - Screenplay by Gary Ross and Suzanne Collins and Billy Ray, based on the novel by Suzanne Collins
Directed by Gary Ross

HURT LOCKER - Written by Mark Boal
Directed by Kathryn Bigelow

HUSTLER (THE) - Written by Sydney Carroll and Robert Rossen, based on the novel by Walter S. Tevis
Directed by Robert Rossen

ICE AGE - Story by Michael J. Wilson, Screenplay by

Michael Berg and Michael J. Wilson and Peter Ackerman
Directed by Chris Wedge, Co-directed by Carlos Saldanha

IMPOSSIBLE (THE) - Story by Maria Belon, Screenplay by Sergio G. Sanchez
Directed by J.A. Bayona

I KNOW WHAT YOU DID LAST SUMMER - Screenplay by Kevin Williamson, based on the novel by Lois Duncan
Directed by Jim Gillespie

IN BRUGES - Written by Martin McDonagh
Directed by Martin McDonagh

INGLOURIOUS BASTERDS - Written by Quentin Tarantino
Directed by Quentin Tarantino

INSIDER (THE) - Written by Eric Roth & Michael Mann, based on the article "The Man Who Knew Too Much," by Marie Brenner
Directed by Michael Mann

IN HARM'S WAY - Screenplay by Wendell Mayes, based on the novel by James Bassett
Directed by Otto Preminger

INHERIT THE WIND - Screenplay by Nedrick Young and Harold Jacob Smith, based on the play by Jerome Lawrence and Robert E. Lee
Directed by Stanley Kramer

INTO THE WILD - Screenplay by Sean Penn, based on the novel by Jon Krakauer
Directed by Sean Penn

INVASION OF THE BODY SNATCHERS - Screenplay by W.D. Richter, from the novel by Jack Finney
Directed by Philip Kaufman

IRON MAN - Screenplay by Mark Fergus & Hawk Ostby and Art Marcum & Matt Holloway
Directed by Jon Favreau

ISHTAR - Written by Elaine May
Directed by Elaine May

IT'S A MAD, MAD, MAD, MAD WORLD - Story by William Rose and Tania Rose, Screenplay by William Rose and Tania Rose
Directed by Stanley Kramer

IT HAPPENED ONE NIGHT - Screenplay by Robert Riskin, based on the short story by Samuel Hopkins Adams
Directed by Frank Capra

JAWS - Screenplay by Peter Benchley and Carl Gottlieb, based on the novel by Peter Benchley
Directed by Steven Spielberg

JEREMIAH JOHNSON - Screenplay by John Milius and Edward Anhalt, based on the story "Crow Killer," by Raymond W. Thorp and Robert Bunker, and the novel "Mountain Man," by Vardis Fisher
Directed by Sydney Pollack

JERRY MAGUIRE - Written by Cameron Crowe
Directed by Cameron Crowe

JUDGEMENT AT NUREMBURG - Written by Abby Mann
Directed by Stanley Kramer

JUMANJI - Story by Jim Taylor and Greg Taylor & Jim Strain, Screenplay by Jonathan Hensleigh and Greg Taylor & Jim Strain
Directed by Joe Johnston

KARATE KID (1984) - Written by Robert Mark Kamen
Directed by John G. Avildsen

KELLY'S HEROES - Written by Troy Kennedy-Martin
Directed by Brian G. Hutton

KILL BILL - Written by Quentin Tarantino
Directed by Quentin Tarantino

KING'S SPEECH (THE) - Screenplay by David Seidler
Directed by Tom Hooper

KRAMER VS KRAMER - Screenplay by Robert Benton, based on the novel by Avery Corman
Directed by Robert Benton

LADY SINGS THE BLUES - Screenplay by Chris Clark and Suzanne De Passe and Terence McCloy, based on the novel by William Duffy and Billie Holiday
Directed by Sydney J. Furie

LAND OF THE LOST - Written by Chris Henchy & Dennis McNicholas
Directed by Brad Silberling

LASSIE COME HOME - Screenplay by Hugo Butler, based on the novel by Eric Knight
Directed by Fred M. Wilcox

LAST KING OF SCOTLAND (THE) - Screenplay by Peter Morgan and Jeremy Brock, based on the novel by Giles Foden
Directed by Kevin Macdonald

LAST STARFIGHTER (THE) - Written by Jonathan R. Betuel
Directed by Nick Castle

LAST TANGO IN PARIS - Story by Bernardo Bertolucci. Screenplay by Bernardo Bertolucci and Franco Arcalli
Directed by Bernardo Bertolucci

LAWRENCE OF ARABIA - Screenplay by Robert Bolt and Michael Wilson, based on the writings of T.E. Lawrence
Directed by David Lean

LEAVING LAS VEGAS - Screenplay by Mike Figgis, based on the novel by John O'Brien
Directed by Mike Figgis

LEGALLY BLOND - Screenplay by Karen McCullah Lutz & Kirstin Smith, based on the novel by Amanda Brown
Directed by Robert Luketic

LES MISERABLES - Screenplay by William Nicholson & Alain Boubilil and Claude-Michel Schonberg & Herbert Kretzmer
Directed by Tom Hooper

LETHAL WEAPON - Written by Shane Black

Directed by Richard Donner

LIBRARIAN, QUEST FOR THE SPEAR (THE) - Written by David M. Titcher
Directed by Peter Winther

LIFE OF BRIAN (THE) - Written by Graham Chapman & John Cleese & Terry Gilliam & Eric Idle & Terry Jones & Michael Palin
Directed by Terry Jones

LINCOLN - Screenplay by Tony Kushner, based on the book "Team of Rivals," by Doris Kearns Goodwin
Directed by Steven Spielberg.

LION KING (THE) - Screenplay by Irene Mecchi and Jonathan Roberts and Linda Woolverton
Directed by Roger Allers and Rob Minkoff

LITTLE CAESAR – Screenplay by Robert Edward Faragoh, based on the novel by W.R. Burnett.
Directed by Mervyn LeRoy

LITTLE MISS SUNSHINE - Written by Michael Arndt
Directed by Jonathan Dayton and Valerie Faris

LITTLE WOMEN - Screenplay by Robin Swicord, based on the novel by Louisa May Alcott
Directed by Gillian Armstrong

LONE RANGER (THE) - Story and Screenplay by Justin Haythe and Ted Elliot & Terry Rossio
Directed by Gore Verbinski

LONGEST DAY (THE) - Screenplay by Cornelius Ryan, based on his novel. Additional episodes written by Romain Gary & James Jones & David Pursall & Jack Seddon.
Directed by Ken Annakin (British exterior episodes) Andrew Marton (American exterior episodes) Bernard Wicki (German episodes)

MAGNIFICENT SEVEN (THE)- Screenplay by William Roberts, based on the film "Seven Samurai," written by Akira Kurosawa & Shinobu Hashimoto & Hideo Oguni

Directed by John Sturges

MALTESE FALCON (THE) - Screenplay by John Huston, based on the novel by Dashiell Hammett
Directed by John Huston

MAN WITH THE GOLDEN ARM (THE) - Screenplay by Walter Newman and Lewis Meltzer, based on the novel by Nelson Algren
Directed by Otto Preminger

MAN WHO WOULD BE KING (THE) - Screenplay by John Huston and Gladys Hill, based on the story by Rudyard Kipling
Directed by John Huston

MARS ATTACKS - Screen story by Johnathan Gems, Screenplay by Johnathon Gems, based on the trading card series by Len Brown & Woody Gelman & Wally Wood & Bob Powell & Norm Saunders
Directed by Tim Burton

M*A*S*H - Screenplay by Ring Lardner, based on the book "MASH: A Novel About Three Army Doctors" by Richard Hooker
Directed by Robert Altman.

MEANING OF LIFE (THE) - Written by Graham Chapman & John Cleese & Terry Gilliam & Eric Idle & Terry Jones & Michael Palin
Directed by Terry Jones & Terry Gilliam (Animation Sequences)

MEN IN BLACK - Story by Ed Solomon, Screenplay by Ed Solomon, based on the comic book series by Lowell Cunningham
Directed by Barry Sonnenfeld

MIDNIGHT COWBOY - Screenplay by Waldo Salt, based on the novel by James Leo Herlihy
Directed by John Schlesinger

MILK - Written by Dustin Lance Black
Directed by Gus Van Sant

MOBY DICK - Screenplay by Ray Bradbury & John Huston, based on the novel by Herman Melville
Directed by John Huston

MONTY PYTHON IN SEARCH OF THE HOLY GRAIL - Written by Graham Chapman & John Cleese & Eric Idle & Terry Gilliam & Terry Jones & Michael Palin
Directed by Terry Gilliam and Terry Jones

MOONSTRUCK - Written by John Patrick Shanley
Directed by Norman Jewison

MR. SMITH GOES TO WASHINGTON - Story by Lewis R. Foster, Screenplay by Sidney Buchman
Directed by Frank Capra

MUSIC MAN (THE) - Screenplay by Marion Hargrove, based on the play by Meredith Wilson and Frank Lacey
Directed by Morton DaCosta

MY BIG, FAT GREEK WEDDING - Written by Nia Vardalos
Directed by Joel Zwick

MY COUSIN VINNIE - Written by Dale Launer
Directed by Johnathan Lynn

MY FAIR LADY - Screenplay by Alan J. Lerner, from his musical play, based on the play "Pygmalion," by George Bernard Shaw
Directed by George Cukor

1984 - Screenplay by Michael Radford, based on the novel by George Orwell
Directed by Michael Radford

NAKED GUN, FROM THE FILES OF POLICE SQUAD - Written by Jerry Zucker & Jim Abrahams & David Zucker & Pat Proft
Directed by David Zucker

NAPOLEON DYNAMITE - Written by Jared Hess & Jerusha Hess
Directed by Jared Hess

NATIONAL TREASURE - Story by Jim Kouf & Orin Aviv &

Charles Segers, Screenplay by Jim Kouf and Cormac Wibberley & Marianne Wibberley
Directed by John Turteltaub

NEVER CRY WOLF - Screenplay by Curtis Hanson and Sam Hamm and Richard Kletter, based on the book by Farley Mowat
Directed by Carroll Ballard

NEVER SAY NEVER AGAIN - Story by Ian Fleming & Kevin McClory &
Jack Whittingham, Screenplay by Lorenzo Semple Jr.
Directed by Irvin Kershner

NIGHT AT THE MUSEUM - Story and Screenplay by Robert Ben Garant & Thomas Lennon, based on the novel by Milan Trenc
Directed by Shawn Levy

NIGHT OF THE GRIZZLY - Written by Warren Douglas
Directed by Joseph Pevney

NIGHTMARE ON ELM STREET - Written by Wes Craven
Directed by Wes Craven

NOBODY'S FOOL - Screenplay by Robert Benton, based on the novel by Richard Russo
Directed by Robert Benton

NORTH BY NORTHWEST - Written by Ernest Lehman
Directed by Alfred Hitchcock

NOW YOU SEE ME - Story by Boaz Yakin & Edward Ricourt, Screenplay by Ed Solomon and Boaz Yakin & Edward Ricourt
Directed by Louis Leterrier

OCEAN'S ELEVEN - (1960) Story by George Clayton Johnson & Jack Golden Russel, Screenplay by Harry Brown & Charles Lederer
Directed by Lewis Milestone

OCEAN'S ELEVEN - (2001) Screenplay by Ted Griffin, based on the 1960 story and screenplay.

Directed by Steven Soderbergh

ODYSSEY (THE) - Greek mythology, written by Homer

OKLAHOMA - Screenplay by Sonya Levian and William Ludwig, adapted from the musical play by Richard Rogers and Oscar Hammerstein
Directed by Fred Zinnemann

OLD SCHOOL - Story by Court Crandall & Todd Phillips & Scot Armstrong, Screenplay by Todd Phillips & Scot Armstrong
Directed by Todd Phillips

PARANORMAL ACTIVITY - Written by Oren Peli
Directed by Oren Peli

PATTON - Story by Francis Ford Coppola and Edmund H. North, Screenplay by Francis Ford Coppola and Edmund H. North, based on the books "Patton: Ordeal and Triumph," by Ladislas Farago and "A Soldier's Story," by Omar N. Bradley
Directed by Franklin J. Schaffner

PERFECT STORM (THE) - Screenplay by Willam D. Wittliff, based on the novel by Sebastian Junger
Directed by Wolfgang Peterson

PHILADELPHIA - Written by Ron Nyswaner
Directed by Johnathan Demme

PHILADELPHIA STORY (THE) - Screenplay by Donald Ogden Stewart, based on the play by Phillip Barry. Contributing writer Waldo Salt (uncredited)
Directed by George Cukor

PINK PANTHER (THE) - Screenplay by Maurice Richland and Blake Edwards
Directed by Blake Edwards

PIRATES OF THE CARIBBEAN: THE CURSE OF THE BLACK PEARL - Story by Ted Elliott & Terry Rosso and Stuart Beattie & Jay Wolpert, Screenplay by Ted Elliott & Terry Rosso
Directed by Gore Verbinski

PLANET OF THE APES (1968) - Screenplay by Michael Wilson & Rod Serling, based on the novel by Pierre Boulle
Directed by Franklin J. Schaffner

PLATOON - Written by Oliver Stone
Directed by Oliver Stone

PORKY'S - Written by Bob Clark
Directed by Bob Clark

POSTMAN (THE) - Screenplay by Eric Roth and Brian Helgeland, based on the novel by David Brin
Directed by Kevin Kostner

PRETTY WOMAN - Written by J. F. Lawton
Directed by Garry Marshall

PRINCESS BRIDE (THE) - Screenplay by William Goldman, based on his novel
Directed by Rob Reiner

PRIZZI'S HONOR - Screenplay by Richard Condon and Janet Roach, from the novel by Richard Condon
Directed by John Huston

PROFESSIONALS (THE) - Screenplay by Richard Brooks, based on the novel by Frank O'Rourke
Directed by Richard Brooks

PSYCHO (1960) - Screenplay by Joseph Stefano, based on the novel by Robert Bloch
Directed by Alfred Hitchcock

PUBLIC ENEMY (THE) – Written by Kubec Glasmon and John Bright, Screen adaptation by Harvey F. Thew
Directed by William A. Wellman

PULP FICTION - Story by Quentin Tarantino & Roger Avary, Screenplay by Quentin Tarantino
Directed by Quentin Tarantino

RAIDERS OF THE LOST ARK - Story by George Lucas and Philip Kaufman, Screenplay by Lawrence Kasdan
Directed by Steven Spielberg

RAIN MAN - Story by Barry Morrow, Screenplay by Ronald Bass and Barry Morrow
Directed by Barry Levinson

RAMBO - Written by Sylvester Stallone and Art Monterastelli
Directed by Sylvester Stallone

RED DAWN - Story by Kevin Reynolds, Screenplay by John Milius and Keven Reynolds
Directed by John Milius

REDS - Written by Warren Beatty & Trevor Griffiths
Directed by Warren Beatty

RESERVOIR DOGS - Written by Quentin Tarantino
Directed by Quentin Tarantino

ROBIN HOOD: MEN IN TIGHTS - Story by J.D. Shapiro & Evan Chandler, Screenplay by Mel Brooks & Evan Chandler & J.D. Shapiro
Directed by Mel Brooks

ROCKY - Written by Sylvester Stallone
Directed by John G. Avildsen

ROMANCING THE STONE - Written by Diane Thomas
Directed by Robert Zemeckis

ROSE (THE) - Story by Bill Kirby, Screenplay by Bo Goldman
Directed by Mark Rydell

RUSSIANS ARE COMING, THE RUSSIANS ARE COMING (THE) - Screenplay by William Rose, based on the novel by Nathaniel Benchley
Directed by Norman Jewison

SAHARA - Screenplay by Thomas Dean Donnely & Joshua Oppenheimer and John C. Richards and James V. Hart
Directed by Breck Eisner

SAVING PRIVATE RYAN - Written by Robert Rodat
Directed by Steven Spielberg

SAW - Story by James Wan and Leigh Whannell, Screenplay by Leigh Whannell
Directed by James Wan

SCARFACE – Screen Story by Ben Hecht, from the novel by Armitage Trail
Directed by Howard Hawks and Richard Rosson

SCARY MOVIE - Written by Shawn Wayans & Marlon Wayans & Buddy Johnson & Phil Beauman and Jason Friedberg & Aaron Seltzer
Directed by Keenen Ivory Wayans

SCHINDLER'S LIST - Screenplay by Steven Zaillian, based on the novel by Thomas Keneally
Directed by Steven Spielberg

SCREAM - Written by Kevin Williamson
Directed by Wes Craven

SEE NO EVIL, HEAR NO EVIL - Story by Earl Barret & Arne Sultan & Marvin Worth, Screenplay by Earl Barrett & Arne Sultan and Eliot Wald & Andrew Kurtzman and Gene Wilder
Directed by Arthur Hiller

SEX, LIES AND VIDEOTAPE - Written by Steven Soderbergh
Directed by Steven Soderbergh

SHANE - Screenplay by A.B. Guthrie, Jr., Additonal dialogue by Jack Sher, based on a novel by Jack Schaefer
Directed by George Stevens

SHAWN OF THE DEAD - Written by Simon Pegg and Edgar Wright
Directed by Edgar Wright

SHE'S GOTTA HAVE IT - Written by Spike Lee
Directed by Spike Lee

SILENCE OF THE LAMBS - Screenplay by Ted Talley, based on the novel by Thomas Harris
Directed by Jonathan Demme

SILVER LININGS PLAYBOOK - Screenplay by David O.

Russell, from the novel by Matthew Quick
Directed by David O. Russell

SISTER ACT - Written by Joseph Howard
Directed by Emile Ardolino

SNAKES ON A PLANE - Story by David Dalessandro and John Heffeman Screenplay by John Heffeman and Sebastian Gutierrez
Directed by David R. Ellis

SIXTH SENSE (THE) - Written by M. Night Shyamalan
Directed by M. Night Shyamalan

SLEEPLESS IN SEATTLE - Story by Jeff Arch, Screenplay by Nora Ephron and David S. Ward and Jeff Arch
Directed by Nora Ephron

SLUMDOG MILLIONAIRE - Screenplay by Simon Beaufoy, based on the novel by Vikus Swarup
Directed by Danny Boyle and Lovleen Tandan

SOUND OF MUSIC (THE)- Screenplay by Ernest Lehman, based on the book by Howard Lindsay & Russel Crouse
Directed by Robert Wise

SPEED - Written by Graham Yost
Directed by Jan de Bont

SPEEDRACER - Written by Andy Wachowski and Lana Wachowski, based on the animated series "Speed Racer," by Tatsuo Yoshida
Directed by The Wachowski Brothers

SPIDERMAN - Screenplay by David Koepp, based on the comic book by Stan Lee and Steve Ditko
Directed by Sam Raimi

STAGECOACH (1939) - Story by Ernest Haycox, Screenplay by Dudley Nichols
Directed by John Ford

STAND BY ME - Screenplay by Raynold Gideon & Bruce A. Evans, based on the novella "The Body," by Stephen King
Directed by Rob Reiner

STAR WARS - Written by George Lucas
Directed by George Lucas

STING (THE) - Written by David S. Ward
Directed by George Roy Hill

STIR CRAZY - Written by Bruce J. Friedman
Directed by Sidney Poitier

SUNSET BOULEVARD - Written by Charles Brackett & Billy Wilder & D.M. Marshman Jr.
Directed by Billy Wilder

SUPERMAN - Story by Mario Puzo, Screenplay by Mario Puzo and David Newman and Leslie Newman & Robert Benton, based on the character created by Jerry Siegel & Joe Shuster
Directed by Richard Donner

SWISS FAMILY ROBINSON - Screenplay by Lowell S. Hawley, based on the novel by Johan Davin Wyss
Directed by Ken Annakin

10 - Written by Blake Edwards
Directed by Blake Edwards

TERMINATOR (THE) - Written by James Cameron and Gale Ann-Hurd
Directed by James Cameron

TEXAS CHAINSAW MASSACRE - Written by Tobe Hooper and Kim Henkel
Directed by Tobe Hooper

THAT THING YOU DO - Written by Tom Hanks
Directed by Tom Hanks

THERE'S SOMETHING ABOUT MARY - Story by Ed Decter & John J. Strauss, Screenplay by Ed Decter & John J. Strauss and Peter Farrelly & Bobby Farrelly
Directed by Peter Farrelly & Bobby Farrelly

THERE WILL BE BLOOD - Screenplay by Paul Thomas Anderson, based on the novel by Upton Sinclair
Directed by Paul Thomas Anderson

THIN RED LINE (THE) - Screenplay by Terrence Malick, based on the novel by James Jones
Directed by Terrence Malick

THIS IS SPINAL TAP - Written by Christopher Guest & Michael McKean & Harry Shearer & Rob Reiner
Directed by Rob Reiner

THOMAS CROWNE AFFAIR (THE) (1968) - Written by Alan Trustman
Directed by Norman Jewison

THREE STOOGES (THE) - Written by Mike Cerrone and Bobby Farrelly and Peter Farrelly
Directed by Bobby Farrelly and Peter Farrelly

THROW MOMMA FROM THE TRAIN - Written by Stu Silver
Directed by Danny DeVito

TITANIC - Written by James Cameron
Directed by James Cameron

TO CATCH A THIEF - Screenplay by John Michael Hayes, based on the novel by David Dodge
Directed by Alfred Hitchcock

TO KILL A MOCKINGBIRD - Screenplay by Horton Foote, based on the novel by Harper Lee
Directed by Robert Mulligan

TOP GUN - Written by Jim Cash & Jack Epps Jr., inspired by the magazine article "Top Guns," by Ehud Yonay
Directed by Tony Scott

TOWER HEIST - Story by Adam Cooper & Bill Collage and Ted Griffin. Screenplay by Ted Griffin and Jeff Nathanson
Directed by Brett Ratner

TRADING PLACES - Written by Timothy Harris and Herschel Weingrod
Directed by John Landis

TROPIC THUNDER - Story by Ben Stiller & Justin Theroux, Screenplay by Ben Stiller & Justin Theroux and Etan Cohen

Directed by Ben Stiller

TRUE GRIT - Screenplay by Ethan Coen & Joel Coen, from the novel by Charles Portis
Directed by Ethan Coen and Joel Coen

TWELVE ANGRY MEN - Written by Reginald Rose
Directed by Sidney Lumet

TWISTER - Written by Michael Chrichton and Anne-Marie Martin
Directed by Jan de Bont

UNSTOPPABLE - Written by Mark Bomback
Directed by Tony Scott

UP IN SMOKE - Written by Tommy Chong & Cheech Marin
Directed by Lou Adler

USUAL SUSPECTS (THE) - Written by Christopher McQuarrie
Directed by Bryan Singer

VERDICT (THE) - Screenplay by David Mamet, based on the novel by Barry Reed
Directed by Sidney Lumet

VOLCANO - Story by Jerome Armstrong, Screenplay by Jerome Armstrong and Billy Ray
Directed by Mick Jackson

WAG THE DOG - Screenplay by Hilary Henkin and David Mamet, from the novel by Larry Beinhart
Directed by Barry Levinson

WAIT UNTIL DARK - Screenplay by Robert Carrington & Jane-Howard Carrington, from the play by Frederick Knott
Directed by Terence Young

WAR OF THE WORLDS (The) (1953) - Screenplay by Barre Lyndon, based on the novel by H.G. Wells
Directed by Byron Haskin

WALK THE LINE - Written by Gill Dennis & James Mangold, based on the books "Cash: The Autobiography," by

Johnny Cash and Patrick Carr and "Man in Black," by Johnny Cash
Directed by James Mangold

WALL STREET - Written by Stanley Weiser and Oliver Stone
Directed by Oliver Stone

WATERWORLD - Written by Peter Rader and David Twohy
Directed by Kevin Reynolds

WEDDING CRASHERS - Written by Steve Faber and Bob Fisher
Directed by David Dobkin

WE NEED TO TALK ABOUT KEVIN - Screenplay by Lynne Ramsay & Rory Kinnear
Directed by Lynne Ramsay

WHEN HARRY MET SALLY - Written by Nora Ephron
Directed by Rob Reiner

WHO'S AFRAID OF VIRGINIA WOOLF? - Screenplay by Ernest Lehman
Directed by Mike Nichols

WILD BUNCH (THE) - Story by Walon Green and Roy N. Sickner, Screenplay by Walon Green and Sam Peckinpah
Directed by Sam Peckinpah

WIZARD OF OZ (THE) - Screenplay by Noel Langley & Florence Ryerson & Edgar Allan Woolf, based on the novel by Frank L. Baum
Directed by Victor Fleming

WRESTLER (THE) - Written by Robert D. Siegel
Directed by Darren Oronofsky

YOUNG FRANKENSTEIN - Story by Gene Wilder and Mel Brooks, Screenplay by Gene Wilder and Mel Brooks, based on the novel "Frankenstein," by Mary Shelley
Directed by Mel Brooks

YOU'VE GOT MAIL - Screenplay by Nora Ephron & Delia Ephron, based on the play "Parfumerie," by Nikolaus Laszlo
Directed by Nora Ephron

The TV Shows:

ALL IN THE FAMILY - Developed by Norman Lear, based on the British sitcom, "Till Death Us Do Part," created by Johnny Speight

BABY MAKES FIVE - Alan Landsburg Productions, ABC TV

BARNEY MILLER - Created by Danny Arnold, Theodore J. Flicker and Chris Hayward

BECKER- Created by Dave Hackel

THE BOB NEWHART SHOW - Created by David Davis and Lorenzo Music.

CHEERS - Created by James Burrows, Glen Charles, Les Charles

COSBY SHOW (THE) - Created by Bill Cosby, Michael Leeson and Ed. Weinberger

CSI: CRIME SCENE INVESTIGATION - Created by Ann Donahue and Anthony E. Zuiker

CURB YOUR ENTHUSIASM - Created by Larry David

GHOST WHISPERER - Created by John Gray

ELEMENTARY - Created by Robert Doherty

HAPPY DAYS - Created by Garry Marshall

HOUSE M.D. - Created by David Shore

LAVERNE AND SHIRLEY - Created by Lowell Ganz, Garry Marshall and Mark Rothman.

LAW AND ORDER - Created by Dick Wolf

MARRIED WITH CHILDREN - Created by Ron Leavitt & Michael G. Moye

THE MARY TYLER MOORE SHOW - Created by James L. Brooks and Allan Burns.

M*A*S*H - Developed by Larry Gelbart, based on the film.

THE MENTALIST - Created by Bruno Heller

xxx

TAXI - Created by James L. Brooks, Stan Daniels, David Davis and Ed. Weinberger.

MEDIUM - Created by Glenn Gordon Caron

MONK - Created by Andy Breckman

MORK AND MINDY - Created by Joe Glauberg, Garry Marshall and Dale McRaven

MR. ED - Created by Walter Brooks

SEINFELD - Created by Larry David and Jerry Seinfeld

SHERLOCK - Created by Mark Gatiss and Steven Moffat

STAR TREK - Created by Gene Roddenberry

WKRP IN CINCINNATI - Created by Hugh Wilson

www.ingramcontent.com/pod-product-compliance
Lightning Source LLC
LaVergne TN
LVHW051541070426
835507LV00021B/2355